T0313358

Production Management
Advanced Models, Tools, and Applications
for Pull Systems

Production Management
Advanced Models, Tools, and Applications
for Pull Systems

Edited by
Yacob Khojasteh

CRC Press
Taylor & Francis Group
Boca Raton London New York

CRC Press is an imprint of the
Taylor & Francis Group, an **informa** business

A PRODUCTIVITY PRESS BOOK

CRC Press
Taylor & Francis Group
6000 Broken Sound Parkway NW, Suite 300
Boca Raton, FL 33487-2742

© 2018 by Taylor & Francis Group, LLC
CRC Press is an imprint of Taylor & Francis Group, an Informa business

No claim to original U.S. Government works

Printed on acid-free paper

International Standard Book Number-13: 978-1-138-03221-7 (Paperback)

International Standard Book Number-13: 978-1-315-39438-1 (eBook)

Visit the Taylor & Francis Web site at
http://www.taylorandfrancis.com

and the CRC Press Web site at
http://www.crcpress.com

Contents

v

Preface

Inventory control is an essential task in production management. An effective inventory control can significantly reduce the holding cost and hence, total production cost. Selecting and implementing a suitable production control system plays an important role in inventory reduction and performance improvement of a production system. Since the introduction of Toyota's just-in-time philosophy, pull control systems have been adopted by numerous companies worldwide, both in the manufacturing and service sectors. The most well-known pull control systems are Kanban, constant work-in-process (CONWIP), and their extensions.

This book provides some recent developments in production management and presents modeling and analysis tools for pull production control systems. It contributes by combining theoretical findings and case study analysis results with a practical and contemporary view on how to effectively manage and control production systems.

Each chapter in this book focuses on a specific topic in production control systems, allowing readers to identify the chapters that relate to their interests. More specifically, the book is presented in three sections. The first section focuses on the design and implementation aspects of the pull production control systems, as well as performance evaluation approaches for pull systems. The second section presents a recent and comprehensive literature review. Three different case studies on implementation of pull production control systems are presented in the last section.

In the first chapter of the book, I briefly discuss the complexity of comparing different production control systems given the fact that selecting and implementing a superior pull production control system has been controversial. By focusing on Kanban and CONWIP as two well-known pull production control systems, I present two simple examples that show how the superiority alters between these two control systems by a small change in the structure of the production system. In Chapter 2, Oladipupo Olaitan, Paul Young, and John Geraghty address the kanban allocation policies of multi-product production control strategies. They compare the performance of the shared and dedicated kanban allocation policies under the application of the Extended and the Generalized Kanban Control Strategies. They investigate the system robustness to measure how well a strategy is able to maintain its optimized service level and inventory control performance when subjected to variability in demand arrival rates and level of machine availability.

In Chapter 3, Paolo Renna addresses a multi-product serial production line and proposes dynamic card control policies in Hybrid Kanban CONWIP and Base-Stock control strategy with shared kanbans. He develops a simulation model to test the proposed policies in steady and dynamic demand conditions. The control policies consider two controllers to capture the demand changes and machine failures in order to improve the performance level. In Chapter 4, Pedro González-R and Marcos Calle examine the effect of reworking in the make-to-order job-shop environments.

Using discrete event simulation, they compare the performance of two production control systems, Kanban and Workload Control, in different job-shop environments with different rework levels. Moreover, they highlight the advantages and disadvantages of those two control systems.

In Chapter 5, Mitchell Millstein and Joseph Martinich present a method called "Takt Time Grouping" for implementing kanban-flow manufacturing. Using a discrete event simulation model, they show the superiority of the proposed method to the other approaches including one-piece flow, CONWIP, and drum-buffer-rope, with a high throughput rate, lower work-in-process inventory, and a faster flow time. In Chapter 6, S. Vinodh, R. Ben Ruben, and P. Asokan discuss the different types of pull systems, and develop a conceptual framework for evaluating performance of pull systems. The developed performance evaluation model is based on the fuzzy logic approach which is capable of handling vagueness and uncertainty that usually exist in conventional performance evaluation models. They conduct a case study to validate the proposed framework and to ensure its practical relevance.

The second section of the book includes a chapter that reviews the literature for CONWIP control system. In this chapter, Mehmet Durmusoglu and Canan Aglan explain the design requirements of CONWIP control system, and then review the related literature for each design requirement. They also evaluate the studies on CONWIP performance comparisons with respect to aims, manufacturing environment, and design parameters.

The last section in the book presents three different case studies on implementation of pull production control systems. In the first chapter of the section, Guodong Huang and Jie Chen propose a CONWIP design framework to make CONWIP scheme in one-of-a-kind production environment (a wire-rope equipment manufacturer). A feasible CONWIP scheme is determined after simulation assessments of the CONWIP alternatives. In Chapter 9, MD Sarder, Mohsen Hosseini, and Mohammad Marufuzzaman discuss a case study to define the push–pull boundary for both continuous and periodic review policies to make the multi-stage supply chain more efficient. They compare the performance of a push-based supply chain and a combined (push–pull)-based supply chain by considering and prioritizing the cost reduction, aggregation of product types, and shipping and transportation methods to set the appropriate push–pull boundaries.

In the last chapter of the book, Chapter 10, Gwendolyn Holowecky and Ratna Babu Chinnam address balancing flexibility and lean in manufacturing environments. They develop a framework for integrating flexibility within a lean environment by logically linking empirical studies in non-lean contexts with the literature on lean manufacturing practices. The framework is based on strategic, operational, and tactical timeframes. A case study is also provided as confirmation for the proposed framework.

This book can be used as an essential source for students and scholars who need to specifically study the pull control systems. Since the superiority of these systems is controversial, this book can also provide an interesting and informative read for practitioners, managers, and employees who need to deepen their knowledge on pull production management systems.

I would like to thank all the authors who have contributed to this book. I express my gratitude to those authors who helped me on early reviewing of some chapters.

I would also like to thank my wife Miya and sons Nima and Yuma for allowing me to devote the time necessary to complete this book. I dedicate this book to them.

Yacob Khojasteh
Tokyo, Japan
May 2017

Editor

Dr. Yacob Khojasteh is an associate professor of operations management at the Graduate School of Global Studies, Sophia University, Tokyo, Japan. He received his PhD in engineering from the University of Tsukuba, Japan. He also received his MSc in policy and planning sciences, and in industrial engineering from the University of Tsukuba and Tarbiat Modares University, respectively. He has several years of professional experience in industry and consulting. His recent books, entitled *Production Control Systems: A Guide to Enhance Performance of Pull Systems* and *Supply Chain Risk Management* were published by Springer in 2016 and 2017, respectively. His research interests include production and operations management, supply chain management, systems modeling and optimization, and lean production systems.

Contributors

Canan Aglan
Faculty of Industrial Engineering
Marmara University
Istanbul, Turkey

P. Asokan
Department of Production Engineering
National Institute of Technology
Tiruchirappalli, India

R. Ben Ruben
Department of Production Engineering
National Institute of Technology
Tiruchirappalli, India

Marcos Calle
Industrial Organization and Business
    Management
University of Seville
Seville, Spain

Jie Chen
School of Economics & Management
Nanjing University of Science & Technology
Nanjing, China

Ratna Babu Chinnam
Industrial & Systems Engineering Department
Wayne State University
Detroit, Michigan

Mehmet Bulent Durmusoglu
Faculty of Industrial Engineering
Istanbul Technical University
Istanbul, Turkey

John Geraghty
Enterprise Process Research Centre
Dublin City University
Dublin, Ireland

Pedro L. González-R
Industrial Organization and Business
    Management
University of Seville
Seville, Spain

Gwendolyn Holowecky
Industrial Engineering and Facilities
TRQSS, Tokai Rika Group North America,
    Quality Safety Systems Company
Tecumseh, Canada
and
Industrial & Systems Engineering Department
Wayne State University
Detroit, Michigan

Mohsen Hosseini
Center for Logistics, Trade and Transportation
University of Southern Mississippi
Long Beach, Mississippi

Guodong Huang
School of Economics & Management
Nanjing University of Science & Technology
Nanjing, China

Yacob Khojasteh
Graduate School of Global Studies
Sophia University
Tokyo, Japan

Mohammad Marufuzzaman
Department of Industrial & Systems
    Engineering
Mississippi State University
Starkville, Mississippi

Joseph S. Martinich
Department of Logistics and Operations
    Management
University of Missouri
St. Louis, Missouri

Mitchell A. Millstein
Department of Logistics and Operations
    Management
University of Missouri
St. Louis, Missouri

Oladipupo Olaitan
Department of Mechanical and Industrial
    Engineering
Norwegian University of Science and
    Technology (NTNU)
Trondheim, Norway

Paolo Renna
School of Engineering, University of Basilicata
Potenza, Italy

M.D. Sarder
Department of Engineering Technologies,
    Bowling Green State University, Bowling
    Green, Ohio

S. Vinodh
Department of Production Engineering
National Institute of Technology
Tiruchirappalli, India

Paul Young
Enterprise Process Research Centre
Dublin City University
Dublin, Ireland

DESIGN, IMPLEMENTATION, AND PERFORMANCE EVALUATION

I

Chapter 1

Pull Production Control Systems: Selection and Implementation Issues

Yacob Khojasteh

Contents

1.1 Introduction

There are many studies regarding the evaluation and comparison of production control systems. Usually, two or more control systems are addressed and the superior system is highlighted, under certain conditions with a set of assumptions. Some studies propose a model or framework to conduct such comparisons. For example, Ghrayeb et al. (2009) compared push, pull, and hybrid control systems in an assemble-to-order manufacturing environment. They showed that in most cases, the hybrid system had the best performance. However, when the cost ratio of delivery lead time and inventory was small, the pull system performed better.

Gaury et al. (2000) compared Kanban, CONWIP, and hybrid control systems in a serial production line, and pointed out that the hybrid control system had the best performance. Pettersen and Segerstedt (2009) compared Kanban and CONWIP control systems through a simulation study over a small supply chain. They showed that the CONWIP control was superior to the

Kanban with a higher throughput rate and the same amount of work-in-process (WIP) inventory. Khojasteh-Ghamari (2012) proposed a model for performance analysis of a production process controlled by Kanban and CONWIP. He showed the impact of initial inventories and card distribution as important parameters on system performance.

According to a survey by Framinan et al. (2003), comparing Kanban and CONWIP, many authors showed that CONWIP is superior to Kanban, when processing times on component operations in production processes are variable. However, a few studies, including Gstettner and Kuhn (1996) and Khojasteh-Ghamari (2009), reached the opposite conclusion. They showed that by choosing an appropriate number of cards at each workstation, Kanban could outperform CONWIP.

Bonvik et al. (1997) compared performance of different production control systems, with respect to WIP and service level, in a serial production line. They showed that CONWIP outperforms Kanban and Base-stock, with a high service level and lower WIP. However, as Framinan et al. (2003) mentioned, this result seems to be contradictory to the findings of Duenyas and Patana-anake (1998) as well as Paternina-Arboleda and Das (2001), which indicated that Base-stock outperforms CONWIP in a serial production line. These differing results highlight the need for more clarification and analysis. In this chapter, we address this controversy in generalizing the superiority among pull production control systems. For more literature reviews on the comparison of pull control systems, see Geraghty and Heavey (2006), Gonzlez-R et al. (2012), and Thürer et al. (2016).

Here, we introduce a comparison method (given in Section 1.2) followed by some numerical examples provided in Section 1.3 to briefly analyze the complexity in comparing the control systems.

1.2 Comparison Method

In this chapter, the framework proposed by Sato and Khojasteh-Ghamari (2012) is used for comparing pull production control systems in the presented example. For more details on the framework, which is based on the theory of token transactions systems, see Sato and Khojasteh-Ghamari (2012). In this section, we present a simple serial production process controlled by CONWIP to support the discussion and the numerical example provided in the next section.

We can consider a simple production process with four workstations. The activity interaction diagram (AID) of this production process controlled by CONWIP is depicted in Figure 1.1. See Sato and Praehofer (1997) for definitions and concepts of the AID.

Raw material R is being processed through p_1 to p_4 and at the end, it is stored in the place b_4 as finished products, while b_i $(i = 1,...,4)$ is the output buffer of station i, and w_i $(i = 1,...,4)$ represents the worker/operator/machine of station i. Queue C contains CONWIP cards. Solid lines represent material flows and dashed lines indicate card/information flows.

The system reaches a steady state after a sufficient period of time. We can show the steady state of the system by referring to the state transition table (Sato and Praehofer, 1997). At steady state, the system shows a periodic behavior. Table 1.1 shows part of the state transition table for the CONWIP controlled production system depicted in Figure 1.1. Processing time at p_1 to p_4 is set to 7, 16, 6, and 5, respectively. Process p_2 has two workers, while the others have one each. Initial inventory in each buffer is set to zero. With this structure, at least four cards are needed to circulate in the entire system to enable maximum throughput. In this table, "—" represents there

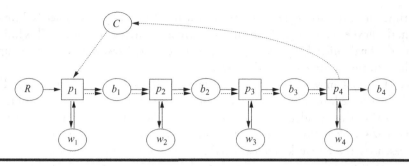

Figure 1.1   A serial production process with four workstations controlled by CONWIP (Sato and Khojasteh-Ghamari, 2012).

Table 1.1   State Transition Table of the CONWIP Example

Time	C	p_1	w_1	b_1	p_2	w_2	b_2	p_3	w_3	b_3	p_4	w_4	b_4
t	0	1(7)	0	1	1(10), 1(3)	0	0	—	1	0	1(5)	0	n
$t+3$	0	1(4)	0	0	1(7), 1(16)	0	0	1(6)	0	0	1(2)	0	n
$t+5$	0	1(2)	0	0	1(5), 1(14)	0	0	1(4)	0	0	—	1	$n+1$
$t+7$	0	—	1	1	1(3), 1(12)	0	0	1(2)	0	0	—	1	$n+1$
$t+9$	0	1(7)	0	1	1(1), 1(10)	0	0	—	1	0	1(5)	0	$n+1$
$t+10$	0	1(6)	0	0	1(16), 1(9)	0	0	1(6)	0	0	1(4)	0	$n+1$
$t+14$	0	1(2)	0	0	1(12), 1(5)	0	0	1(2)	0	0	—	1	$n+2$
$t+16$	0	1(7)	0	1	1(10), 1(3)	0	0	—	1	0	1(5)	0	$n+2$

is no part being processed, that the corresponding worker is idle. For example, "1(7)," shows that one part is being processed and it will finish after 7 time units.

The numbers and symbols in the first row of the state transition table, given in Table 1.1, can be interpreted as follows. At time t, there is no available card in the card buffer C ($C = 0$). One part is being processed at p_1, which will finish after 7 time units. Since a part is being processed at p_1, the corresponding worker w_1 is busy and is not available ($w_1 = 0$). There is one part in the first output buffer ($b_1 = 1$), and two parts are being processed at p_2, one will finish after 10 time units and the other after 3 time units. Hence, none of the respective workers is available ($w_2 = 0$). No part is in the output buffer of the second and third stations ($b_2 = b_3 = 0$), also no part is being processed at p_3. Therefore, the respective worker is idle ($w_3 = 1$). One part is being processed in p_4 with a remaining time of 5 time units causing its worker to be busy ($w_4 = 0$). In the last output buffer b_4 waiting to be delivered to the customer, n finished products are available.

After 3 time units (which is the smallest remaining time at time t), p_2 finishes one part. This means that the current time is now $t + 3$, as shown in the second row of the table. At this point, the finished part in p_2 moves to its output buffer b_2, but it is then immediately taken by the downstream station p_3, since it was idle. Therefore, p_3 starts its new job and will continue the process for the next 6 time units. In turn, p_2 takes a new part, while the other part still needs 7 time units to finish. Then, the next event is on p_4. It finishes its current job after 2 time units. This finished good will move to the final buffer b_4 by adding one to its inventory. Now, the numbers are updated, as shown in the next row, at time $t+5$ in the table.

The state of the system will evolve in the same way such that after a certain period all numbers in a row will be repeated. In this example, this happens every 16 $[(t+16)-t]$ time units.

The system WIP can be calculated for a period using the state transition table. As it is seen in Table 1.1, at time t, six tokens (four of them are being processed at p_1, p_2 and p_4, one is in output buffer b_1, and one representing the idle worker) remain in the system for 3 time units $[(t+3)-t=3]$. At the next event time (i.e., $t+3$), five tokens remain in the system, but for 2 time units $[(t+5)-(t+3)=2]$. Similarly, 5, 6, 6, 5, and 5 tokens remain in the system for the next 2, 2, 1, 4, and 2 time units, respectively. This yields $(6\times3)+(5\times2)+(5\times2)+(6\times2)+(6\times1)+(5\times4)+(5\times2)=86$ (tokens×time units) as the total holding and waiting times for a period. Since the period is 16 time units, the system WIP is 5.375 (=86/16) tokens.

1.2.1 Analytical Comparisons

Khojasteh-Ghamari and Sato (2011) characterized the comparison between Kanban and CONWIP control systems in serial production lines. They proved that a CONWIP system outperforms a Kanban if and only if the total number of cards circulated in the CONWIP is less than in the Kanban. Additionally, they have an identical performance if and only if the same number of cards is employed in both systems. It should be noted that the total number of cards here refers to the optimum number of cards employed in the system; in other words, the least number of cards that enables the system to attain the maximum throughput. The proofs also are supported by numerical examples. In another study, Khojasteh and Sato (2015) formulated a comparison between the three control systems, Kanban, CONWIP, and Base-stock, in both serial and assembly production processes. They provided supportive numerical examples as well.

In the following section, we show the controversy on the superiority of pull production control systems through a simple example.

1.3 Numerical Experiments

The following example shows the complexity in comparing Kanban and CONWIP as two pull production control systems.

1.3.1 An Example

Consider an assembly production process where the finished product is assembled from two distinctive subassemblies, and each subassembly is made up of two distinctive parts. The product is assembled from one unit of each subassembly, and each of the subassemblies is fabricated by using one unit of each part. A schematic figure is depicted in Figure 1.2, where p_{ij} ($i=1,2$ and $j=1,2$), p_i ($i=1,2$), and p are the processes, b_{ij} ($i=1,2$ and $j=1,2$) and b_i ($i=1,2$) are the output buffers for the corresponding process, and b is the final buffer for the finished goods. The AIDs for these production processes, controlled by Kanban and CONWIP, are depicted in Figures 1.3 and 1.4, respectively. In the Kanban system, K_{ij}, K_i, and K are card buffers that contain the kanban cards. Card buffers in CONWIP system are shown by C_{ij} (Figure 1.4).

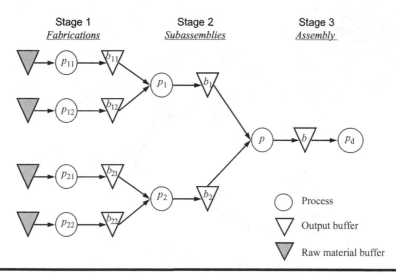

Figure 1.2   A simple assembly production process with three stages (Khojasteh, 2016).

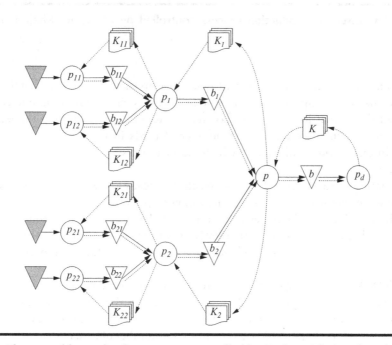

Figure 1.3   The assembly production process controlled by Kanban (Khojasteh and Sato, 2015).

1.3.1.1 Scenario 1

In Figure 1.2, assume that the processing times of p_{11}, p_{12}, p_{21}, p_{22}, p_1, p_2, and p are set to 10, 11, 12, 20, 10, 10, and 1 time units, respectively. The process p_{22} has two operators/machines/workers, while each of the others has only one. Also, initial inventory for every part is set to zero, and assume that enough raw materials are always available.

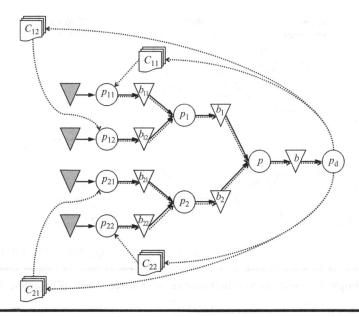

Figure 1.4 The assembly production process controlled by CONWIP (Khojasteh and Sato, 2015).

In the Kanban control system, one card is assigned to each card buffer, therefore the total number of cards circulating in the entire system becomes eight. Assigning one card to each station allows the system to attain the maximum throughput with having the least WIP in the system. In fact, this is the optimum number of cards in the system because allocating more cards in any station will cause an increase in the system WIP without changing the throughput.

The simulation is run until the system reaches a steady state, at which time the system begins to show a periodic behavior. The system shows a periodic behavior every 12 time units. The throughput is 1/12 products per time unit, and the system WIP is equal to 10.833. It can be verified that the amount of system WIP is minimum to attain the throughput 1/12. Table 1.2 shows the state transition table for a period of the production process with Kanban control.

In the CONWIP control system, nine cards in total are needed in order for the system to attain the maximum throughput of 1/12 products per time unit (as in the Kanban system). The optimal card distribution is to assign two cards to each of C_{11}, C_{12}, and C_{21}, and three cards to C_{22}. That is, nine cards in total, which is the minimum number of cards to attain the maximum possible throughput. The system shows a periodic behavior every 12 time units. However, the system WIP is equal to 9.750, which is the minimum value to attain the throughput. The state transition table for a period of the production process controlled by CONWIP system is given in Table 1.3.

The CONWIP control system is superior to Kanban system here because it attains the same system throughput, but with a lower amount of the WIP (9.750 vs. 10.833).

Table 1.2 State Transition Table of Kanban for a Period in Scenario 1

Time	K_{11}	p_{11}	b_{11}	K_{12}	p_{12}	b_{12}	K_1	p_1	b_1	K_{21}	p_{21}	b_{21}	K_{22}	p_{22}	b_{22}	K_2	p_2	b_2	K	p	b	p_d
t	0	1(10)	0	0	1(11)	0	0	1(10)	0	0	1(2)	0	0	—, 1(10)	1	1	—	0	0	1(1)	0	1(1)
$t+1$	0	1(9)	0	0	1(10)	0	0	1(9)	0	0	1(1)	0	0	—, 1(9)	1	1	—	0	1	—	0	1(12)
$t+2$	0	1(8)	0	0	1(9)	0	0	1(8)	0	0	1(12)	0	0	1(20), 1(8)	0	0	1(10)	0	1	—	0	1(11)
$t+10$	0	—	1	0	1(1)	0	0	—	1	0	1(4)	0	0	1(12), —	1	0	1(2)	0	1	—	0	1(3)
$t+11$	0	—	1	0	—	1	0	—	1	0	1(3)	0	0	1(11), —	1	0	1(1)	0	1	—	0	1(2)
$t+12$	0	1(10)	0	0	1(11)	0	0	1(10)	0	0	1(2)	0	0	1(10), —	1	1	—	0	0	1(1)	0	1(1)

Table 1.3 State Transition Table of CONWIP for a Period in Scenario 1

Time	C_{11}	p_{11}	b_{11}	C_{12}	p_{12}	b_{12}	p_1	b_1	C_{21}	p_{21}	b_{21}	C_{22}	p_{22}	b_{22}	p_2	b_2	p	b	p_d
t	0	1(10)	0	0	1(11)	0	1(9)	0	1	1(1)	0	0	1(20), 1(8)	1	—	0	—	0	1(12)
$t+1$	0	1(9)	0	0	1(10)	0	1(8)	0	0	1(12)	0	0	1(19), 1(7)	0	1(10)	0	—	0	1(11)
$t+8$	0	1(2)	0	0	1(3)	0	1(1)	0	0	1(5)	0	0	1(12), —	1	1(3)	0	—	0	1(4)
$t+9$	0	1(1)	0	0	1(2)	0	—	1	0	1(4)	0	0	1(11), —	1	1(2)	0	—	0	1(3)
$t+10$	0	—	1	0	1(1)	0	—	1	0	1(3)	0	0	1(10), —	1	1(1)	0	—	0	1(2)
$t+11$	0	—	0	0	—	0	1(10)	0	0	1(2)	0	0	1(9), —	1	—	0	1(1)	0	1(1)
$t+12$	0	1(10)	0	0	1(11)	0	1(9)	0	1	1(1)	0	0	1(8), 1(20)	1	—	0	—	0	1(12)

1.3.1.2 Scenario 2

In the example above, we apply a small change in processing time of a process. We only change the processing time at p from 1 to 6 time units, while all the other processing times remain unchanged. That is, the processing times at p_{11}, p_{12}, p_{21}, p_{22}, p_1, p_2, and p is 10, 11, 12, 20, 10, 10, and 6 time units, respectively. Also, as before, the process p_{22} has two workers, while each of the others have only one, and the initial inventory for every part is set to zero.

In the Kanban control system, assigning one card to each card buffer enables the system to attain the maximum throughput with the least system WIP. Therefore, the total number of cards in the entire system is eight. The simulation is run until the system begins to show a periodic behavior. The system shows a periodic behavior every 12 time units with the throughput rate of 1/12 products per time unit, but the system WIP drops to 10.417. A part of its state transition table for a period is shown in Table 1.4.

However, in the CONWIP control system, at least 13 cards in total are needed in order for the system to attain the maximum throughput of 1/12 products per time unit (same throughput rate in the Kanban system). In other words, the maximum throughput cannot be achieved by the same card distribution. In order to attain the maximum throughput, the minimum number of additional cards should be added into the appropriate card buffers in the system. To do so, three cards are needed in each of C_{11}, C_{12}, and C_{21}, and four cards in C_{22}, that is, 13 cards in total. This card distribution increases the system WIP to 11.50, which is more than that in the Kanban system. This makes the CONWIP an inferior control system. Therefore, the Kanban system outperforms the CONWIP. The state transition table for this case is given in Table 1.5.

In fact, changing only one processing time in the system requires a different card distribution for the CONWIP, which causes an increase in the total number of cards in the system, hence an increase in the system WIP. One can see that a small change in the production structure (increasing processing time of one station from 1 to 6 time units) requires the CONWIP system to have four more cards in total (13 compared to 9 in Scenario 1) to reach the maximum throughput.

For more analyses and examples on Kanban, CONWIP, and Base-stock control systems in different production structures, see Khojasteh and Sato (2011, 2015) and Khojasteh (2016).

1.4 Conclusions

Selecting and implementing a suitable, and best, pull production control system has been a challenge for managers. By using numerical experiments and comparing Kanban and CONWIP as two pull control systems in different scenarios, we showed that the superiority of a control system may change, if the structure of the production system changes. In the example provided, we saw that by changing only the processing time of a station, the superiority between CONWIP and Kanban switched.

Therefore, we can conclude that none of the Kanban or CONWIP controls are always the superior system. In fact, a configuration of parameters, such as processing time of activities, number of workers, and number of cards employed in the whole process decides the superior system in each situation (Khojasteh and Sato, 2015; Khojasteh, 2016).

The other chapters in this book will present more cases and analyses on pull production control systems.

Table 1.4   State Transition Table of Kanban for a Period in Scenario 2

Time	K_{11}	p_{11}	b_{11}	K_{12}	p_{12}	b_{12}	K_1	p_1	b_1	K_{21}	p_{21}	b_{21}	K_{22}	p_{22}	b_{22}	K_2	p_2	b_2	K	p	b	p_d
t	0	1(10)	0	0	1(11)	0	0	1(10)	0	0	1(2)	0	0	−, 1(10)	1	1	−	0	0	1(6)	0	1(6)
$t+2$	0	1(8)	0	0	1(9)	0	0	1(8)	0	0	1(12)	0	0	1(20), 1(8)	0	0	1(10)	0	0	1(4)	0	1(4)
$t+6$	0	1(4)	0	0	1(5)	0	0	1(4)	0	0	1(8)	0	0	1(16), 1(4)	0	0	1(6)	0	1	−	0	1(12)
$t+10$	0	−	1	0	1(1)	0	0	−	1	0	1(4)	0	0	1(12), −	1	0	1(2)	0	1	−	0	1(8)
$t+11$	0	−	1	0	−	1	0	−	1	0	1(3)	0	0	1(11), −	1	0	1(1)	0	1	−	0	1(7)
$t+12$	0	1(10)	0	0	1(11)	0	0	1(10)	0	0	1(2)	0	0	−, 1(10)	1	1	−	0	0	1(6)	0	1(6)

Table 1.5 State Transition Table of CONWIP for a Period in Scenario 2

Time	C_{11}	p_{11}	b_{11}	C_{12}	p_{12}	b_{12}	p_1	b_1	C_{21}	p_{21}	b_{21}	C_{22}	p_{22}	b_{22}	p_2	b_2	p	b	p_d
t	0	1(10)	0	0	1(11)	0	1(9)	1	1	1(8)	0	0	1(20), 1(8)	1	1(6)	0	—	0	1(12)
$t+6$	0	1(4)	0	0	1(5)	0	1(3)	0	1	1(2)	0	0	1(14), 1(2)	1	—	0	1(6)	0	1(6)
$t+8$	0	1(2)	0	0	1(3)	0	1(1)	0	0	1(12)	0	0	1(12), —	1	1(10)	0	1(4)	0	1(4)
$t+9$	0	1(1)	0	0	1(2)	0	—	1	0	1(11)	0	0	1(11), —	1	1(9)	0	1(3)	0	1(3)
$t+10$	0	—	1	0	1(1)	0	—	1	0	1(10)	0	0	1(10), —	1	1(8)	0	1(2)	0	1(2)
$t+11$	0	—	0	0	—	0	1(10)	1	0	1(9)	0	0	1(9), —	1	1(7)	0	1(1)	0	1(1)
$t+12$	0	1(10)	0	0	1(11)	0	1(9)	1	1	1(8)	0	0	1(8), 1(20)	1	1(6)	0	—	0	1(12)

References

Bonvik, A.M., Couch, C.E., and Gershwin, S.B. (1997) A comparison of production-line control mechanisms. *International Journal of Production Research*, 35(3), 789–804.

Duenyas, I. and Patana-anake, P. (1998) Base-stock control for single product tandem make-to-stock systems. *IIE Transactions*, 30, 31–39.

Framinan, J.M., Gonzalez, P.L., and Ruiz-Usano, R. (2003) The CONWIP production control system: Review and research issues. *Production Planning and Control*, 14, 255–265.

Gaury, E.G.A., Pierreval, H., and Kleijnen, J.P.C. (2000) An evolutionary approach to select a pull system among Kanban, Conwip and hybrid. *Journal of Intelligent Manufacturing*, 11, 157–167.

Geraghty, J. and Heavey, C. (2006). A review and comparison of hybrid and pull-type production control strategies. In G. Liberopoulos, C.T. Papadopoulos, B. Tan, J. MacGregor Smith, and S.B. Gershwin (Eds.), *Stochastic Modeling of Manufacturing Systems*, Springer: Berlin.

Ghrayeb, O., Phojanamongkolkij, N., and Tan, B.A. (2009) A hybrid push/pull system in assemble-to-order manufacturing environment. *Journal of Intelligent Manufacturing*, 20(4), 379–387.

Gonzlez-R, P.L., Framinan, J.M., and Pierreval, H. (2012) Token-based pull production control systems: An introductory overview. *Journal of Intelligent Manufacturing*, 23(1), 5–22.

Gstettner, S. and Kuhn, H. (1996) Analysis of production control systems Kanban and CONWIP. *International Journal of Production Research*, 34(11), 3253–3274.

Khojasteh, Y. (2016) *Production Control Systems: A Guide to Enhance Performance of Pull Production Systems*, Springer, Tokyo.

Khojasteh, Y. and Sato, R. (2015) Selection of a pull production control system in multi-stage production processes. *International Journal of Production Research*, 53(14), 4363–4379.

Khojasteh-Ghamari, Y. (2009) A performance comparison between Kanban and CONWIP controlled assembly systems. *Journal of Intelligent Manufacturing*, 20(6), 751–760.

Khojasteh-Ghamari, Y. (2012) Developing a framework for performance analysis of a production process controlled by Kanban and CONWIP. *Journal of Intelligent Manufacturing*, 23(1), 61–71.

Khojasteh-Ghamari, Y. and Sato, R. (2011) Managing an assembly production process with a proper control policy. *International Journal of Manufacturing Technology and Management*, 22(1), 2–25.

Paternina-Arboleda, C.D. and Das, T.K. (2001) Intelligent dynamic control policies for serial production lines. *IIE Transactions*, 33(1), 65–77.

Pettersen, J.A. and Segerstedt, A. (2009) Restricted work-in-process: A study of differences between Kanban and CONWIP. *International Journal of Production Economics*, 118(1), 199–207.

Sato, R. and Khojasteh-Ghamari, Y. (2012) An integrated framework for card-based production control systems. *Journal of Intelligent Manufacturing*, 23(3), 717–731.

Sato, R. and Praehofer, H. (1997) A discrete event model of business system: A systems theoretic for information systems analysis—Part 1. *IEEE Transactions on Systems, Man, and Cybernetics*, 27, 1–10.

Thürer, M., Stevenson, M., and Protzman, C.W. (2016) Card-based production control: A review of the control mechanisms underpinning Kanban, ConWIP, POLCA and COBACABANA systems. *Production Planning and Control*, 27(14), 1143–1157.

Chapter 2

Kanban Allocation Policies of Multi-product Production Control Strategies

Oladipupo Olaitan, Paul Young, and John Geraghty

Contents

2.1 Introduction: Pull Production Control Strategies

The aim of this chapter is to compare the performance of the shared and dedicated kanban allocation policies under the application of the EKCS and the GKCS. The EKCS and the GKCS are two of the many production control strategies that have been categorized as Pull Production Control Strategies (PPCS). Other strategies that exist in this category are the traditional Kanban Control Strategy (KCS) (Ohno 1982), the Base-Stock Control Strategy (BSCS) (Kimball 1988), the Constant Work-in-Process (CONWIP) (Spearman et al. 1990), and others. These strategies are so categorized because of the way they pull products through a manufacturing system in response to customer orders.

2.1.1 Extended Kanban Control Strategy (EKCS)

The EKCS is a combination of the BSCS and the KCS, and described as combining the advantage of immediate response to demands offered by the BSCS, with tight WIP control of the KCS (Dallery and Liberopoulos 2000).

As shown in Figure 2.1 for a single product serial line, customer demands for finished products that arrive to the system are duplicated and transmitted as demand information to each of the manufacturing stages. The demand information that arrives to each stage—except the last stage—is then synchronized with a kanban before being used to authorize the release of a finished part downstream. At the last stage, demand information is used to release a part from the finished goods buffer to satisfy the customer demand.

2.1.2 Generalized Kanban Control Strategy (GKCS)

The GKCS (Zipkin 1989) requires setting the base-stock level and the number of kanbans per manufacturing stage, similarly to the EKCS (Baynat et al. 2002). However, its own approach to demand information transmission is not global, and the timing of its kanban detachment differs. As shown in Figure 2.2 for a single product serial line, when demand information arrives, it is duplicated and transmitted to the last and penultimate stages only. From the penultimate stage, the demand information is transmitted locally upstream one stage at a time.

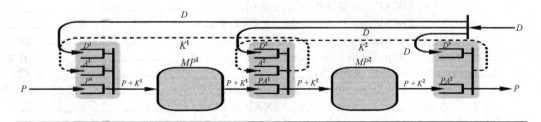

Figure 2.1   The extended kanban control strategy (Baynat et al., 2002).

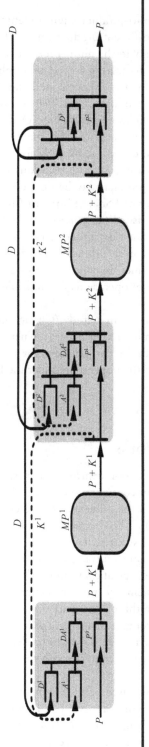

Figure 2.2   The generalized kanban control strategy (Baynat et al., 2002).

2.1.3 *Kanban Allocation Policies*

Applying some pull strategies in multi-product environments poses the question of how the kanbans are allocated between the different product types. The most natural extension of the single product kanban control strategy to the multi-product environment is to treat each product as if it constituted its own line, dedicating a specific number of kanbans to each product. This number would be optimized for the expected demand profile to share the production capacity of the system between the products, effectively allowing each product equal opportunity to meet its demand. Such policies are considered Dedicated Kanban Allocation Policy (DKAP). The alternative is to set the kanban level for the system and allow products to claim a kanban, based on whatever queue discipline (usually first in, first out or FIFO) is applied between stations. This ensures that the processing stations operate at their maximum level, but leads to the potential that one product may be delayed as the capacity is all claimed by another product. Such policies are termed Shared Kanban Allocation Policy (SKAP). It should be noted that apart from the FIFO discipline, other possible disciplines can also be applied in the release of kanbans to the parts. Such disciplines could prioritize the release of kanbans to parts based on their current numbers of unfulfilled demands at a particular stage, or even globally using the current levels of customer demand backlogs at the last stage. Such approaches have been applied in the scheduling of operations for multiple parts to minimize set-up times (Gurgur and Altiok 2007).

These two policies were first outlined in a study (Chang and Yih 1994), however their first detailed analysis was presented in a more recent paper (Baynat et al. 2002), and this contributed to the subsequent increased interest in the two policies. The two policies are described in better detail in Section 2.4.3 with respect to their operation under the EKCS and the GKCS in a multi-product serial line.

2.2 Review of Related Works

Studies have been conducted on production control strategies, and their corresponding policies, under different manufacturing system configurations, which include systems of various lengths, numbers of products, as well as, under the influence of different experimental factors (Khojasteh and Sato 2015, Gurgur and Altiok 2007, Yavuz and Satir 1995).

Although, these studies have investigated how system conditions and product parameters affect the performance of production control strategies, there are none that have shown how these factors influence system performance, specifically under the DKAP and the SKAP. Therefore, in addition to investigating how system and product factors affect production control strategy performance, the research reported in this chapter will aim to investigate how dedicating or sharing kanbans between the multiple products in a system will affect their respective SLs. How the different products fare in the SKAP has been shown to be dependent upon factors pertaining to a particular product, and how such factors compare with the other products with which it shares cards (Olaitan et al. 2013).

A study with closely related research used perturbation analysis to dynamically vary the number of kanbans allocated to the different part types in a multi-product system, as a means of counteracting undesirable effects of changes in product mix on system throughput (Liberatore et al. 1995). This appears to be the first work to have recognized the impact products attributes can have on one another under the DKAP.

Another more closely related work proposes the dynamic adjustment of the number of kanbans initially allocated to the two products of a system, in response to their respective current levels of demand backlog and inventory (Martinelli and Valigi 1998). Other related studies have observed the effect the number of product types can have on the performance of a system. For instance, it has been reported that having a high number of product types results in a lower customer SL, and this was attributed to the production time lost when changing over from the processing of one product to another (Yavuz and Satir 1995). In contrast, another study observed that manufacturing systems with fewer products suffer a more significant decline in SL when there is an increase in demand arrival rate (Gurgur and Altiok 2007). This was attributed to the fact that a system with more products is likely to have a higher ratio of production capacity to an individual product's demand. An increase in demand arrival rate for a single product consumes a lesser proportion of the overall production capacity.

It also is worth reviewing the observations of existing research primarily focused on the effects of product related and system level factors on its performance. In this chapter, such studies may help to differentiate outcomes that are due to product interaction from those resulting from system level factors. In studying the effects of demand variability, production time, backlog cost, and inventory holding cost, on the kanban size and the SL of a single-stage-multi-product system, one study concluded that a manufacturing system is able to adjust itself accordingly to offset the changes that occur to most of these parameters (Murino et al. 2009). However, a contrary observation was made in another study which suggests that even a well-designed pull system is hardly able to avoid starvation and overproduction that result from large and unpredictable fluctuations in demand (Krajewski et al. 1987). For processing time variability, its increase has been reported to cause shortages, and consequently, significant decrease in SL (Gurgur and Altiok 2007). However, it is reported to have no significant impact on system WIP (Grosfeld-Nir et al. 2000).

2.3 Methodology

The research reported in this chapter will achieve its goal of comparing the performances of DKAP and SKAP of the EKCS and the GKCS in a manufacturing system that is subjected to internal and external sources of variability by first modeling the manufacturing system and optimizing it for a base setting of product and system parameters. This is followed by introducing variability in the parameters to determine how well the production control strategies and their policies sustain the original optimized performance.

The performance measures of interest are the average amount of system WIP and the service level (SL) achieved for the products. These are combined into an optimization objective that seeks to achieve a target SL with the least amount of WIP possible through a trade-off (Geraghty and Heavey 2005, Khojasteh-Ghamari 2009). In this chapter, SL is defined as the proportion of demands that are satisfied immediately when they arrive to the finish goods buffer, without being backlogged. Research works that assume an unlimited arrival of demands to the system measure throughput, instead of SL (Khojasteh 2016). Thus, they set the optimization objective to determine the least possible amount of WIP needed to achieve maximum system throughput (Khojasteh 2016, Khojasteh and Sato 2015). Other commonly applied performance measures in research are cycle time, stability of throughput rate, average wait time of backlogged demands, and the average duration and frequency of demand backlog (Gurgur and Altiok 2007, Spearman et al. 1990).

2.3.1 Manufacturing System Optimization

The essential parameters in the design of a kanban controlled manufacturing system are the number of kanbans needed to link the processes together, the number of machines, and the appropriate unit of lot size (Shahabudeen et al. 2003). A range of techniques have been adopted for the optimization of manufacturing systems, mostly from other fields of application. Some of these techniques are Perturbation Analysis (Liberatore et al. 1995), Mathematical Programming (Alfieri and Matta 2012), Genetic Algorithms (Sivakumar and Shahabudeen 2008), Simulated Annealing (Geraghty and Heavey 2004), Tabu Search (Alabas et al. 2000), and Ant Colony Optimization (Becker and Szczerbicka 2005).

One approach that is widely adopted is the simulation-based optimization (Koulouriotis et al. 2010), which, according to Bowden and Hall (1998), is "the practice of linking an optimization method with a simulation model to determine appropriate settings of certain input parameters so as to maximize the performance of the simulated system." The system's performance is usually expressed in the form of an objective function that would assign penalty costs or benefits to a statistical measure, which can be outputted directly from the simulation model.

Due to the effectiveness of this simulation-based optimization approach, some simulation software have inbuilt optimization blocks that are based on some of these algorithms. For example, ExtendSim™, which is described in this chapter, uses a Genetic Algorithm to which an objective function and the parameters for optimization can be specified. The Genetic Algorithm (Holland and Reitman 1977) has been expressed as a mechanism that imitates the genetic evolution of species (Pirlot 1996). It operates by reproduction, crossover, and mutation of populations; the population being the solution space to the specified problem (Sivakumar and Shahabudeen 2008). The reproduction operator selects an initial population of solutions, evaluates them for fitness, and ranks them. Individuals with good fitness are combined as parents to produce offspring, with the hope that the offspring will retain some of the desirable traits of the parents. The offspring then go through mutation and evaluation to see if they can evolve into even better individuals. In the context of optimizing pull strategies, an individual can be seen as a particular setting of kanbans and/or base-stocks for all the manufacturing stages, and its mutation would involve interchanging these settings.

Multi-product systems are even more complicated to optimize and, as such, some techniques have been devised to solve the intractability that results from the volume of parameters involved in them. One of such approaches, which is called a "decomposition-based approximation," involves breaking the multi-stage-multi-product system into smaller multi-stage-single product systems and/or single-stage-multi-product systems. These smaller systems are then analyzed separately and their outcomes are used to approximate the larger more complicated systems (Gurgur and Altiok 2007).

Another study suggests that the search for optimal kanban and base-stock could start with a zero base-stock and seek to determine the number of kanbans that would maximize the throughput using single stages in isolation. This would be followed by gradually increasing the base-stock level and reducing the kanban number sequentially (Dallery and Liberopoulos 2000). It is also useful to conduct a preliminary solution space evaluation to predetermine reasonable ranges for the parameters (Karrer 2011).

2.3.2 Sensitivity Analysis for Robustness of Pull Production Control Strategies

Sensitivity analysis, which has been described as "the systematic investigation of the reaction of the simulation response to extreme values of the model's input or to drastic changes in the model's structure" (Kleijnen 1995), has been applied in conducting robustness tests, and it has provided a different perspective to comparing strategies. For instance, the outcomes of a study (Kleijnen and Gaury 2003) conducted on an existing work (Bonvik et al. 1997) show disparity between the conclusion derived from conducting the experiments on an optimized base scenario and when the robustness of the different strategies to variability are considered through sensitivity analysis. Other studies have made similar observations (Onyeocha et al. 2015, Olaitan and Geraghty 2013, Gaury and Kleijnen 1998), and their outcomes show that lesser effort should be placed on trying to obtain absolutely optimal parameter settings. Rather, most of the effort should be concentrated on comparing the robustness of the near optimal outcomes obtained from minimal optimization efforts. This comparison will be achieved by creating new sets of realizations of a manufacturing system, different from the base settings for which it was originally optimized, and re-running its simulation without re-optimizing it. A stochastic dominance test will then be conducted on the newly simulation outcomes to determine how well a strategy was able to maintain its previously optimized performance when subjected to the variation in the system factor settings. This can form the basis for selecting the strategy to apply in a manufacturing system based on its suitability to the inherent conditions of the system.

Importantly, a sensitivity analysis outcome, which this research would benefit from, is that it can be used to understand the relationship between variables (Kleijnen 1995). It can measure the level of impact product related factors and system level factors have on a strategy's performance.

2.3.3 Latin Hypercube Sampling for Design of Experiments for Sensitivity Analysis

Latin Hypercube Sampling (LHS) (McKay et al. 1979) is the preferred method for this research because of the number of factors involved in the sensitivity analysis of manufacturing systems simulation models. Often, it is difficult to use classical design experiment techniques, such as Factorial designs (full or fractional) and Central Composite Designs, for the design of simulation experiments because of the large number of design factors involved. If a full factorial experiment was used for the 10 factor experiments conducted in this research, it would necessitate conducting 1024 experimental runs, and yet these would only evaluate the factors at their lowest and highest levels. However, LHS offers a more flexible approach to the number of runs for any number of simulation factors. It allows specification of a desired number of runs, N, into which each factor is equally divided. N can be decided irrespective of the number of experimental factors involved (Kleijnen 2005). For example, in a study that recommends taking a minimum LHS sample size of 100, they were able to achieve sufficient coverage for a 17 factor experiment (Gaury and Kleijnen 1998).

As shown in Table 2.1, a sample is randomly taken from each division for all the factors to form different factor level combinations in the N experimental runs.

2.3.3.1 Stochastic Dominance Test of Robustness

Stochastic dominance tests (Fishburn 1975) on the system SL performance will give indications of how well a strategy/policy is able to remain close to the original target SLs when the previously anticipated system condition changes. The tests are conducted on the LHS outputs and the test results can be of first-order, second-order, or inconclusive, depending on the level of difference between the outputs from the options (strategies) being compared.

Table 2.1 LHS factor division and sampling

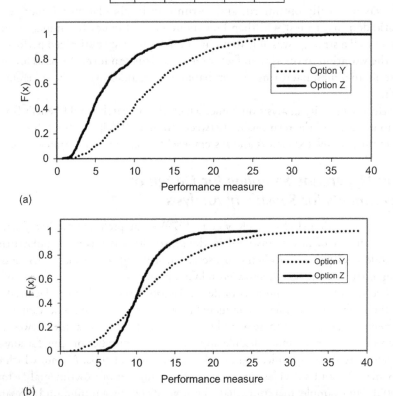

Figure 2.3 Types of stochastic dominance test outcomes. (a) First-order dominance. (b) Second-order dominance (Vose, 2014).

As shown in Figure 2.3a, a first-order dominance is often recognizable by visual observation because the cumulative density function (CDF) curves of the two options being compared do not intersect.

Mathematically expressed, it implies that for two options Y and Z with CDFs $F_Y(x)$ and $F_Z(x)$ where the objective is to maximize the value of x.

Option Y first-order stochastically dominates Z, if

$$F_Y(x) \leq F_z(x) \quad \text{for all } x \tag{2.1}$$

However, as shown in Figure 2.3b, a second-order dominance is not visually identifiable, and it requires the use of the area under the CDF curve to identify the dominant option. Thus, Option Y second-order stochastically dominates Z, if

$$\int\limits_{min}^{k} F_Y(x)dx \leq \int\limits_{min}^{k} F_z(x)dx \quad \text{for all } k \tag{2.2}$$

Vose™ Software's MS Excel™ plugin, named Model Risk, is used in this research to compute the areas under the CDF curves and identify the level of dominance between sets of raw data.

2.4 Set-up of Manufacturing System and Experiments

In the following sub-sections, a two-product system is set up and used to compare the ability of DKAP and SKAP of the EKCS and the GKCS to maintain their optimized levels of performance under different sources of variability. These include machine unreliability, product demand variability, and having to cope with multiple products of disparate demand profiles. The latter scenario is particular to the semiconductor manufacturing sector, which often must manufacture newly introduced, mature, soon to be phased out, and legacy products, that simultaneously would have different demand profiles.

2.4.1 System Description

The manufacturing system used in this chapter is a two-product, three-stage serial line, which has been used in a previous study for research on EKCS (Olaitan and Geraghty 2013). Product 1 requires 1.5 h processing time at each of the manufacturing stages, while Product 2 requires twice as much time at the three stages. For the two products, it is assumed that raw materials are always available to begin production at the first stage, once it has been authorized (Khojasteh and Sato 2015). The products' mean times between demands are specified with a normal distribution because of its suitability for modeling distributions that represent a combination of events (Law and Kelton 2000). In this case, the demand events are from different customer sources. Moreover, this distribution has been chosen because of the ease in setting the variability level with a combination of standard deviation, σ, and mean, μ, values (Hopp and Spearman 1996). The coefficient of variation (CV) of a normal distribution is defined as shown in Equation 2.3:

$$CV = \frac{\sigma}{\mu} \tag{2.3}$$

The demand standard deviation values for this system are set to 0.1 and 0.5 of the mean values to represent low and high CV levels, respectively, as shown in Table 2.2.

It should be noted that the normal distribution is truncated by setting any negative variate it generates for the time between two consecutive demands to zero to represent that such demands arrived simultaneously (Moeeni et al. 1997). It was observed from the inspection of the truncated data that the high CV levels are effectively 0.47, while the low CV levels remain 0.1.

With the low and high levels of demand CVs for the two products, a full factorial design of experiments is developed to create four scenarios that correspond to varying levels of disparity in the demand profiles of the products, as shown in Table 2.3.

Table 2.2   Demand CV Levels for the Products

| Product | Fixed Mean | Demand CV Levels | |
		Low (0.1)	High (≈0.47)
1	μ = 5.61	σ = 0.561	σ = 2.805
2	μ = 5.72	σ = 0.572	σ = 2.860

Table 2.3   Experimental Scenarios

Scenario	Product 1 Demand CV	Product 2 Demand CV
1	High	Low
2	Low	Low
3	Low	High
4	High	High

Finally, reflective of a corrective maintenance policy (Shaaban et al. 2013) in which the time of occurrence and the nature of the next breakdown are unpredictable, the three manufacturing stages have exponentially distributed Mean Time to Failure (MTTF) and Mean Time to Repair (MTTR) with means of 90 and 10 h, respectively, resulting in 90% availability for each of them.

2.4.2 Simulation Modeling

Discrete event simulation has been recommended as a preferred method for studying the complex dynamics of stochastic manufacturing systems because of its ability to handle the unpredictability of such systems (Kochel and Nielander 2002). It has been widely applied in existing literature and a lot of the present understandings of manufacturing systems have stemmed from it, mostly because it allows for an offline representation and experimentation of a system without tampering with it physically (Onyeocha et al. 2015, Geraghty and Heavey 2005, Spearman et al. 1990).

The steps necessary for successful conduct of the non-terminating type of simulation of this chapter, as outlined in (Law and Kelton 2000), have been taken to determine the system warm-up period, number of replications, and the simulation run length. System initialization bias has been removed by first ensuring that the system is not started empty, but with the buffers filled with base-stock items and then deleting data from a 15,000 h warm-up period that was determined through Welch's procedure (Welch 1983). Welch's method is generally considered acceptable, and studies that have compared different methods often recommend its use (Alexopoulos 2000, Robinson and Ioannou 2007).

After the initialization bias data is deleted, the simulation is subsequently run for a 35,000 h run time over which the performance measures (SL and WIP) statistics are then collected. The initialization-bias-deleted run is replicated 30 times with different random number seeds across which the SL and WIP statistics are recorded and averaged. The run length and the number of replications are determined through a sequential approach until confidence interval half-widths that are within 3% of their respective mean. Statistics are achieved for the two performance measures, that is, a 3% precision in the measured statistics (Robinson 2005).

2.4.3 Logic of Operation of DKAP and SKAP under the EKCS and the GKCS

The logic of a policy differs slightly, depending on the pull strategy under which it is being operated. Therefore, the following sub-sections will provide further descriptions of how policies operate under the EKCS and the GKCS in a two-product, two-stage serial line. The two manufacturing stages used for these descriptions are sufficient to illustrate all the elements of kanban and demand transmission and synchronization logics of any multi-stage-multi-product serial system, including the two-product, three-stage system used in this chapter.

2.4.3.1 DKAP and SKAP under the EKCS

A DKAP policy operates in a multi-product system as a direct extension of the single product system. As shown in Figure 2.4, each part type has its own demand information and sets of stage kanbans, which are synchronized and transmitted independently of the other products in the system, as described earlier in Section 2.1.3. The only points of contact are at the manufacturing stages where parts that have been authorized for processing are queued in the input buffer and processed in a FIFO discipline, based on their order of arrival to the input buffer. It should be noted, that the FIFO discipline pays no attention to when the demand actually arrived for a part, instead it recognizes when it was able to synchronize with a kanban and a part for processing.

As shown in Figure 2.4, the order of processing of Parts, P_1 and P_2, at Stage MP^2, will be based strictly on the order in which they arrived at its input buffer, without any consideration for when their respective demand information, D_1 and D_2, arrived to their demand buffers, D_1^2 and D_2^2. Other disciplines, as described in Section 2.1.3, might handle this differently.

The SKAP would use the same FIFO discipline as the DKAP to order parts for processing at the manufacturing stage. However, additionally in the SKAP, the parts must be prioritized for accessing the shared pool of kanban. As shown in Figure 2.5, there is a shared buffer to which the kanbans, detached from the parts are returned for use by any of them. A kanban will be released to the parts based on time of arrival of their demand to a stage, provided there is a part available to be released downstream.

For instance, at Stage MP^2 in Figure 2.5, when a demand, D_1, for Part Type 1 arrives to buffer, D_1^2, a kanban is assigned from the buffer, A^2, to that part type to merge with it, provided there is a part in the buffer, $\mathbf{PA}_1^1$, that can be immediately released downstream. If there is no part, D_1 is queued in D_1^2 until one becomes available. But, if while D_1 is waiting a demand arrives to buffer, D_2^2, for the other Part Type 2 and there is a part in its own buffer, $\mathbf{PA}_2^1$, then a kanban is immediately assigned from the buffer, A^2, to Part Type 2 so that a part, P_2, can be released downstream. The release of a kanban to Part Type 2 will not be affected by the fact that Part Type 1 had a waiting demand in its own demand buffer. Therefore, the kanban buffer does not recognize the individual time of arrival of a part or a demand to their separate buffers, it only recognizes the time they become merged.

2.4.3.2 DKAP and SKAP under the GKCS

Similar to the EKCS DKAP, the GKCS DKAP is a direct extension of the single product system. As shown in Figure 2.6, each part type has its own demand information and set of stage kanbans which are synchronized and transmitted independently of the other products in the system, as described earlier in Section 2.1.3.

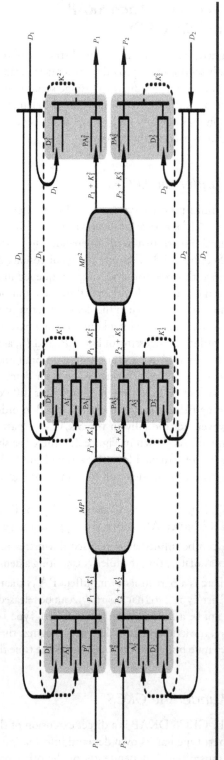

Figure 2.4 Operation of the DKAP under the EKCS (Baynat et al., 2002).

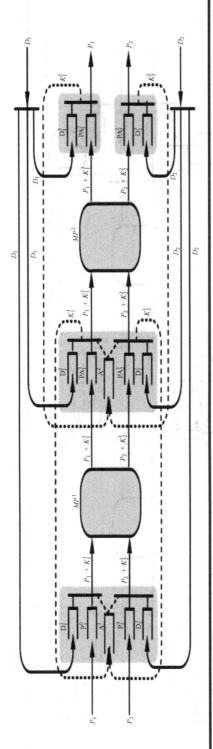

Figure 2.5   Operation of the SKAP under the EKCS (Baynat et al., 2002).

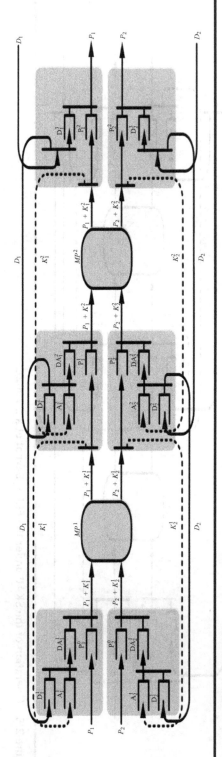

Figure 2.6   Operation of the DKAP under the GKCS (Baynat et al., 2002).

The parts only come into contact at the input buffer of the manufacturing stages where their processing is again done based on a FIFO discipline. The FIFO discipline also is entirely based on the order in which the parts arrived at a stage's input buffer, without any consideration for when their respective demand information arrived at the stage.

Although, the GKCS SKAP follows the same FIFO discipline in the processing of parts from the input buffer of the manufacturing stages, its rule for assigning the shared pool of kanbans differs. As shown in Figure 2.7, the kanbans that are detached from parts downstream are returned to a common buffer, from which they can be used to authorize the release of any of the parts downstream. The kanbans are assigned to parts based on the order of arrival of their demands.

As shown in Figure 2.7, at Stage MP^2, when a demand, D_1, for Part Type 1 arrives to buffer, $D_1{}^2$, a kanban is assigned from the buffer, A^2, to merge with it before the merged pair is added to the queue, $DA_1{}^2$. The pair, $D_1 + K^2$, then seek a corresponding part from the buffer, P_1^1, to release downstream. If there is no part available in P_1^1, $D_1 + K^2$ remains queued in $DA_1{}^2$ until a part becomes available. Demands that arrive to this stage subsequently for both part types will have kanbans released to them from A^2 in the order in which they arrive.

2.4.4 System Optimization

A Genetic Algorithm library offered by the simulation modeling software is applied to determine the stage-by-stage optimal settings of the base-stock (S) and the kanbans (K) for the strategies. The solution search space for each stage's setting is predetermined by conducting preliminary evaluations to identify the reasonable ranges within which to carry out their optimization evaluations. An objective function is then specified to the genetic algorithm library, which generates alternative settings, simulate and evaluate them until a 95% target SL for both products is achieved with the lowest average system WIP level.

The minimization-type objective function was formulated as follows:

$$\text{Min Cost} = \begin{cases} \text{WIP} & \text{if SL1 and SL2} \geq 0.95 \\ X & \text{otherwise} \end{cases} \rightarrow \qquad (2.4)$$

where:

X is a penalty cost for not meeting the target SL

In the objective function in Equation 2.4, it is verified if a parameter setting achieved up to the target SL of 95% for both products. If it does, its objective function is calculated based on the WIP. Otherwise, a penalty cost, X, is assigned to the objective function. The value of X is chosen to be significantly greater than the maximum possible WIP so that such parameter setting becomes an unattractive candidate for further evaluation. The same optimization approach is followed for both strategies, and their policies.

It should be noted that because the philosophy of the EKCS is to keep kanbans attached to the base-stock parts while they wait in a stage's output buffers, the simulation model has been implemented such that the initialized finished parts of the set base-stock level, S, have a corresponding number of kanbans, K. Therefore, the kanban number being optimized for the EKCS's DKAP and SKAP are the extra unattached kanbans, AK, where

$$AK = K - S \qquad (2.5)$$

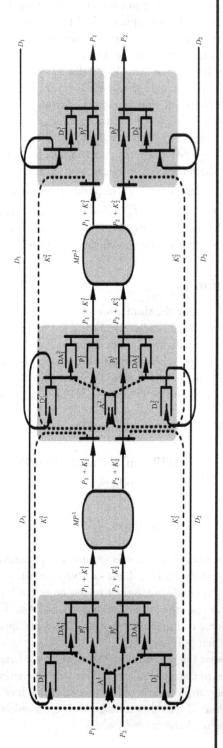

Figure 2.7 Operation of the SKAP under the GKCS (Baynat et al., 2002).

2.4.5 Design of Experiments for Sensitivity Analysis

In the sensitivity analysis, factors that are usually susceptible to environmental changes, that is, factors that are not within the control of production-line designers or managers, are selected and varied within the range of ±5% to simulate different experimental scenarios. The following environmental variables are chosen to reflect the possibility of an increase or decrease in the demand arrival rate and its variability, as well as the in-process variability which could create bottlenecks within the system.

■ Mean and standard deviation of the demand distributions of the two products; a total of four factors.
■ MTTF and MTTR for the three stages of the system give a total of six factors.

In total there are 10 factors, and the LHS technique is applied in setting up the sensitivity analysis experiments. As recommended in a previous study (Gaury and Kleijnen 1998), 100 experimental runs are derived from combinations of factor levels that are sampled from within ±5% of their base values shown in Table 2.4. The LHS experiments are designed in JMP® software.

Similar to the base settings experiments, each LHS run is replicated 30 times. Stochastic dominance tests are then conducted on the results obtained from the LHS experiments. The LHS results also are applied in investigating the impacts of the variabilities in the levels of machine availability on the products' SLs and the system WIP under different strategies and their policies. It should be noted, the systems are not re-optimized for the LHS run settings, since the aim is to investigate their robustness to variations that were unforeseen during their optimization.

Table 2.4   Part One Experiments: LHS Ranges for Sensitivity Analysis

	Product 1				*Product 2*		
	−5%	*Base*	*+5%*		*−5%*	*Base*	*+5%*
Demand	**Low CV**				**Low CV**		
Mean (h)	5.540	5.610	5.681	Mean	5.648	5.720	5.792
S.D. (h)	0.281	0.561	0.842	S.D.	0.286	0.572	0.858
Demand	**High CV**				**High CV**		
Mean (h)	5.258	5.610	5.962	Mean	5.361	5.720	6.079
S.D. (h)	2.525	2.805	3.086	S.D.	2.574	2.860	3.146
Workstations 1–3							
MTTF (h)	78.50	90.00	103.00				
MTTR (h)	8.72	10.00	11.50				

2.5 Analyses and Discussion of Results

This section presents the results obtained from the stochastic dominance (robustness) tests of the strategies and their policies, as well as the outcomes of the sensitivity analysis of the strategies to variability in the levels of availability of the machines. The stochastic dominance tests compared the results obtained for the strategies and policies across the 100 LHS experiments in each of the four scenarios.

It should be noted that the interpretation of stochastic dominance test results differs for a maximization and minimization-type objective. In a maximization objective, such as SL, a stochastically dominant option is favorable. However, the reverse is true for a minimization objective, such as WIP.

2.5.1 Robustness of SL and WIP under EKCS and GKCS

The results of the stochastic dominance tests that were conducted on DKAP and SKAP of the EKCS and the GKCS are presented in Tables 2.5 and 2.6. The tables show that in all four scenarios, the EKCS's SL for Products 1 and 2 stochastically dominated that of the GKCS on a like-for-like DKAP or SKAP comparison. The expectation that the GKCS's localized kanban transmission—as described in Section 2.1.2—would make it have a tighter WIP control was only evident in two scenarios. Therefore, it can be concluded that the EKCS provides a better trade-off for SL and WIP robustness than the GKCS.

2.5.2 Robustness of SL and WIP under SKAP and DKAP

The results obtained from the robustness tests indicate that the DKAP offers better SL robustness than the SKAP, as presented in Tables 2.7 and 2.8. In the 16 robustness comparisons conducted across the four scenarios for each of the two products' SLs under both strategies, the DKAP was stochastically dominant in 12 of them, out of which two were first-order dominance. Three of the tests were inconclusive, while the SKAP dominated in one of them.

However, the WIP control robustness comparison results for the two policies show that the SKAP is more effective at controlling WIP than the DKAP under the two strategies. This can be explained by the fact that the SKAP often requires a lower number of total shared kanbans than the total kanbans dedicated across the products under the DKAP. However, this seems to have a corresponding effect on the SL robustness as the SKAP is not able to summon extra kanbans to raise production in demand surge situations (Dallery and Liberopoulos 2000). This observation also might be related to those of previous studies that propose simultaneous and independent kanban control

Table 2.5 Stochastic Dominance Comparison of GKCS and EKCS (DKAPs)

DKAP	SL1		SL2		WIP	
Scenario	EKCS	GKCS	EKCS	GKCS	EKCS	GKCS
1	2nd order		2nd order		1st order	
2	2nd order		2nd order		Inconclusive	Inconclusive
3	2nd order		2nd order		Inconclusive	Inconclusive
4	2nd order		2nd order		Inconclusive	Inconclusive

Table 2.6   Stochastic Dominance Comparison of GKCS and EKCS (SKAPs)

SKAP	SL1		SL2		WIP	
Scenario	EKCS	GKCS	EKCS	GKCS	EKCS	GKCS
1	1st order		2nd order		1st order	
2	2nd order		2nd order		Inconclusive	Inconclusive
3	2nd order		2nd order		Inconclusive	Inconclusive
4	2nd order		2nd order		Inconclusive	Inconclusive

Table 2.7   Stochastic Dominance Comparison of EKCS DKAP and SKAP

EKCS	SL1		SL2		WIP	
Scenario	DKAP	SKAP	DKAP	SKAP	DKAP	SKAP
1	Inconclusive	Inconclusive	2nd order		2nd order	
2	1st order		Inconclusive	Inconclusive	1st order	
3	2nd order			2nd order	2nd order	
4	2nd order		2nd order		2nd order	

Table 2.8   Stochastic Dominance Comparison of GKCS DKAP and SKAP

GKCS	SL1		SL2		WIP	
Scenario	DKAP	SKAP	DKAP	SKAP	DKAP	SKAP
1	Inconclusive	Inconclusive	2nd order		1st order	
2	2nd order		2nd order		1st order	
3	2nd order		1st order		2nd order	
4	2nd order		2nd order		2nd order	

approaches (Chaouiya et al. 2000, Matta et al 2005). The independent approach, which is logically close to the DKAP, is reported to be more responsive to customer demands (Chaouiya et al. 2000, Matta et al. 2005), especially at high system capacity load (Matta et al. 2005). Also, it is reported to be more susceptible to keeping higher amount of inventory (Chaouiya et al. 2000).

2.5.3 Impact of Demand and Kanban Synchronization Logic on Products' SL Robustness

It was observed that the application of a SKAP between the two products often leads to the products achieving similar SL performances, irrespective if one of them has a less variable demand, which should make it achieve a relatively more robust SL. Under the DKAP, on the other hand, each product would achieve a SL performance that corresponds to its level of demand variability, as reported in a previous study (Olaitan et al. 2013). Operating a SKAP between the two products seems to cause the demand variability of one product to affect the SL of the other product, with which it shares kanbans. This was observed to be more pronounced under GKCS than under EKCS.

As shown in Table 2.7, under the EKCS, SL robustness achieved by the SKAP for Product 1 or 2 was at least as good as that of the DKAP in three scenarios, that is, in Scenarios 1, 2, and 3. However, as evident in Table 2.8, under the GKCS the robustness of the two products' service levels were consistently worse under SKAP than under DKAP. Scenario 1 was an exception, as there was no clear superiority between the two policies. This shows that the service level robustness of a product is more likely to become negatively affected when it shares kanbans under the GKCS than under the EKCS.

As a result, the EKCS would be a better strategy under which to operate the SKAP than under the GKCS. This can be explained by the differences in the logic of kanban and demand synchronization under the two policies. As explained in Section 2.4.3, a shared kanban becomes assigned to a particular part type as soon as it is synchronized with a demand or a part, since those two are already synonymous with a particular part type. This takes place in different ways under the EKCS and the GKCS, as illustrated in Figure 2.8.

In the two-product system illustrated in Figure 2.8, under the GKCS, the kanban assignment at Stage MP^1, takes place as soon as a kanban, K, from the shared buffer, A^1, becomes merged with a demand, D_1, for Part Type 1. The merged pair, $D_1 + K$, then seek a corresponding part from the buffer, P_1^0, to release downstream. If there is no part available in P_1^0, $D_1 + K$ remains queued in DA_1^1 until a part becomes available. During this time, K cannot be detached and reassigned to another part type. Therefore, if K was the only available free kanban at MP^1, a subsequent demand, D_2, for Part Type 2 will have to wait until $D_1 + K$ obtains a Part Type 1 and completes its processing, even if there was a Part Type 2 in P_2^0 that can be authorized for processing immediately. This would result in avoidable machine idle times that could otherwise be spent processing other part types. It seems the assignment of kanbans to a part type under the GKCS takes place prematurely and this would have significant effect in cases whereby the products' demand attributes differ significantly.

On the other hand, the EKCS does not assign a kanban to a part type without a corresponding part type being available for processing. As shown in Figure 2.8, a demand, D_1, for a Part Type 1 must have been synchronized with a part that is available for processing from P_1^0 before a kanban, K, is assigned from the shared buffer, A^1, to it. As such, there cannot be any subsequent delay in the use of the kanban to release a part for processing. It is worth mentioning that an alternative interpretation of the EKCS, which does not seem probable, is if the demands are merged with kanbans as they arrive, without regard for the availability of a part for processing. Such minor difference in interpretation would lead to significant variation in performance, similar to the difference between a minimal blocking or blocking policy could make in a pull strategy, as observed in a study (Bonvik et al. 1997).

It also might be argued that in the EKCS, a kanban can become stuck to a part type in the finished parts buffer, but it should be remembered that the EKCS already sets a separate base-stock level with attached kanbans for each part type, as described in Section 2.4.4. To some extent, the set base-stock levels limit the number of parts that can be in the finished parts buffer. Having extra parts beyond the base-stock level would only occur during demand surges. Such parts usually end up being moved downstream as soon as they arrive into the finished parts buffer. Therefore, it won't happen for too long that extra number of kanbans beyond a part type's set base-stock level will remain in its finished parts buffer.

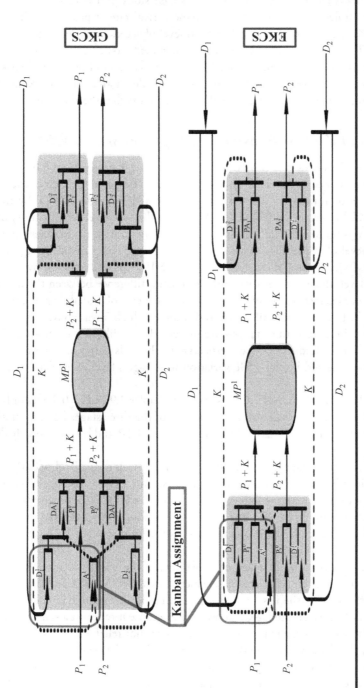

Figure 2.8   SKAP demand, part, and kanban synchronization (Baynat et al., 2002).

The initial sets of kanbans that are attached to each product's base-stock parts under EKCS ensure that the different part types will have a balanced level of access to the shared pool of kanbans. A kanban that was initialized on a product's base-stock part is very likely to be reused by the same product, unless there is a lopsided demand arrival rate or processing time between the products. The GKCS does not have such balanced level of access because the base-stock parts are not initialized with any kanbans. However, a possible remedy to achieve the same outcome in the GKCS would be to set aside certain proportions of the shared pool of unattached kanbans and strictly dedicated them to specific products. It would provide for an interesting research to investigate how these proportions can be determined and the factors that should influence that decision.

2.5.4 Impact of Kanban Transmission Logic on SL and WIP

In this sub-section, the impacts of the variation in level of availability of each of the manufacturing stages on the products' SLs and the system WIP are investigated for each of the experimental scenarios. The level of availability of a stage is derived by dividing its MTTF by the sum of its MTTR and its MTTF [i.e., MTTF/(MTTR+MTTF)]. The base level of availability of each manufacturing stage was set to 90% in Section 2.4.1. Therefore, the aim is to determine if the ±5% variation in the level of availability of a manufacturing stage has statistically significant impact on the products' service levels and the average system WIP. This was achieved by calculating if, at 95% confidence level, there was a statistically significant difference between the SLs and average system WIP achieved across the set of runs, in which the level of availability of a manufacturing stage was below the base level of availability, and those in which it was above.

The results obtained from this analysis are presented in Tables 2.9 through 2.12 for DKAP and SKAP of the EKCS and the GKCS, respectively. The cells corresponding to a performance measure that is not affected by the ±5% variation in a stage's level of availability are shaded in the tables.

Under DKAP and SKAP of the EKCS, as shown in Tables 2.9 and 2.10, it was only in Scenario 1 that the variation in the levels of availability of any of the three stages had any statistically significant impact on the products' SLs or the average system WIP, and this was mostly due to Stages 1 and 2.

However, unlike under the EKCS, the variations in the levels of availability of the manufacturing stages—specifically the first two stages—had statistically significant impact on at least one of the performance measures in all the four scenarios under the GKCS, as shown for the DKAP and the SKAP, respectively, in Tables 2.11 and 2.12. The variation in the level of availability of Stage 3 did not have any statistically significant impact on the products' service levels and the system WIP across the four scenarios.

In general, the variations in the levels of availability of the stages was more likely to have statistically significant impact on the performance measures under the GKCS than under the EKCS. This is particularly true for the first two stages, and could be explained as follows. Firstly, the impact of stage availability on the GKCS shows that, because it relies on a stage-by-stage demand information transmission, if the manufacturing stages are not reliable to complete the processing of parts on time, the demand information frequently will be delayed waiting for kanbans to be detached from parts that complete processing. Secondly, under the GKCS, the first two stages are more crucial because the last stage is by-passed in the transmission of demand information upstream. As described in Section 2.1.2, when a customer demand arrives to the last stage, it is transmitted directly to the penultimate stage without having to first couple with a free kanban, as done at the other stages. Therefore, even if the last stage is less available than anticipated, the

Table 2.9 Impact of Stage Availability Level under EKCS DKAP

Scenario	Performance Measures	Stage 1 Availability		Stage 2 Availability		Stage 3 Availability	
		Below Base	Above Base	Below Base	Above Base	Below Base	Above Base
1	SL1 (95% C.I)	0.897 ± 0.023	0.945 ± 0.011	0.903 ± 0.022	0.941 ± 0.013	0.904 ± 0.021	0.941 ± 0.013
	SL2 (95% C.I)	0.902 ± 0.018	0.941 ± 0.010	0.894 ± 0.017	0.950 ± 0.008	0.909 ± 0.016	0.937 ± 0.013
	WIP(95% C.I)	46.056 ± 0.250	47.066 ± 0.136	46.378 ± 0.257	46.776 ± 0.215	46.790 ± 0.231	46.364 ± 0.239
2	SL1 (95% C.I)	0.951 ± 0.002	0.950 ± 0.002	0.951 ± 0.002	0.951 ± 0.002	0.951 ± 0.002	0.950 ± 0.002
	SL2 (95% C.I)	0.944 ± 0.002	0.948 ± 0.003	0.945 ± 0.003	0.944 ± 0.002	0.945 ± 0.002	0.944 ± 0.003
	WIP(95% C.I)	33.573 ± 0.038	33.570 ± 0.042	33.573 ± 0.039	33.570 ± 0.040	33.576 ± 0.040	33.568 ± 0.040
3	SL1 (95% C.I)	0.941 ± 0.005	0.941 ± 0.005	0.940 ± 0.005	0.942 ± 0.005	0.941 ± 0.005	0.941 ± 0.005
	SL2 (95% C.I)	0.921 ± 0.018	0.913 ± 0.019	0.911 ± 0.020	0.924 ± 0.017	0.918 ± 0.017	0.916 ± 0.020
	WIP(95% C.I)	32.916 ± 0.256	32.822 ± 0.290	32.802 ± 0.288	32.942 ± 0.255	32.883 ± 0.266	32.860 ± 0.280
4	SL1 (95% C.I)	0.922 ± 0.017	0.923 ± 0.016	0.923 ± 0.017	0.922 ± 0.016	0.923 ± 0.016	0.922 ± 0.016
	SL2 (95% C.I)	0.918 ± 0.018	0.922 ± 0.017	0.920 ± 0.018	0.920 ± 0.017	0.923 ± 0.017	0.917 ± 0.018
	WIP(95% C.I)	32.659 ± 0.205	32.660 ± 0.218	32.667 ± 0.214	32.651 ± 0.210	32.682 ± 0.213	32.637 ± 0.210

Table 2.10   Impact of Stage Availability Level under EKCS SKAP

Scenario	Performance Measures	Stage 1 Availability		Stage 2 Availability		Stage 3 Availability	
		Below Base	Above Base	Below Base	Above Base	Below Base	Above Base
1	SL1 (95% C.I)	0.894 ± 0.023	0.943 ± 0.011	0.891 ± 0.022	0.947 ± 0.010	0.903 ± 0.021	0.936 ± 0.015
	SL2 (95% C.I)	0.891 ± 0.022	0.941 ± 0.010	0.887 ± 0.021	0.946 ± 0.010	0.901 ± 0.020	0.934 ± 0.015
	WIP(95% C.I)	44.738 ± 0.463	46.600 ± 0.260	45.121 ± 0.481	46.270 ± 0.356	45.880 ± 0.442	45.527 ± 0.454
2	SL1 (95% C.I)	0.947 ± 0.003	0.945 ± 0.003	0.945 ± 0.003	0.945 ± 0.003	0.945 ± 0.003	0.944 ± 0.003
	SL2 (95% C.I)	0.946 ± 0.003	0.946 ± 0.003	0.946 ± 0.003	0.946 ± 0.003	0.947 ± 0.003	0.946 ± 0.003
	WIP(95% C.I)	31.417 ± 0.080	31.421 ± 0.091	31.425 ± 0.086	31.412 ± 0.084	31.429 ± 0.084	31.407 ± 0.086
3	SL1 (95% C.I)	0.932 ± 0.013	0.927 ± 0.014	0.925 ± 0.014	0.934 ± 0.012	0.930 ± 0.013	0.929 ± 0.014
	SL2 (95% C.I)	0.926 ± 0.015	0.920 ± 0.017	0.917 ± 0.017	0.928 ± 0.014	0.924 ± 0.015	0.922 ± 0.017
	WIP(95% C.I)	32.700 ± 0.405	32.548 ± 0.450	32.505 ± 0.456	32.752 ± 0.393	32.649 ± 0.410	32.606 ± 0.446
4	SL1 (95% C.I)	0.909 ± 0.023	0.915 ± 0.020	0.912 ± 0.023	0.911 ± 0.022	0.914 ± 0.022	0.909 ± 0.022
	SL2 (95% C.I)	0.908 ± 0.024	0.914 ± 0.021	0.911 ± 0.024	0.910 ± 0.022	0.913 ± 0.023	0.908 ± 0.023
	WIP(95% C.I)	32.078 ± 0.554	32.156 ± 0.553	32.132 ± 0.568	32.090 ± 0.550	32.190 ± 0.553	32.033 ± 0.564

Table 2.11 Impact of Stage Availability Level under GKCS DKAP

Scenario	Performance Measures	Stage 1 Availability		Stage 2 Availability		Stage 3 Availability	
		Below Base	Above Base	Below Base	Above Base	Below Base	Above Base
1	SL1 (95% C.I)	0.863 ± 0.037	0.935 ± 0.016	0.872 ± 0.036	0.927 ± 0.018	0.879 ± 0.035	0.922 ± 0.020
	SL2 (95% C.I)	0.884 ± 0.024	0.938 ± 0.011	0.876 ± 0.023	0.947 ± 0.009	0.895 ± 0.022	0.931 ± 0.015
	WIP(95% C.I)	41.385 ± 0.853	44.579 ± 0.475	41.950 ± 0.890	44.099 ± 0.600	42.735 ± 0.872	43.370 ± 0.727
2	SL1 (95% C.I)	0.913 ± 0.012	0.960 ± 0.008	0.912 ± 0.013	0.955 ± 0.009	0.924 ± 0.015	0.942 ± 0.010
	SL2 (95% C.I)	0.915 ± 0.013	0.959 ± 0.008	0.915 ± 0.014	0.954 ± 0.009	0.922 ± 0.015	0.947 ± 0.010
	WIP(95% C.I)	34.088 ± 0.416	36.381 ± 0.332	34.282 ± 0.484	35.867 ± 0.421	34.843 ± 0.530	35.306 ± 0.469
3	SL1 (95% C.I)	0.911 ± 0.013	0.951 ± 0.011	0.911 ± 0.014	0.949 ± 0.010	0.920 ± 0.015	0.941 ± 0.011
	SL2 (95% C.I)	0.879 ± 0.036	0.918 ± 0.028	0.862 ± 0.041	0.933 ± 0.019	0.888 ± 0.033	0.908 ± 0.033
	WIP(95% C.I)	34.203 ± 0.682	36.079 ± 0.602	34.296 ± 0.804	35.873 ± 0.485	34.979 ± 0.683	35.203 ± 0.717
4	SL1 (95% C.I)	0.877 ± 0.037	0.935 ± 0.019	0.880 ± 0.039	0.924 ± 0.024	0.883 ± 0.039	0.921 ± 0.025
	SL2 (95% C.I)	0.862 ± 0.042	0.932 ± 0.021	0.870 ± 0.041	0.915 ± 0.031	0.883 ± 0.042	0.901 ± 0.032
	WIP(95% C.I)	34.960 ± 1.006	37.438 ± 0.672	35.282 ± 1.024	36.768 ± 0.867	35.879 ± 1.055	36.171 ± 0.878

Table 2.12 Impact of Stage Availability Level under GKCS SKAP

Scenario	Performance Measures	Stage 1 Availability		Stage 2 Availability		Stage 3 Availability	
		Below Base	Above Base	Below Base	Above Base	Below Base	Above Base
1	SL1 (95% C.I)	0.858 ± 0.034	0.931 ± 0.014	0.856 ± 0.033	0.934 ± 0.013	0.874 ± 0.032	0.919 ± 0.019
	SL2 (95% C.I)	0.866 ± 0.032	0.937 ± 0.012	0.863 ± 0.031	0.941 ± 0.011	0.881 ± 0.030	0.925 ± 0.018
	WIP(95% C.I)	39.859 ± 1.025	43.523 ± 0.548	40.328 ± 1.051	43.144 ± 0.655	41.395 ± 1.030	42.148 ± 0.849
2	SL1 (95% C.I)	0.889 ± 0.018	0.950 ± 0.010	0.887 ± 0.020	0.944 ± 0.012	0.898 ± 0.021	0.932 ± 0.013
	SL2 (95% C.I)	0.891 ± 0.018	0.952 ± 0.010	0.889 ± 0.020	0.945 ± 0.012	0.901 ± 0.020	0.934 ± 0.014
	WIP(95% C.I)	32.247 ± 0.658	35.359 ± 0.495	32.321 ± 0.726	34.850 ± 0.581	33.086 ± 0.787	34.085 ± 0.677
3	SL1 (95% C.I)	0.836 ± 0.049	0.901 ± 0.038	0.806 ± 0.057	0.926 ± 0.020	0.856 ± 0.044	0.878 ± 0.048
	SL2 (95% C.I)	0.832 ± 0.051	0.896 ± 0.040	0.802 ± 0.058	0.923 ± 0.022	0.852 ± 0.045	0.874 ± 0.049
	WIP(95% C.I)	32.457 ± 1.520	35.365 ± 1.344	31.855 ± 1.765	35.792 ± 0.895	33.626 ± 1.395	34.047 ± 1.623
4	SL1 (95% C.I)	0.812 ± 0.059	0.914 ± 0.026	0.824 ± 0.058	0.889 ± 0.045	0.836 ± 0.060	0.876 ± 0.043
	SL2 (95% C.I)	0.811 ± 0.060	0.914 ± 0.026	0.822 ± 0.059	0.888 ± 0.045	0.837 ± 0.060	0.874 ± 0.044
	WIP(95% C.I)	31.987 ± 1.678	35.695 ± 1.115	32.353 ± 1.656	34.809 ± 1.462	33.262 ± 1.693	33.900 ± 1.494

upstream transmission of the demand information is not delayed. The same logic can be applied to understanding why the EKCS's global demand information transmission ensured that the levels of availability of the stages had lesser impacts on the system's performance.

Furthermore, it can be concluded from these observations that the statistically significant impacts of the variations in the levels of availability of the stages on the GKCS's system WIP also is the result of a delay in the demand information transmission, especially due to low levels of availability of Stages 1 and 2. The GKCS's release of new parts into the system only occurs after the demand information has passed through all the stages to reach the upstream raw parts buffer. In contrast, the EKCS's demand information reaches the upstream raw parts buffer as soon as it arrives to the last stage, and it can release new parts into the system as soon as a first stage kanban is available.

Based on these findings, it seems a study that proposes a flexible routing of information transmission to create entirely new controls as needed is very promising for the customization of pull strategies to suit specific manufacturing systems (Gaury et al. 2001). Such approach can be used to by-pass the localized flow of demand information through an unreliable manufacturing stage.

2.6 Conclusions and Recommendations

The research reported in this chapter investigated the SL robustness of DKAP and SKAP of the EKCS and the GKCS in situations where changes occur to the original system conditions, for which they were optimized. It also compared the effectiveness of their inventory control in such situations. It found that the less restrictive kanban and demand coupling of the EKCS shows it offers a more robust SL performance than the GKCS, but this also makes it slightly less effective in inventory control than the GKCS. However, if the pros and cons were considered, the EKCS can be said to offer a better SL and inventory trade-off than the GKCS overall.

This chapter also found that the logic of kanban and demand transmission in a strategy determines its susceptibility to variabilities emanating from machine breakdowns. Specifically, it found that because the GKCS operated a localized demand information transmission upstream—unlike the EKCS's global transmission, it was more susceptible to machine breakdowns affecting its SL performance due to the delays that they might cause to the transmission of the demand information upstream.

Additionally, it found that this kanban and demand transmission approach and their synchronization logic also have implications on the level of impact products can have on one another's SL performance if a SKAP was operated between them. Under the GKCS, products in a kanban sharing group were more likely to suffer from the effect of one another's demand variability than under the EKCS. This was found to be due to the GKCS attributing kanbans too early to a particular product type. Also, when each product had its own set of dedicated kanbans under the EKCS and the GKCS, the products could maintain SLs that correspond to their respective levels of demand variability. Similarly, it found that the products generally achieved more robust SLs under the DKAP than under the SKAP, but the SKAP can maintain a lower amount of WIP.

Although, this chapter only focused on researching the application of the DKAP and the SKAP under the EKCS and the GKCS, the two kanban allocation policies also can be applied and researched in a similar way in some of the other pull and hybrid push–pull strategies. It would be worth researching them using a system that has a higher number of products and/or manufacturing stages, and which is unbalanced with products having different processing time requirements at the manufacturing stages.

Acknowledgment

The research leading to these results has received funding from the European Union Seventh Framework Programme (FP7/2007-2013) under grant agreement no 314364.

References

Alabas, C., Altiparmak, F. and Dengiz, B., 2000. The optimization of number of kanbans with genetic algorithms, simulated annealing and Tabu search. *Proceedings of the Congress Evolutionary Computation*, La Jolla, CA, 16–19 July, IEEE, vol. 1, pp. 580–585.

Alexopoulos, C., 2000. Output analysis: output analysis for simulations. In Joines, J.A., Barton, R.R., Kang, K. and Fishwick, P.A., eds. *Proceedings of the 32nd Conference on Winter Simulation*, Orlando, FL, 10–13 December, IEEE Computing Society, Piscataway, NJ, vol. 1, pp. 101–108.

Alfieri, A. and Matta, A., 2012. Mathematical programming representation of pull controlled single-product serial manufacturing systems. *Journal of Intelligent Manufacturing*, 23(1), 23–35.

Baynat, B., Buzacott, J.A. and Dallery, Y., 2002. Multiproduct Kanban-like control systems. *International Journal of Production Research*, 40(16), 4225–4255.

Becker, M. and Szczerbicka, H., 2005. Parameters influencing the performance of ant algorithms applied to optimisation of buffer size in manufacturing. *Industrial Engineering and Management Systems*, 4(2), 184–191.

Bonvik, A.M., Couch, C.E. and Gershwin, S.B., 1997. A comparison of production-line control mechanisms. *International Journal of Production Research*, 35(3), 789–804.

Bowden, R.O. and Hall, J.D., 1998. Simulation optimization research and development. In Medeiros, D.J., Watson, E.F., Carson, J.S. and Manivannan, M.S., eds. *Proceedings of the Winter Simulation Conference*, Washington, DC, 13–16 December, IEEE, vol. 2, pp. 1693–1698.

Chang, T.M. and Yih, Y., 1994. Generic kanban systems for dynamic environments. *International Journal of Production Research*, 32(4), 889–902.

Chaouiya, C., Liberopoulos, G. and Dallery, Y., 2000. The extended kanban control system for production coordination of assembly manufacturing systems. *IIE Transactions*, 32(10), 999–1012.

Dallery, Y. and Liberopoulos, G., 2000. Extended kanban control system: combining kanban and base stock. *IIE Transactions*, 32(4), 369–386.

Fishburn, P.C., 1975. Stochastic dominance: theory and applications. In White, D.J., and Bowen, K.G., eds. *The Role and Effectiveness of Theories of Decision in Practice*. Hodder and Stonghton, London, UK, pp. 60–72.

Gaury, E.G.A. and Kleijnen, J.P.C., 1998. Risk analysis of robust system design. In Medeiros, D.J., Watson, E.F., Carson, J.S. and Manivannan, M.S., eds. *Proceedings of the Winter Simulation Conference*, Washington, DC, 13–16 December, vol. 2, pp. 1533–1540.

Gaury, E.G.A., Kleijnen, J.P.C. and Pierreval, H., 2001. A methodology to customize pull control systems. *Journal of the Operational Research Society*, 52(7), 789–799.

Geraghty, J. and Heavey, C., 2004. A comparison of hybrid push/pull and CONWIP/pull production inventory control policies. *International Journal of Production Economics*, 91(1), 75–90.

Geraghty, J. and Heavey, C., 2005. A review and comparison of hybrid and pull-type production control strategies. *OR Spectrum*, 27(2), 435–457.

Grosfeld-Nir, A., Magazine, M. and Vanberkel, A., 2000. Push and pull strategies for controlling multistage production systems. *International Journal of Production Research*, 38(11), 2361–2375.

Gurgur, C.Z. and Altiok, T., 2007. Analysis of decentralized multi-product pull systems with lost sales. *Naval Research Logistics*, 54(4), 357–370.

Holland, J.H. and Reitman, J.S., 1977. Cognitive systems based on adaptive algorithms. *ACM SIGART Bulletin*, 1(63), 49–49.

Hopp, W. and Spearman, M., 1996. *Factory Physics: Foundations of Factory Management*. McGraw-Hill, Chicago, IL.

Karrer, C., 2011. Engineering production control strategies for complex discrete manufacturing-with a case study in electronics assembly. Ph.D. Thesis, Berlin Technische Universitat, Berlin, Germany.

Khojasteh, Y., 2016. *Production Control Systems: A Guide to Enhance Performance of Pull Systems.* Springer, Tokyo.

Khojasteh-Ghamari, Y., 2009. A performance comparison between Kanban and CONWIP controlled assembly systems. *Journal of Intelligent Manufacturing*, 20(6), 751–760.

Khojasteh, Y. and Sato, R., 2015. Selection of a pull production control system in multi-stage production processes. *International Journal of Production Research*, 53(14), 4363–4379.

Kimball, G.E., 1988. General principles of inventory control. *Journal of Manufacturing and Operations Management*, 1(1), 119–130.

Kleijnen, J.P.C., 1995. Sensitivity analysis and optimization in simulation: design of experiments and case studies. In Alexopoulos, C., Kang, K., Lilegdon, W.R. and Goldsman, D., eds. *Proceedings of the 27th Winter Simulation Conference*, Arlington, VA, 3–6 December, IEEE Computer Society, pp. 133–140.

Kleijnen, J.P., 2005. An overview of the design and analysis of simulation experiments for sensitivity analysis. *European Journal of Operational Research*, 164(2), 287–300.

Kleijnen, J.P.C. and Gaury, E., 2003. Short-term robustness of production management systems: A case study. *European Journal of Operational Research*, 148(2), 452–465.

Kochel, P. and Nielander, U., 2002. Kanban optimization by simulation and evolution. *Production Planning and Control: The Management of Operations*, 13(8), 725–734.

Koulouriotis, D.E., Xanthopoulos, A.S. and Tourassis, V.D., 2010. Simulation optimisation of pull control policies for serial manufacturing lines and assembly manufacturing systems using genetic algorithms. *International Journal of Production Research*, 48(10), 2887–2912.

Krajewski, L.J., King, B.E., Ritzman, L.P. and Wong, D.S., 1987. Kanban, MRP, and shaping the manufacturing environment. *Management Science*, 33(1), 39–57.

Law, A.M. and Kelton, D.M., 2000. *Simulation Modeling and Analysis* (3rd ed.). McGraw-Hill Higher Education, Boston, MA.

Liberatore, G., Nicosia, S. and Valigi, P., 1995. Dynamic allocation of kanbans in a manufacturing system using perturbation analysis. *Proceedings of Symposium on Emerging Technologies and Factory Automation (ETFA' 95)*, Paris, France, 10-13 October, INRIA/IEEE, vol. 2, pp. 595–603.

Martinelli, F. and Valigi, P., 1998. A dynamic control problem for a two part-type pull manufacturing system. *Proceedings of the IEEE International Conference on Robotics and Automation*, Leuven, Belgium, 16–20 May, IEEE, vol. 3, pp. 2753–2758.

Matta, A., Dallery, Y. and Di Mascolo, M., 2005. Analysis of assembly systems controlled with kanbans. *European Journal of Operational Research*, 166(2), 310–336.

McKay, M.D., Beckman, R.J. and Conover, W.J., 1979. Comparison of three methods for selecting values of input variables in the analysis of output from a computer code. *Technometrics*, 21(2), 239–245.

Moeeni, F., Sanchez, S.M. and Vakha RIA, A.J., 1997. A robust design methodology for Kanban system design. *International Journal of Production Research*, 35(10), 2821–2838.

Murino, T., Naviglio, G., Romano, E. and Zoppoli, P., 2009. Single stage multi product kanban system. optimization and parametric analysis. *Proceedings of the 8th WSEAS International Conference on System Science and Simulation in Engineering*, Genova, Italy, 17–19 October, pp. 313–318.

Ohno, T., 1982. The origin of Toyota production system and kanban system. *Proceedings of the International Conference on Productivity and Quality Improvement*, Tokyo, Japan, 20–22 October.

Olaitan, O.A. and Geraghty, J., 2013. Evaluation of production control strategies for negligible-setup, multi-product, serial lines with consideration for robustness. *Journal of Manufacturing Technology Management*, 24(3), 331–357.

Olaitan, O., Rotondo, A., Young, P. and Geraghty, J., 2013. Performance evaluation of production control strategies in a serial manufacturing system with two products having disparate demand profiles, with consideration for robustness. In Tempelmeier, H., Kuhn, H. and Furmans, K. eds. *Proceedings of the 9th Conference on Stochastic Models of Manufacturing and Service Operations*, Kloster Seeon, Germany, May 25–30.

Onyeocha, C.E., Khoury, J. and Geraghty, J., 2015. Robustness analysis of pull strategies in multi-product systems. *Journal of Industrial Engineering and Management*, 8(4), 1125–1161.

Pirlot, M., 1996. General local search methods. *European Journal of Operational Research*, 92(3), 493–511.

Robinson, S., 2005. Automated analysis of simulation output data. In Kuhl, M.E., Steiger, N.M., Armstrong, F.B. and Joines, J.A., eds. *Proceedings of the Winter Simulation Conference*, Orlando, FL, 4–7 December, IEEE, pp. 763–770.

Robinson, S. and Ioannou, A., 2007. The problem of the initial transient: Techniques for estimating the warm-up period for discrete-event simulation models. Technical Paper, Warwick Business School, University of Warwick, Coventry, UK.

Shaaban, S., Mcnamara, T. and Hudson, S., 2013. The effects of unbalancing operation time variability on the performance of unreliable lines. *Journal of Manufacturing Technology Management*, 24(3), 428–447.

Shahabudeen, P., Krishnaiah, K. and Thulasi Narayanan, M., 2003. Design of a two-card dynamic Kanban system using a simulated annealing algorithm. *The International Journal of Advanced Manufacturing Technology*, 21(10), 754–759.

Sivakumar, G. and Shahabudeen, P., 2008. Design of multi-stage adaptive kanban system. *The International Journal of Advanced Manufacturing Technology*, 38(3), 321–336.

Spearman, M.L., Woodruff, D.L. and Hopp, W.J., 1990. CONWIP: A pull alternative to kanban. *International Journal of Production Research*, 28(5), 879–894.

Vose Software, 2014. *Model Risk Industrial User Manual*, Vose Software, Gent, Belgium.

Welch, P.D., 1983. The statistical analysis of simulation results. In *Lavenberg, S.S., ed.Computer Performance Modeling Handbook*. Academic Press, New York, vol. 22, pp. 268–328.

Yavuz, I.H. and Satir, A., 1995. A kanban-based simulation study of a mixed model just-in-time manufacturing line. *International Journal of Production Research*, 33(4), 1027–1048.

Zipkin, P., 1989. A Kanban-like production control system: analysis of simple models. Research Working Paper No. 89-1, Graduate School of Business, Columbia University, New York.

Chapter 3

BK-CONWIP Adaptive Control Strategies in a Multi-Product Manufacturing System

Paolo Renna

Contents

3.1　Introduction

The control approaches to release orders in production systems can follow a pull or push control. Spearman et al. (1990), Spearman and Zazanis (1992), and Hopp and Spearman (1996) discussed the advantages of pull systems over the push systems. Several pull control mechanisms were proposed: Kanban policy (Monden 1983, Ohno 1988, Shingo 1989, Rees et al. 1987, Philipoom et al. 1987, and Berkley 1992), base-stock policy (Clark and Scarf 1960, Kimball 1988), and CONWIP control system proposed by Spearman et al. (1990). Buzacott (1989) proposed a hybrid control system, called Generalized Kanban control system, while Dallery and Liberopoulos (2000) introduced a new pull type control mechanism called Extended Kanban control system, which is a mixture of base-stock and Kanban systems. Bonvik et al. (1997) highlighted how the CONWIP and Kanban-CONWIP mechanisms are more robust with respect to changes in demand rate. Onyeocha et al. (2013) proposed an approach based on Base-Stock Kanban CONWIP in Shared Kanban Allocation Policy (SKAP) able to operate in a multi-product environment. SKAP uses a shared resource pool to allocate Production Authorization Card (PAC) to all the product type based on the availability of PAC and demand information (Duenyas 1994). The approach was implemented on Hybrid Kanban-CONWIP (HK-CONWIP), and they developed a new pull production control strategy called base-stock Kanban CONWIP (BK-CONWIP) control strategy. Table 3.1 reports the parameters to set for each pull control approach and for a single stage of the production system.

As shown in Table 3.1, the number of parameters to set increases with the number of manufacturing stages considering one product typology; therefore, the parameters increase with the number of product typologies. This leads to more complex optimization techniques to determine the optimal setting of the parameters.

The choice of the production control strategy (and optimization of its parameters) is relevant for effectiveness and efficiency of the manufacturing system. The main performance measures of manufacturing systems can be classified in three sets: quality, cost, and delivery of products (Drew et al. 2004).

A production control strategy controls the authorization and flow of material in the system and it is directly related to the work-in-process (WIP). WIP influences the productivity of a manufacturing system, the cost of production and the lead time. Moreover, the WIP can influence the product quality if the product quality depends on the amount of time materials spend in queue. The control parameter setting is important to obtain the effectiveness and efficiency of the manufacturing system. The optimization of parameters of a specific control policy under given constraints or objectives was addressed in several works. The fluctuations in demand that lead to the adjustment of control parameters have been studied (Tardif and Maaseidvaag 2001, Takahashi 2003).

The research proposed in this chapter concerns the adaptive control of the number of cards and the base-stock level of the buffers in as SKAP combined with BK-CONWIP to keep a high level of performance when demand fluctuation and machine failures occur. A controller has been developed to adapt the base-stock level and number of cards, to avoid setting parameters in advance. The controller uses the information on demand, final stock level and failures, to decide whether to add or remove extra cards. A simulation environment based on the Extendsim programme has been developed to test the proposed controller in-static and dynamic demand conditions. The performance measures are compared to a model proposed in literature to highlight the benefits of the proposed approach.

Table 3.1 Parameters to Set

	Parameters for a Stage	*Parameters for the Entire System*
Kanban system	One	—
CONWIP	—	One
CONWIP-Kanban	One	One
BK-CONWIP-shared	One (Kanban) One (stock level)	One
BK-CONWIP-dedicated	One (Kanban for each product) One (for each stock level)	One

The remainder of this chapter is organized as follows. Section 3.2 presents an overview of the production authorization cards policies and the production control strategies under investigation. The proposed control policies are presented in Section 3.3. The simulation model and experimental results are discussed in Section 3.4. Finally, Section 3.5 provides the study conclusions.

3.2 Literature Review

Several works have been proposed on the adaptive card control for Kanban and CONWIP with only product type cases, but little research has focused on the HK-CONWIP and base-stock control strategies with cards to share among the product types. One research path is related to the method of adding extra cards to the manufacturing system.

Framinan et al. (2006) presented two adaptive policies based on the standard CONWIP strategy system plus a queue with extra cards. The service level or throughput is monitored to decide the number of extra cards that are available. Renna et al. (2013) presented a dynamic card control methodology to maintain a high level of performance measures. The proposed methodology is based on the observation of customer demand to detect fluctuations and adjust the number of cards. The simulation experiments conducted in several scenarios highlight the better performance obtained using the controller. The controller was improved, including demand fluctuations and throughput rate, supported by a fuzzy engine (Renna 2015).

Belisario and Pierreval (2015) proposed a simulation-based genetic programming approach to learn how to decide, that is, to generate a decision logic that specifies under which circumstances it is worth modifying the number of cards. It aims at eliciting the underlying knowledge through a decision tree that uses the current system state as input and returns the suggested modifications of the number of cards as output. This knowledge is expressed under the form of a decision tree that can be understood and exploited by the decision maker, or by an automated on-line decision support system providing a self-adaptation component to the manufacturing system.

The effect of the policies to determine the number of cards in the case of multi-products has been studied in recent works. Gurgur and Altiok (2008) examined the implementation of a two-card Kanban control policy in a multi-stage, multi-product-system. They proposed an approximation algorithm based on: (1) characterization of the delay by a product type before receiving the processor's attention at each stage and (2) creation of subsystems for all the storage activity and phase-type modeling of the remaining system's behavior. Olaitan and Geraghty (2013) investigated Kanban-like production control strategies operating dedicated and, where applicable, shared Kanban card allocation policies in a multi-product system with negligible set-up times and with consideration for robustness to uncertainty. The control parameters are optimized by discrete event simulation and a genetic algorithm. Park and Lee (2013) studied a multi-product CONWIP assembly system in which individual components are made to stock, but a final product is assembled from different components to meet a customer order. They developed an approximation algorithm based on a decomposition method and an iterative procedure was then used to determine the unknown parameters of each subsystem. Ajorlou and Shams (2013) considered a multi-product, multi-machine serial production line operated under a CONWIP protocol. A mathematical model for the system was first presented, and then an artificial bee colony optimization algorithm was applied to simultaneously find the optimal work-in-process inventory level as well as job sequence order, in order to minimize the overall makespan time.

Romagnoli (2015) presented a methodology for the design and integration of CONWIP in a make-to-order firm. The proposed approach was applied directly to the flexible job shop of a real manufacturing firm in order to assess the validity of the methodology. The comparison between the two systems achieved excellent results, and showed that CONWIP is a very interesting tool for planning and controlling a complex flexible job shop.

Korugan and Gupta (2014) considered a hybrid production system with two distinct production lines, where one of them undertakes remanufacturing activities, while the other executes traditional manufacturing tasks. In order to control such production systems, they proposed a single-stage pull type control mechanism with adaptive Kanban and state independent routing of demand information. They proposed an adaptive Kanban control mechanism using stochastic queue network.

Onyeocha et al. (2015b) evaluated the performance of the HK-CONWIP control strategy and BK-CONWIP control strategy operating SKAP and Dedicated Kanban Allocation Policy (DKAP) in a multi-product serial flow line. According to their results, the BK-CONWIP outperforms the HK-CONWIP in a serial manufacturing system. Onyeocha et al. (2015a) showed that the SKAP uses lower production authorization cards and base-stock level than the DKAP in a multi-product lean manufacturing environment with erratic demand profiles. Also, the SKAP responds to demand variations quicker than the DKAP because the production authorization cards are interchangeable and can be used by any available demand, rather than waiting for a corresponding production authorization card before releasing a product-type into a system.

Al-Baik and Milelr (2015) aim to provide insight into the Kanban approach and its elements (concepts, principles, practices, techniques, and tools) that have been empirically reported by scholars and practitioners. Their study concludes that there is limited research that gives practitioners guidelines to set the parameters of the software that supports the Kanban approach.

Based on the above literature review, the following limitations can be highlighted:

■ Little research concerns adaptive card control for BK-CONWIP or HK-CONWIP that outperforms other approaches considering variable demand.
■ The adaptive control of the number of cards is often based on complex approaches, such as genetic algorithms, mathematical models, or heuristic processes with several parameters to be set.
■ The dynamic condition is often considered limited to demand profiles, while other conditions as failures were not considered.

The research proposed in this chapter overcomes the above limits:

■ The proposed control policies concern the adaptive control of cards number and base-stock level for BK-CONWIP and HK-CONWIP. The control policies are based on the demand observation and machine failure events.
■ The number of parameters to set are drastically reduced, because the number of cards for each production stage, while the number of cards for CONWIP and the base-stock level are not set in advance. The performance of a pull controlled manufacturing system depends primarily on the control parameter settings. Therefore, configuring a system using the best control parameter settings will produce the best performance of the system for comparative analysis (Koulouriotis et al. 2010).
■ Several demand profiles are considered to test the robustness of the proposed policies.

3.3 Proposed Policies

The proposed policies are based on the development of a controller that decides the release of extra cards in the manufacturing system. The developed controller works with any parameters being set, while the approaches proposed in the literature work with some parameters set as buffer levels or maximum number of available extra cards.

The controller works following a periodic review policy. It evaluates a set of signals from the manufacturing system and customer demand to decide if the level of the buffers should be increased or decreased. Figure 3.1 shows the main signals considered: buffer level (for each product type) at the last stage, the demand, and the cycle time of the products (for each product typology) through the production stages.

Figure 3.2 shows the signals considered for the buffer level. Signal 1 is the weighted moving average of the buffer level, while Signal 3 is the buffer level at the decision time considered.

Finally, Figure 3.3 shows the signals of the customer demand: average demand, standard deviation demand, and throughput time of the manufacturing system. Signal 2 is computed as the average demand (items/time) multiplied ("×" symbol) by the average throughput time (time) of the manufacturing system. Signal 2 evaluates the volume necessary to satisfy the demand considering the lead time of the manufacturing system. Signal 4 (dimensionless) is computed as the ratio ("/" symbol) between the standard deviation and the mean of the to evaluate the demand fluctuations degree.

The above signals are combined to decide on the necessary increment or decrement of the number of cards available and the release of extra demand to increase/decrease the buffer level of the final products.

3.3.1 Increasing Rule (Policy 1)

The increment of the number of cards and release of an extra production order considers the weighted moving average of the buffer (items) and the buffer level at time of the decision (items) combined with two weights α and β. The sum of the weighted moving average and the buffer level is reduced by the value of ratio between the standard deviation and mean of the demand (K dimensionless) multiplied by the average demand for average throughput time. The first term estimates the buffer level, while the second term evaluates the demand of items. The parameter K takes into account the demand fluctuations to improve the service level (K is the coefficient of variation of the demand).

If Expression 3.1 is true, then a new card is available to the manufacturing system with a request to increase the final buffer stock by a production order released. Therefore, the production order is released in the production system

$$(\alpha \cdot \text{signal}\,1 + \beta \cdot \text{signal}\,3) - K \cdot (\text{signal}\,4 \cdot \text{signal}\,2) < \text{signal}\,2 \text{ AND } (\text{signal}\,3 > 1) \qquad (3.1)$$

Figure 3.1 Manufacturing system information.

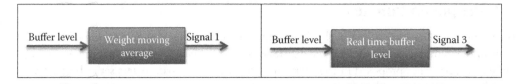

Figure 3.2   Buffer level signal.

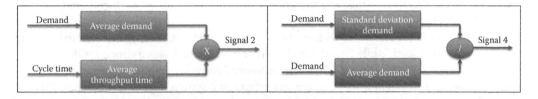

Figure 3.3   Demand signals.

Expression 3.1 uses the "AND" logical operator to combine two conditions. The first condition evaluates the trend of buffer level, reducing a quantity (evaluated by the parameter K) to consider the demand fluctuations compared to the forecast demand (Signal 2). If the condition is true, then the buffer will not satisfy demand, therefore the card increases. Signal 3 verifies that the buffer is not empty.

3.3.2 Decreasing Rule (Policy 1)

If Equation 3.2 is true, then the number of available cards is reduced by one (if the number of cards are grater or equal to 2)

$$(\alpha \cdot \text{signal}1 + \beta \cdot \text{signal}3) - K \cdot (\text{signal}4 \cdot \text{signal}2) > \text{signal}2 \text{ AND } (\text{signal}3 > 1) \qquad (3.2)$$

Expression 3.2 uses the "AND" logical operator to combine two conditions; The first condition evaluates the trend of buffer level reducing a quantity (evaluated by the parameter K) to consider the demand fluctuations compared to the forecast demand (Signal 2). If the condition is true, then the buffer is enough to satisfy demand, therefore the card decreases. Signal 3 verifies that the buffer is not empty.

The value of K considers that the combinations of Signals 1 and 3 can follow a normal distribution. In this case, the first part of Equations 3.1 and 3.2 considers the probability to stock-out of the final buffers. A normal distribution exhibits the following: 68.3% of the population is contained within 1 standard deviation from the mean ($K = 1$); 95.4% of the population is contained within 2 standard deviations from the mean ($K = 2$); 99.7% of the population is contained within 3 standard deviations from the mean ($K = 3$). Therefore, increasing K reduces the probability of stock-out.

3.3.3 Failure Control (Policy 2)

In this case, the control approach evaluates the failures of the machines. The information "signals" used from the machines are as the following (see Figure 3.4):

- total number of failures of the machines (number)
- the utilization of the machines in terms of total processing time (time)
- the utilization of the machine from the last failure in terms of processing time (time)

Figure 3.4 shows the signals evaluated from the machines, while Figure 3.5 shows how the signals are combined among them. Signal 4 evaluates the average time between two failures monitoring the failures of the machines by the ratio between the number of failures observed. Signal 5 over estimates the average time between two failures with a constant, considering that the Mean Time Between Failures (MTBF) and Mean Time To Repair (MTTR) follow a particular statistical distribution (this will be discussed in Section 3.4). Finally, Signal 5 is a binary value; if Signal 5 (average time between failures with over-estimation) is greater than Signal 3 (the total processing time of the machine accumulated from the last failure), then Signal 6 is 1, and a card is released to the stage and upstream stages in order to consider the higher probability of failure of the machines of this stage. Otherwise, if Signal 6 is 0, then the number of cards does not change.

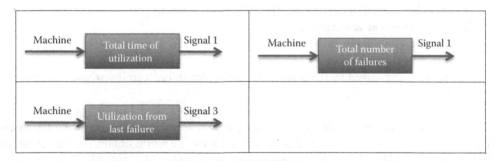

Figure 3.4   Machine signals.

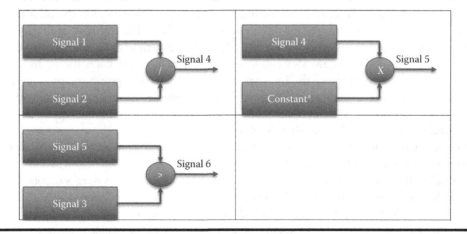

Figure 3.5   Failure signals.

The constant* for the computation of Signal 5 concerns the estimation of the failures. This constant is used to limit the cards added due to the failures estimate. In this chapter, the failures follow an exponential distribution with a coefficient of variation of 1; then, the constant takes into account this high coefficient of variation.

The periodic review time of the controller is not fixed for all products; the periodic review time is related to the product typology considering the cycle time. In this chapter, the periodic review time is three times of the cycle time observed during the simulation. This means that the periodic review time changes during the simulation of the production system.

3.4 Simulation Environment and Numerical Results

The manufacturing system considered is the same as tested by Onyeocha et al. (2015b), which was first proposed by Olaitan and Geraghty (2013). The manufacturing system produces two product types in a three-stage serial line, with the same manufacturing process. The demand follows a normal distribution and an unsatisfied demand is logged as a backlog and served before the next demand. The machines can breakdown considering only working status. Moreover, the following assumptions are considered.

- The set-up is included in the process time of the three stages.
- The information flow is instantaneous.
- Operations cannot be pre-empted.
- Each machine can process only one task at once.
- The queues are managed by the first-in first-out policy in order to investigate only the proposed strategy.

Table 3.2 reports the production system configuration and the parameters set by Onyeocha et al. (2015b). This configuration is used as a benchmark for the results obtained by the proposed policies. Moreover, Table 3.2 reports the simulation cases tested.

The cases 1–3 are the same obtained by the optimization proposed in Onyeocha et al. (2015b) and used as a benchmark. The simulations have been conducted for the three cases of the benchmark (designed in Onyeocha et al. [2015b]), and for the five of combinations of the value α and β. The five combinations are replicated for three values of K (1, 2, 3). The constant* is fixed, because the distribution of the failures' distributions are fixed for all experiments conducted.

The described simulations are also conducted in case of demand fluctuations. In order to emulate a dynamic environment, the inter-arrival demand changes during the production run consisting of three alternating stages. The inter-arrival parameter changes every stage with three different values of the stage length (5000, 2500, and 1000). If the length of the stage is lower, then the demand changed more times during the simulation.

The last scenario (Demand 4) concerns the scenario of temporary increment of the demand (a step). The experiments concern the following cases: 5 demand cases × 3 (cards and buffer stock parameters) = 15 for the benchmark cases and 5 demand cases × 5 (α and β combinations) × 3 (K-values) × (2 policies) = 150 cases for the policies with a total of 165 cases simulated. The simulation length is 50,000 h as in Onyeocha et al. (2015b), but the analysis is conducted considering termination simulation analysis [for detail see Banks (1998)]. For each experiment, a number of replications able to assure a 5% confidence interval and 95% of confidence level for each performance measure have been conducted. This leads to a number of replications higher than the replications proposed in Onyeocha et al. (2015b).

Table 3.2 System Configuration

Stage	Product 1 Processing Time (h)	Product 2 Processing Time (h)	MTBF Exponential Distribution Mean (h)	MTTR Exponential Distribution Mean (h)
1	1.5	3	90	10
2	1.5	3	90	10
3	1.5	3	90	10
Demand	$N(5.61, 2.81)$	$N(5.72, 0.57)$		

Benchmark Parameters

	Card 1	Card 2	CONWIP	Base-tock 1	Base-stock 2
Case1	13	13	32	16	14
Case 2	13	13	32	18	14
Case 3	13	13	32	25	24

Experimental Classes

	α	β	K	Constant*
Comb 1	0	1	1, 2, 3	4
Comb 2	1	0	1, 2, 3	
Comb 3	0.2	0.8	1, 2, 3	
Comb 4	0.8	0.2	1, 2, 3	
Comb 5	0.5	0.5	1, 2, 3	

(Continued)

Table 3.2 (Continued) System Configuration

Stage	Product 1 Processing Time (h)		Product 2 Processing Time (h)	MTBF Exponential Distribution Mean (h)	MTTR Exponential Distribution Mean (h)	
	Demand Fluctuations					
	Demand 1, 2, 3				**Demand 4**	
	Demand	Period Time		Demand	Demand	Period Time
	N(5.61, 2.81)	5,000/2,500/10,000			N(5.61, 2.81)	20,000
	N(4, 2.81)	5,000/2,500/10,000			N(4, 2.81)	10,000
	N(7, 2.81)	5,000/2,500/10,000			N(5.61, 2.81)	20,000

The average number of replications is over 1000 for each class simulated. Therefore, the results of this research are more general than the research proposed in the literature. The performance measures investigated are the following:

- Throughput of the production system. This performance allows the evaluation of the level of the throughput for each policy considered.
- WIP, it is considered the work in process in the production system except the final products in the final buffers.
- Service level, it is the average percentage of orders satisfied without any delay.
- Lateness, it is the average delay time of the products satisfied in delay.
- Average backorders, it is the average that waits to be satisfied in queue.
- CONWIP cards utilization (*Ut Con*) average utilization of the cards of the CONWIP control system.
- Kanban cards utilization (*Ut Kan*) average utilization of the cards of the Kanban control system.
- Total buffer; average level of product buffers stock level.
- Average utilization of the workstations of the production system.
- Sum of the WIP and final buffers stock level to evaluate the entire WIP.

Table 3.3 reports the simulation results for the benchmark and the two policies proposed. For each case and *K*-parameter of the proposed policies, it is reported that the combination of α and β leads to the better performance measures. The simulation results of the three benchmark cases lead to the same service levels of Onyeocha et al. (2015b), and these results validate the simulation environment developed.

In static demand, the benchmark leads to better results (Case 3); the first policy with higher value of *K*-parameter leads to service level close to the benchmark (−2.59%) with relevant reduction of final buffer (−16.22%). However, the average backorders and lateness are higher than the benchmark. The second policy with failure inclusion leads to the same service level as the benchmark, but a dramatic increase of the product buffer stock level.

The results show how the first policy without any parameter in advance and optimization of the parameters leads to result very similar to the benchmark. The proposed policy reduces the buffer stock level and WIP, but with higher lateness and backorders.

Figure 3.6 shows the simulation results for the four cases of demand fluctuations. The demand fluctuations are characterized by the inter-arrival change every 2,500, 5,000 and 10,000 h. The results reported regard the best cases for the combination of α and β.

In each figure, the number denotes the value of *K*, while the "F" denotes the Policy 2 that includes failures evaluation. For example, the case "3s F" denotes the case with *K* = 3 and the failures of the machines, while the case "3s" denotes the case with *K* = 3 without failures.

Figure 3.6a shows the percentage differences compared to the benchmark case of the service level. The control approach with failure leads to the better service level. When the *K*-value changes from 3 to 1, the performance level of the proposed control policies is worst Moreover, when the demand is stable (demand changes every 10,000 h) the proposed control policies don't improve the performance. Therefore, the proposed policies work better when the demand fluctuation is higher (demand change every 2500 or 5000 h).

Table 3.3 Benchmark Models

Performance	Case 1	Case 2	Case 3	Policy 1 (α–β)			Policy 2 (α–β)		
				20–80	80–20	50–50	50–50	20–80	20–80
				K = 3	K = 2	K = 1	K = 3	K = 2	K = 1
Throughput (parts/h)	0.35	0.35	0.35	0.35	0.35	0.35	0.35	0.35	0.35
WIP (parts)	12.49	12.50	12.51	14.28	14.22	14.32	24.38	24.38	24.34
Service level (%)	92.71	95.42	99.24	96.67 (−2.59%)	95.39	95.28	98.63 (−0.61%)	98.30	97.60
Lateness (h/part)	1.75	1.07	0.17	0.76	1.07	1.61	0.33	0.39	0.59
Average backorders	0.31	0.19	0.03	0.14	0.19	0.29	0.06	0.07	0.11
CONWIP cards utilization (%)	40.35	40.34	40.35	44.74	44.03	43.45	62.56	62.42	62.21
Total buffer (parts)	17.24	21.01	35.69	29.90 (−16.22%)	24.92	20.15	49.68 (39.20%)	41.68	34.10
Average utilization work stations (%)	79.04	79.04	79.03	79.08	79.05	79.05	79.33	79.29	79.24
Kanban cards utilization (%)	29.44	29.34	29.35	35.32	34.66	35.02	79.19	79.26	79.10
WIP + final buffers	29.73	33.51	48.19	44.18 (−8.32%)	39.14	34.33	74.06 (53.68%)	66.06	58.44

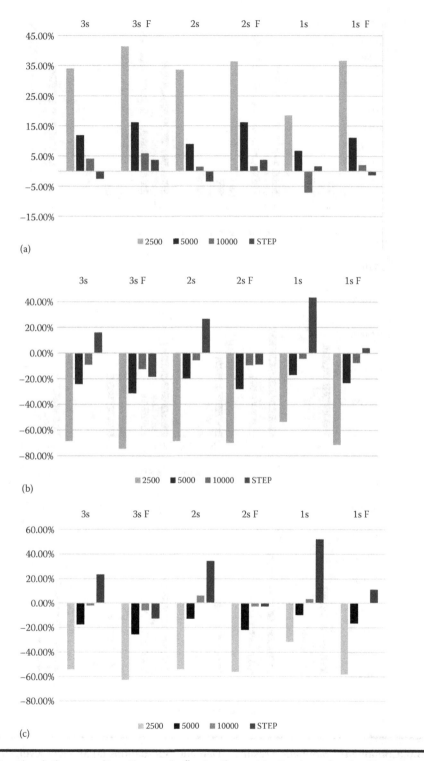

Figure 3.6 Simulation results—Demand fluctuations (a) Services level, (b) Lateness, (c) Backorders, (d) WIP, (e) Buffer level, (f) WIP + Buffer level.

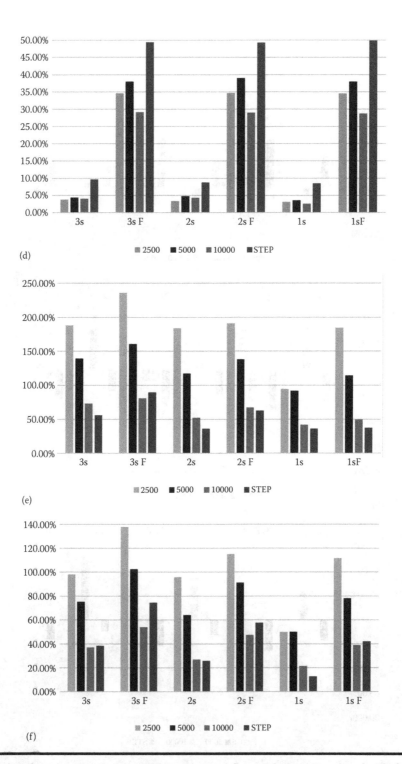

Figure 3.6 (Continued) Simulation results—Demand fluctuations (a) Services level, (b) Lateness, (c) Backorders, (d) WIP, (e) Buffer level, (f) WIP + Buffer level.

Figure 3.6b,c shows the lateness of the orders that wait to be satisfied and the average number of backorders, respectively. This performance has the same behavior of the service level. The better service levels are obtained with the increment of WIP and final buffer levels as shown in Figure 3.6d–f.

The first control policy allows to improve the performance with limited increment of WIP and buffer. The *K*-parameter can be used to control the trade-off between improvements of service level and increment of WIP and buffer. Appendix reports all the numerical results for the cases tested. The main performance measures are affected about 10% by the choice of the weights α and β

3.5 Conclusions and Future Developments

The proposed research concerns the control strategy of HK-CONWIP and base-stock. Two policies are proposed without any parameters to set (e.g., the Kanban cards, CONWIP cards, and base-stock levels) as the policies proposed in the literature. Two parameters for each product typology should be set for the policies proposed.

A simulation model is developed to test the proposed policies in steady and dynamic demand conditions. The simulation experiments are conducted with terminating simulations methodology to obtain more general results. This research highlights the following issues:

- The policies proposed allow to improve the service level in steady conditions and when the demand changes rapidly. The control policies are worst when the demand changes slowly. The main advantage in steady condition is to set a limited number of parameters. In fact, as shown in Onyeocha et al. (2015b), the design of the parameters is a multi-objective optimization with important time consumption.
- The policy with failure included leads to better results, but increases the WIP and final buffer stock level dramatically. Therefore, the policy proposed without failure leads to better trade-off between service level and WIP/final buffer stock level.
- The simulation experiments allow to provide a map of the main performance measures of the production system. The managerial implication concerns the decision maker that can make the decision considering the costs related to the WIP and final buffer stock levels with improvements gained in the service level, lateness, and backorders. The evaluations of the costs can drive choice of the parameters of the policies (as the *K*-parameter).

Further research should include maintenance activities into the policies proposed. The study can be extended to more complex production systems to highlight if the number of stages can influence the performance of the proposed policies. Moreover, the introduction of a fuzzy engine to control the parameters can improve the performance in more complex production systems.

Appendix

	Period Time = 2,500 (Demand 1)					
	Policy 1 (Best α–β)			Policy 2 (Best α–β)		
	0.2–0.8 K = 3	0.5–0.5 K = 2	0.5–0.5 K = 1	0–1 K = 3	0.5–0.5 K = 2	0.2–0.8 K = 1
WIP (%)	3.84	3.38	3.07	34.60	34.71	34.53
Service level (%)	34.05	33.56	18.47	41.29	36.37	36.64
Lateness (%)	−68.52	−68.50	−53.46	−74.51	−69.97	−71.26
Average backorders (%)	−54.28	−54.31	−31.72	−62.89	−56.26	−58.29
Total buffer (%)	188.18	184.12	94.58	236.17	191.34	184.80
WIP + base-stock (%)	98.19	95.89	49.91	137.78	114.88	111.44
	Period Time = 5,000 (Demand 2)					
	Policy 1 (Best α–β)			Policy 2 (Best α–β)		
	0.5–0.5 K = 3	0.5–0.5 K = 2	0.5–0.5 K = 1	0.5–0.5 K = 3	0.2–0.8 K = 2	0.5–0.5 K = 1
WIP (%)	4.40	4.82	3.59	37.97	39.00	38.00
Service level (%)	11.89	9.02	6.76	16.13	13.60	11.13
Lateness (%)	−24.05	−19.75	−16.92	−31.42	−28.22	−23.32
Average backorders (%)	−17.66	−12.84	−9.59	−25.51	−21.89	−16.39
Total buffer (%)	139.25	117.54	92.15	160.77	138.35	114.39
WIP + base-stock (%)	75.22	64.02	50.11	102.47	91.18	78.12
	Period Time = 10,000 (Demand 3)					
	Policy 1 (Best α–β)			Policy 2 (Best α–β)		
	0.8–0.2 K = 3	0–1 K = 2	0.8–0.2 K = 1	0.8–0.2 K = 3	0.2–0.8 K = 2	0.8–0.2 K = 1
WIP (%)	4.04	4.33	2.57	29.19	29.01	28.80
Service level (%)	4.16	1.46	−0.33	5.92	3.90	2.13
Lateness (%)	−9.04	−5.63	−4.44	−12.42	−9.49	−7.48

(Continued)

Average backorders (%)	−2.21	6.06	3.34	−6.03	−2.86	−0.33
Total buffer (%)	72.85	52.09	41.81	80.93	67.23	49.83
WIP + base-stock (%)	37.17	27.13	21.47	54.11	47.42	38.93
	Step (Demand 4)					
	Policy 1 (Best α–β)			Policy 2 (Best α–β)		
	0.5–0.5 $K = 3$	0–1 $K = 2$	0–1 $K = 1$	0.2–0.8 $K = 3$	1–0 $K = 2$	0.5–0.5 $K = 1$
WIP (%)	9.69	8.81	8.51	49.43	49.28	49.85
Service level (%)	−2.59	−4.40	−7.15	3.76	1.64	−1.36
Lateness (%)	16.11	26.45	43.16	−18.30	−8.89	4.18
Average backorders (%)	23.36	34.44	52.26	−12.68	−2.78	11.23
Total buffer (%)	55.90	36.25	15.61	89.72	62.83	37.58
WIP + base-stock (%)	38.45	25.89	12.93	74.50	57.71	42.21

References

Ajorlou, S. and Shams, I. 2013. Artificial bee colony algorithm for CONWIP production control system in a multi-product multi-machine manufacturing environment. *Journal of Intelligent Manufacturing*, 24, 1145–1156.

Al-Baik, O. and Miller, J. 2015. The Kanban approach, between agility and leanness: A systematic review. *Empirical Software Engineering*, 20(6), 1861–1897.

Banks, J. 1998. *Handbook of Simulation: Principles, Methodology, Advances, Applications, and Practice*. Hoboken, NY: John Wiley & Sons, Inc.

Belisario, L.S. and Pierreval, H. 2015. Using genetic programming and simulation to learn how to dynamically adapt the number of cards in reactive pull systems. *Expert System with Applications*, 42, 3129–3141.

Berkley, B.J. 1992. A review of the Kanban production control research literature. *Production and Operations Management*, 1(4), 393–411.

Bonvik, A.M., Couch, C.E. and Gershwin, S.B. 1997. Comparison of production-line control mechanisms. *International Journal of Production Research*, 35(3), 789–804.

Buzacott, J.A. 1989. Queuing models of Kanban and MRP controlled production systems. *Engineering Cost and Production Economics*, 17, 3–20.

Clark, A.J. and Scarf, H. 1960. Optimal policies for the multi-echelon inventory problem. *Management Science*, 6(4), 475–490.

Dallery, Y. and Liberopoulos, G. 2000. Extended Kanban control system: Combining Kanban and base-stock. *IEEE Transactions*, 32, 369–386.

Drew, J., McCallum, B. and Roggenhofer, S. 2004. *Journey to Lean: Making Operational Change Stick*. Basingstoke, UK: Palgrave Macmillan.

Duenyas, I. 1994. A simple release policy for a network of queues with controllable inputs. *Operations Research*, 42(6), 1162–1171.

Framinan, J.M., Gonzalez, P.L. and Ruiz-Usano, R. 2006. Dynamic card controlling in a Conwip system. *International Journal of Production Economics*, 99, 102–116.

Gurgur, C.Z. and Altiok, T. 2008. Decentralized multi-product multi-stage systems with backorders. *IIE Transactions*, 40, 238–251.

Hopp, W.J. and Spearman, M.L. 1996. *Factory Physics*. New York, NY: McGraw-Hill.

Kimball, G. 1988. General principles of inventory control. *Journal of Manufacturing and Operations Management*, 1(1), 119–130.

Korugan, A. and Gupta, S.M. 2014. An adaptive CONWIP mechanism for hybrid production systems. *International Journal of Advanced Manufacturing Technology*, 74(5), 715–727.

Koulouriotis, D.E., Xanthopoulos, A.S. and Tourassis, V.D. 2010. Simulation optimisation of pull control policies for serial manufacturing lines and assembly manufacturing systems using genetic algorithms. *International Journal of Production Research*, 48(10), 2887–2912.

Monden, Y. 1983. *Toyota Production System: Practical Approach to Production Management*. Boca Raton, FL: Taylor & Francis.

Ohno, T. 1988. *Toyota Production System: Beyond Large Scale Production*. Cambridge, MA: Productivity Press.

Olaitan, O.A. and Geraghty, J. 2013. Evaluation of production control strategies for negligible-setup, multi-product, serial lines with consideration for robustness. *Journal of Manufacturing Technology Management*, 24, 331–357.

Onyeocha, C.E., Khoury, J. and Geraghty, J. 2013. Evaluation of the effect of erratic demand on a multiproduct basestock Kanban-CONWIP control strategy. Proceedings of the 9th Conference on Stochastic Models of Manufacturing and Service Operations, Kloster Seeon.

Onyeocha, C.E., Khoury, J. and Geraghty, J. 2015a. Evaluation of multi-product lean manufacturing systems with setup and erratic demand. *Computers and Industrial Engineering*, 87, 465–480.

Onyeocha, C.E., Wang, J., Khoury, J. and Geraghty, J. 2015b. A comparison of HK-CONWIP and BK-CONWIP control strategies in a multi-product manufacturing system. *Operations Research Perspectives*, 31(2), 137–149.

Park, C.-W. and Lee, H.-S. 2013. Performance evaluation of a multi-product CONWIP assembly system with correlated external demands. *International Journal of Production Economics*, 144, 334–344.

Rees, L.P., Philipoom, P.R., Taylor III , B.W. and Huang, P.Y. 1987. Dynamically adjusting the number of Kanbans in a just-in-time production system using estimated values of lead time. *IEEE Transactions*, 19(2), 199–207.

Renna, P. 2015. A fuzzy control system to adjust the number of cards in a CONWIP–based manufacturing system. *International Journal of Services and Operations Management*, 20(2), 188–206.

Renna, P., Magrino, L. and Zaffina, R. 2013. Dynamic card control strategy in pull manufacturing systems. *International Journal of Computer Integrated Manufacturing*, 26(9), 881–894.

Romagnoli, G. 2015. Design and simulation of CONWIP in the complex flexible job shop of a make-to-order manufacturing firm. *International Journal of Industrial Engineering Computations*, 6, 117–134

Shingo, S. 1989. *A Study of the Toyota Production System from an Industrial Engineering Viewpoint*. Cambridge, MA: Productivity Press.

Spearman, M.L., Woodruff, D.L. and Hopp, W.J. 1990. CONWIP: A pull alternative to Kanban. *International Journal of Production Research*, 28(5), 879–894.

Spearman, M.L. and Zazanis, M.A. 1992. Push and pull production systems: Issues and comparisons. *Operation Research*, 40(3), 521–532.

Takahashi, K. 2003. Comparing reactive Kanban systems. *International Journal of Production Research*, 41(18), 4317–4337.

Tardif, V. and Maaseidvaag, L. 2001. An adaptive approach to controlling Kanban systems. *European Journal of Operational Research*, 1332(16), 411–424.

Chapter 4

Impact of Reworking in Job-Shop Environments Controlled by Kanban System

Pedro L. González-R and Marcos Calle

Contents

4.1 Introduction

Pull systems have proven to be, beyond their just-in-time (JIT) origins, an effective alternative to production controlling, based on the flow of cards (kanbans). Card-based production control systems (PCSs) such as constant work-in-process (CONWIP) (Spearman et al. 1990) and Kanban (Sugimori et al. 1977) have shown to be applicable to a great variety of manufacturing environments. These environments range from the simplest production lines in tandem, to more complex job-shops, or have even been applied to the coordination of the different nodes involved in the supply chain (Hopp 2007, Xiaobo et al. 2007, González-R et al. 2013). Although these systems are widespread, on a practical level, there are still no clear rules about the yield of such systems in specific scenarios. Practitioners' selection of a particular control policy is strongly conditioned by performance of the system working in specific conditions. One of the aspects that has been insufficiently addressed in the literature is the impact of reworking on pull systems. In many industrial contexts, the reprocessing or rework phenomena appears. We find this issue in the aeronautical sector, where after completing the process of a composite part, it can be necessary to repeat some of the steps. This fact makes the workload, balancing, and materials flow difficult, since a new rework on the system can modify the predefined schedule for the shop.

The influence of reworks in pull systems operating in a flow shop has been previously addressed in González-R et al. (2010). That study showed the advantages of using local control systems in respect to global flow control. A simulation study concluded that Kanban system (KS) performed better than CONWIP in a great variety of scenarios.

However, to the best of our knowledge, the effect of reworks in made-to-order (MTO) job-shop systems has not been tackled. Job-shop systems are much more complex to manage, and it can be expected that a small breaking event may have a very large impact. Therefore, the need to select the most appropriate PCS for reworking is particularly important, given that the implementation of a new system is costly and requires a change of culture, philosophy, and working practices (Stevenson et al. 2005).

Wein (1988) showed in an extensive series of experiments that the most important feature affecting the performance of a PCS was the input control. By building queuing models, he proved that improvements around 35% and 45% can be obtained by regulating the input of jobs in the stations. The rest of the decisions (such as priority/dispatching rules) have a smaller influence on the performance of the system. To manage the production planning and control, different approaches can be used. The selection of which type of PCS to implement depends upon the specific context in which it must operate, as each may have some particularities that makes one type of system perform better than another. One of these peculiarities is the occurrence of reworking (also termed in the related literature as re-entrant flow or reprocessed).

Our main issue is to understand the implications in the management features of complex systems (as in job-shops) upon the occurrence of reprocessing at a station, depending on the chosen PCS. For this purpose, we have selected two different approaches. First, the stations load limit by the workload control (WLC), widely used in MTO environments. Second, the stations inventory control by the KS (less used in these types of environments, but more efficient in limiting the amount of inventory in each station, and therefore with better prospects in the reprocessing).

Although we are aware that the KS has greater meaning and applicability in MTS environments and under the JIT philosophy, we use a simplistic version of KS for the MTO environment. This limits the amount of inventory at each station on the shop floor, but outside the JIT application, for which this system was originally conceived. More details are given later.

In this chapter, we study the influence of rework in the two aforementioned PCSs, under an MTO job-shop context. We conducted the research via a discrete event simulation and performed statistical analysis on the data. For each scenario, a simulation-optimization process has been performed, with the systems tested under the most favorable conditions for each operation. The results show the advantages and disadvantages of the KS with respect to the WLC approach in an MTO job-shop environment subject to reworking.

The rest of this chapter is organized as follows: Section 4.2 presents a review of the literature on the two PCSs compared, stressing the applicability in an MTO and the impact of re-entrant flow on the performance of the systems. Section 4.3 describes the implementations of the WLC and KS used in this chapter. Section 4.4 provides a detailed description of the shop floor under study, given that several degrees of directionality are evaluated in the job-shop. Section 4.5 describes the computational experience by simulation analyses, as well as a subsequent discussion of statistical results. Finally, the last section is devoted to drawing conclusions and pointing out possible research directions.

4.2 Literature Review

4.2.1 Systems in MTO and Job-Shop

The most widely used method for production controlling in MTO and job-shop environments is the WLC (Stevenson et al. 2005). The system has a long history, both in research and in practice. Thürer et al. (2011b) provides a review of the conceptual, analytical, empirical, and simulation-based WLC literature. The main objective is to deliver orders on time, while keeping the queue on the shop floor at stable levels. According to Gershwin's classification (Gershwin 2000) the WLC system is a surplus-based system, given that their triggering mechanisms are based on the difference between the cumulative demands and aggregated planning. However, the release of jobs to the shop floor is performed at regular time intervals, from the pre-shop pool of orders, which contains a list of pending orders. Accordingly, we can say that the release of jobs is time-based. If we expand the classification of the pull systems proposed by González-R et al. (2012) to push systems, the WLC can be considered a hybrid, as the system combines different types of release mechanisms: time and surplus. The release mechanism in WLC is determined by the workload level (norm). There are different types of load norms, so the performance is affected by the relevant choice. Regarding the different approaches of workload norms, Thürer et al. (2011a) studied the main aggregate load-oriented WLC approaches (classical load and corrected load methods) and concluded that the corrected load approach is considered a better and more robust option for implementation in practice. The WLC system continues to present potential for improvement and development, as shown in recent studies, such as Yan et al. (2016) and Thürer et al. (2012), which aim at improving approaches that combine continuous with periodic release.

A different approach to production control is through the use of kanban-type PCSs. The KS is a PCS that arises from the application of JIT philosophy at the production control level. One of the earliest descriptions of the system can be found in Sugimori et al. (1977), although we can find reviews on the KS in Uzsoy and Martin-Vega (1990), Berkley (1992), Huang and Kusiak (1996), Akturk and Erhun (1999), Kumar and Panneerselvam (2007), and recently by Lage and Godinho Filho (2010), or González-R et al. (2012). Usually, the kanban success is accomplished in repetitive manufacturing environments (MTS flow shops) with a continuous flow or production in reduced batches. The main objective is to keep a high utilization rate while maintaining the WIP at low levels. Rarely has the KS been found in research discussions or applications in job-shop environments, and its use in an MTO context is much less documented. We can only find some discussion regarding the interaction and integration with the material-requirements-planning (MRP) system operating at a higher level in the hierarchical planning scheme. For example, the KS has been applied in MTO (operating at the production control level) to meet the centralized plans established at a higher level in the planning scheme by an MRP tool (see e.g., Ding and Yuen 1991, Smet and Gelders 1998, Benton and Shin 1998, or recently Gong et al. 2014). We also can find their application in purely MTO environments, outside the guidance of an advanced planning system. However, there are only a few references, and the applications are limited to simpler assembly systems (Gravel and Price 1988). Stevenson et al. (2005) were skeptical about the applicability of such systems in MTO environments, but in Harrod and Kanet (2013) a KS was implemented in a job-shop environment.

The input control in the KS is mainly based on the flow control by a blocking mechanism that limits the maximum amount of WIP at each station with the use of cards. There are several pull systems that use cards, and in particular, different types of KS. For example, there is the single kanban, which considers only production cards. While the dual kanban uses two different sets of cards for each station, with one for production tasks and the other for transportation operations between stations. Each card is usually attached to a particular part (job) or batch of jobs at a station. The setting of the appropriate number of cards to the specific production environment is the most strategic issue, balancing the WIP, materials flow, and machine utilization (see Khojasteh 2016, Khojasteh and Sato, 2015).

4.2.2 Systems under Rework

In some core processes, it is considered more economic to rework those products that have not reached the required quality levels, than to produce a new unit. Reworking is often performed in the current station in the route, or visiting upstream stations on the route. The rate of defective products, and therefore the percentage of reworking, depends greatly on the type of industry in which it is produced (Lee and Zipkin 1992).

At the production level, the reworking has a negative impact on the system performance, since the lead time, WIP level, and the number of tardy jobs, are increased. The existence of reworkings often are signs of a deficiency in product design or perhaps poor execution at production level. In many cases the defects are not detected in a simple manner, so it can be interesting to determine the optimal inspection policy (Duri et al. 2000). These works are the basis on which to cope with defects in the design stage and to enhance the manufacturing process. However, there are certain products or jobs that are very difficult to improve, and they still have a high probability of being reprocessed somewhere in the shop.

The negative effect of reprocessing has been previously studied by González-R et al. (2010) in pull systems and by Thürer and Stevenson (2016) in WLC systems. González-R et al. (2010) observed (in an MTS environment), that systems managing local information (such as the KS) also manage the WIP more efficiently, compared with other systems using a global information system (such as CONWIP).

Thürer and Stevenson (2016) showed that the performance of the WLC system is significantly affected by reprocessing. The WLC system basically uses local information from stations, but also handles non-local information, being influenced by the workload levels of the stations in the route of the jobs.

It must be taken into consideration that the KS has the advantage of directly limiting the WIP at each station, so it may be able to limit overstock at the station where reworking occurs. However, the KS draws its maximum advantage from repetitive environments, and therefore, plays at a disadvantage in MTO environments compared to the WLC system. However, the resilience of the WLC system under reworked jobs is limited and smoothed by the difficult coordination between the local and non-local information in a bottleneck station. The main advantage of the WLC system is that has proven very effective in job-shops under MTO production.

To our knowledge, there are no works related to a comparison of WLC versus kanban working under reprocessing conditions. Since the input control method of both systems have a different nature, the fundamental objective, and main contribution of this work, is to test the performance of these two strategies, limiting the load of jobs on the shop floor (stations workload vs. WIP cap), by means of a comparison between the KS and the WLC system. Unlike Thürer and Stevenson (2016), who studied the impact of reworking in a WLC system with consecutive visits prohibited, our study focuses on the case in which consecutive visits are allowed, given that they resemble more closely the production and assembly of parts made of composite material (so important today in the aeronautical industry). Details and assumptions used in the experiments are given in Sections 4.4 and 4.5.

4.3 Workload versus WIP Cap

The detailed operation of the two compared systems is described below.

4.3.1 The Workload Control Operation

Customer orders are stored in the pre-shop, waiting to be released to the shop floor for processing. This list of orders is sorted according to a given criterion, usually related to the urgency of the work, by the planned release time. Jobs must wait until they are released into the shop. The release occurs when the current load level of the stations that must visit the job (route) is below a maximum load limit.

It must be considered that the job should neither stay a long time in the pre-shop P (to avoid delaying orders), nor should it be released very early (to avoid an overload in stations). It is documented how the pre-shop attenuates the effect of the variability of orders (Bertrand and Van Ooijen 2002). This releasing mechanism R simplifies the rest of the decisions in the shop, and therefore justifies the use of the FIFO dispatching rule in the intermediate buffers (Kingsman 2000). Figure 4.1 shows a basic outline of the WLC system operation, where ST_i denotes the station i, and B_i the input buffer of station i.

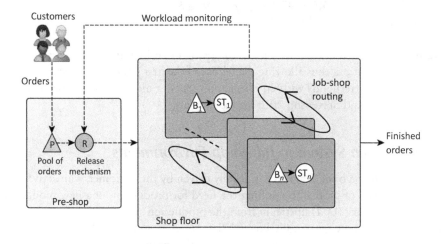

Figure 4.1   WLC system.

The majority of WLC concepts use periodic release where the period length must be less than the smallest slack of the jobs in the pool, to avoid delay. For a more complete description of WLC see Land and Gaalman (1996), Bergamaschi et al. (1997), and Kingsman (2000).

For a correct operation, it is necessary to select the workload norm correctly. There are different approaches for the workload, but in Thürer et al. (2011a) the appropriateness of the use of the so-called "Corrected Aggregate Load" is argued, because it is more robust and more easily applicable in practice. Therefore, our focus is on the Corrected Aggregate Load measure for the workload. The workload of a station is calculated as the total amount of time that a station is processing jobs during the release period T.

Let S_j be the set of stations that compose the route of a specific job j. A job j may be processed if each of the stations $s \in S_j$ fulfills that the sum of the current workload W_s and the load of processing the job j is less than the workload norm N_s^C. The load of processing the job j in station s, that is, the processing time p_{js}, is corrected according to the position of the station on the route of the corresponding job (in Corrected Aggregate Load method). Thus, for a job j with a route formed by s_a, s_b and s_c, the factors that correct the charge (depreciation factors) to each of the stations are: $d_{ja} = 1$, $d_{jb} = 1/2$, $d_{jc} = 1/3$. This allows consideration of the current workload along the route. Obviously, depreciation values are closely linked to the review period. The procedure for the WLC is as follows:

Every T time units:

1. Compute the planned release date t_j^R, for each job j in the pre-shop, according to the following expression: $t_j^R = DD_j - \sum_{s \in S_j} T_{js}$, where T_{js} is the planned throughput time of job j in station s.
2. Let $J:=$ Sorted set of jobs according to t_j^R, in ascending order.
3. Select j', first job in the list.
4. While j' does not fit norms (i.e., $W_s + d_{j's} \cdot p_{j's} > N_s^C$ for some $s \in S_{j'}$):
   a. Update $J := J - \{j'\}$.
   b. Select j', first job in the list
   c. If job j' is selected:
      i. Update Load: $W_s := W_s + d_{j's} \cdot p_{j's}$, $\forall s \in S_{j'}$
      Else: wait until next T period

There are other recent, and less studied methods that consider an additional release of jobs to avoid the station starvation, thus allowing the release of the first job in the pre-shop where the first station in the route corresponds with an idle station. Such a method has not been considered in this work (see Thürer and Stevenson 2016 for more detail).

4.3.2 The Kanban System in Job-Shop Environments

The implementation of a basic Single KS is usually driven by the customer, who activates the need to manufacture a type of product by pulling the need for production of a new product from the finished-goods-inventory (FGI) upstream from the production system.

In Figure 4.2, we show graphically how a KS operates in a tandem flow shop under an MTS environment, where ST_i denotes the station i, and B_i the input buffer of station i. The solid lines represent the flow of jobs, while dotted lines represent the flow of cards.

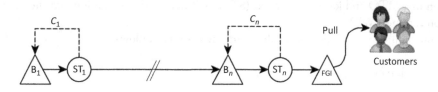

Figure 4.2   Single kanban system in flow shops.

Station i initially has c_i cards that are, at the beginning of production, available in a control panel. When a new job enters the station, a card is removed from the control panel, and is then attached to the job. A new job can enter the station whenever there are cards available in the control panel. When the process is finished, the card is released and sent back to the control panel, waiting to be attached to a new job. Therefore, the WIP at that station i must be less than or equal to the number of cards associated with that station.

Here, the considered KS consists of a pre-shop with the same function as the WLC. Jobs are sorted according to a particular criterion. In our case, we use the FIFO rule in the pre-shop, due to its practical simplicity, and as we will see in the results (see Section 4.5.3), it does not have a particular impact on the results. The release mechanism is responsible for monitoring and checking the number of cards available in each control panel of each station, at each moment. Unlike the WLC implementation of Thürer et al. (2011a), the system presented has an instantaneous release, provided it complies with the availability of cards. As a result, a job can enter the system if there are cards available in the first station of its route. Once the job is finished in one station, the card attached returns to the control panel where it will be available for another job as required. The job coming out of a station passes to the next station on its route, provided that it has cards available. In the case of no availability of cards in the control panel, the job remains in its source station, blocking the machine. Once there are cards available at the station, the job continues its established route and the source machine is unlocked. Figure 4.3 shows a basic outline of the KS

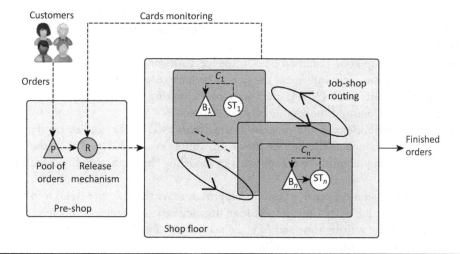

Figure 4.3   Single kanban system in job-shop.

operation in a MTO and job-shop context (ST_i and B_i denote the ith station and the input buffer of station i, respectively).

The procedure for the job-shop kanban order release is as follows:

On every Job event:

1. Let $J := $ Sorted set of jobs in the pre-shop pool according the FIFO rule.
2. For every station i:
   a. Set $NCi := $ number of cards available in the control panel of station i, S_i.
3. Select j', first job in the list, and set j'_0 the first station of the route of j'.
4. While $NC_{S_{j_0}} > 0$:
   a. Update $J := J - \{j'\}$.
   b. Select j', first job in the list, and set j'_0 the first station of the route of j'.
   c. If job j' is selected:
      i. Update $NC_{S_{j_0}} := NC_{S_{j_0}} - 1$
      Else: wait until next job event

4.4 Job-Shop Description

The different configurations of the shops affect the performance of the PCS. The level of flow direction is related to the existence of one or more dominant flows. At one extreme of the flow direction scale is the General Flow Shop (fully directed routing or 100% directed routing) where the elements of the routing vector (which represent the stations) are sorted in ascending order (see Figure 4.4a). Thus, if Stations 1 and 2 are part of the routing vector, the Station 1 will always be visited just before the Station 2. At the other extreme of the flow direction scale is found the Pure Job-shop (undirected routing or 0% directed routing), where the routing vector is completely random (see Figure 4.4b). Thus, all stations have the same probability of being visited in any step. The routing vectors can be directed at any degree between 0% and 100%, by sorting the routing vector. The sorting procedure used by Thürer et al. (2011a) consists of generating a random number to decide whether a work station moves to a new (sorted) position in the routing of a job or whether it maintains its old uniformly distributed position.

Regarding the shop floor, common sizes in the literature range from 4–12 stations (Thürer et al. 2011a). Another issue that influences the system performance is the length of the routing vector. As shown in Thürer et al. (2011a), the length of the routing vector usually follows a uniform distribution between one and the total number of stations.

Among the distributions of the processing time most used in the studies are the Uniform, Exponential, Gamma and 2-Erlang. As shown in Thürer et al. (2011a, 2012), the truncated 2-Erlang distribution presents a better approach to modeling the processing times found in real-life shops.

Regarding the customer's order, a common approach to set the due date (DD) is to add a random allowance to the job entry time to include an urgency variation range among jobs, where m is the minimum value of waiting time and M is the maximum value (see Thürer et al. [2011a], Land [2004, 2006], and Oosterman et al. [2000]).

$$DD = \text{Job entry time} + \text{allowance} \qquad (4.1)$$

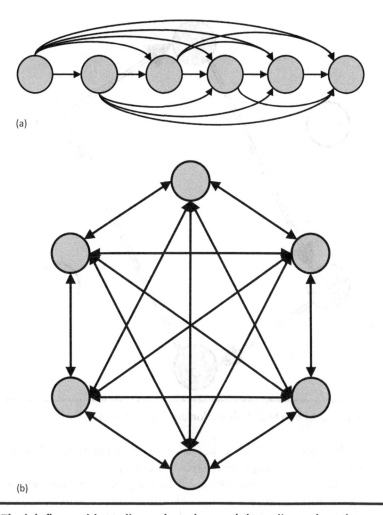

(a)

(b)

Figure 4.4   The job flows with (a) directed routings and (b) undirected routings.

In addition to the above issues, another factor that can influence the performance of the PCS is the reworking of production orders.

Finally, we should mention the Lockup phenomenon (Harrod and Kanet 2013) that occurs in the KS when the flow is not fully directed. In the KS, a station is blocked when there are no available cards in the next station of the routing vector. When this phenomenon occurs the set of blocked stations form a closed loop, in which each station is blocked by a single station and, at the same time, this station blocks another station (see Figure 4.5).

4.5 Computational Experience

4.5.1 Shops Model

This chapter considers a shop floor composed of eight work stations. As in other works (see Thürer et al. 2010, Land 2006, and Oosterman et al. 2000), the routing length is uniformly distributed between one and the total number of stations (eight stations in this study). It will be assumed that

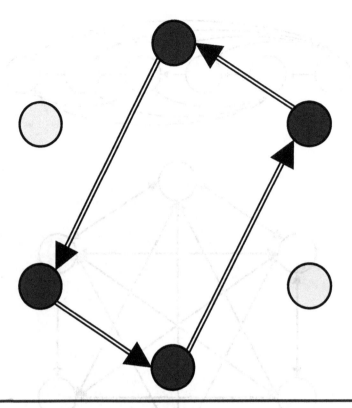

Figure 4.5   Closed loop of blocked stations (lockup phenomena).

a manufacturing order does not visit the same station twice and all stations have an equal probability of being visited (the reworking issue is explained below).

As in recent studies (Thürer et al. 2011a, 2012), the processing times follow a truncated 2-Erlang distribution with a non-truncated mean of 1 time unit and a maximum of 4 time units. In this work, set-up times have not been considered.

To avoid shop congestion, the shop floor occupation rate is set to 80%. Thus, none of the stations will exceed the utilization level of 90% in any scenario of this study, including scenarios with reworking. The inter-arrival times is distributed exponentially, with a mean time set to 0.703125 time units, whose mean value has been adjusted by Equation 4.2 (see Thürer et al. [2011a] for more details):

$$\text{Occupation} = \frac{\text{mean processing time} \times \text{mean routing length}}{\text{inter-arrival time} \times \text{capacity of the shop floor}} \tag{4.2}$$

As in many other studies (see Thürer et al. 2011a and Land 2004), a FIFO dispatching rule is used on the shop floor.

The WLC model studied in this work implements the Corrected Aggregate Load approach (see description in Section 4.3.1) for accounting the workload of a job to the backlog of each station, and as in Thürer et al. (2011a), the system performs a periodic release every $T = 5$ time units. In the release procedure of the WLC model, the planned throughput time, T_{js}, of job j in station s is set to 5, according to Thürer et al. (2010).

Regarding the adjustment process of WLC and KS, the optimization software [OptQuest, developed by Glover et al. (1996)] is used to find (1) the optimum values for the workload norm for each station, in the WLC model; and (2) the optimum number of cards for each station, in the KS model. In this chapter, the optimization procedure is stopped after 200 iterations. Equation 4.3 defines the objective function used:

$$\text{Objective function} = \text{Shop-floor throughput time} + \text{gross throughput time} \qquad (4.3)$$

where,

$$\text{Gross throughput time} = \text{Shop-floor throughput time} + \text{pool delay} \qquad (4.4)$$

As in Thürer et al. (2011a), the objective function used in this study aims to reduce the amount of time that a job waits on the shop floor. Therefore implying a reduction of the WIP level, and making lead times more predictable. This objective function is considered the most adequate and simple, aiding reliability, and allowing us to interpret the results with more confidence.

The DD is set by simply adding a random allowance to the job entry time to include an urgency variation range among jobs, according to Land (2004) procedure:

$$\text{DD} = \text{Job entry time} + \text{allowance}; \quad \text{allowance} \sim U[m, M] \qquad (4.5)$$

A minimum waiting time allowance (m) time units and a maximum (M) of 50 time units have been used. The minimum is set to cover a station throughput time of 5 time units for the maximum of eight operations plus a waiting time before release of 5 time units. The value of the maximum waiting time allowance (M) is chosen in order that the basic set of experiments result in a percentage tardy between 5% and 20%.

The KS modeled in this chapter implements a mechanism to prevent the lockup phenomenon. This mechanism consists of triggering a checking procedure of closed loops on every job event. If a closed loop is detected, this mechanism throws an unblocking signal to all stations which constitute the loop.

4.5.2 Analysis of Results

In this chapter, we use simulation to study the performance of the KS and the WLC systems in multiple scenarios. Specifically, we use ARENA®, a discrete event simulation software. Simulation studies have been carried out following a full factorial design of experiments. The design of experiments contains three factors. The first factor includes the different PCSs compared in this research. The PCS factor considers that the low level (–1) corresponds to the WLC system. At the same time, the high level (+1) corresponds to the KS. To take into account the influence on different shop floor configurations, the second factor includes the different levels of flow direction. The low level (–1) corresponds to the 0% directed routing (Pure Job-shop). The central level (0) corresponds to the 50% directed routing. And the high level (+1) corresponds to the 100% directed routing (general flow shop). Finally, the third factor contains different levels of reworking. The central position in the route (Station 5) is the only station with random reworking (consecutive visits are allowed). Therefore, the low level (–1) corresponds to the rework ratio of 0% of the orders processed in Station 5. The central level (0) corresponds to the rework ratio of 1% of the orders processed in Station 5. And the high level (+1) corresponds to the rework ratio of 5% of the orders processed in Station 5.

As in Thürer et al. (2010, 2011a), for each one of the resulting scenarios 100 replicates have been performed (Law and Kelton 2000). In order to capture the real system performance, in all cases, a warm-up period of 3000 time units is considered. The run length of simulations is set to 10,000 time units.

4.5.3 Discussion of Results

The responses of the systems studied in the different scenarios have been measured by the following indicators: percentage tardy, pre-shop inventory level, WIP level, gross throughput time, pre-shop time, and shop-floor throughput time. The three main hypotheses to use the ANOVA parametric technique (normality, homoscedasticity, and independence of the residuals) have been checked and no remarkable alterations were observed. Consequently, the influence that the factors studied in this work exert on the performance were evaluated by using ANOVA analysis. Table 4.1 presents the results of the Factorial ANOVA (i.e., a single-factor analysis of variance). A summary of the simulation results is shown in Table 4.2.

Alternatively, the progress of responses for the different levels of each factor has been tracked using an analysis of means (ANOM) technique (see Figures 4.6 through 4.11), showing the confidence intervals (Upper and Lower Decision Limits).

Regarding the tardy jobs, the ANOVA results show that the three factors studied in this work exert a significant influence on it. As shown in Figure 4.6, KS outperforms the WLC. Furthermore, Figure 4.6 shows a significant difference between the performances of the different levels of direction routing. Finally, Figure 4.6 shows that although an increase of the reworking level causes an increase in the number of tardy jobs; this variation range has on average the lowest impact of the three studied factors.

Regarding the WIP level, the ANOVA results also show that the three studied factors also exert a significant influence on the WIP level. Figure 4.7 shows that the WIP levels achieved by the KS are higher than the WLC levels. This is because the pre-shop is practically empty in the KS. Nevertheless, the magnitude of orders of both systems are close. Regarding the influence of the flow direction, Figure 4.7 shows a decrease of the WIP level when the flow direction level increases, and an increase of the WIP level when the rework ratio increases.

The ANOVA of the pre-shop inventory level shows that the three studied factors exert a significant influence. As shown in Figure 4.8 the mean values are practically zero in KS, while they are clearly non-zero in WLC. Therefore, the impact of the dispatching rule in the pre-shop is negligible, and the use of the FIFO rule is justified. The influence that the flow direction exerts on the pre-shop is like the influence exerted on the tardy jobs. Figure 4.8 shows an appreciable difference between the performance of the undirected routing and the directed routing, and an insignificant difference between levels dissimilar to the 100% directed flow. Although a decrease of the pre-shop level occurs when the rework ratio increases, the variation range due to the rework factor is the narrowest, as can be seen in Figure 4.8 and can be deduced by the lowest F-ratio of the ANOVA results.

Regarding gross throughput time, the ANOVA results show that the three factors studied in this work exert a significant influence on it. As in the analysis of tardy jobs, Figure 4.9 shows that KS outperforms the WLC. In a similar manner, Figure 4.9 shows a significant difference between the performance of the undirected routing, and the directed routing, while the levels achieved by the different degrees of undirected routing (i.e., 0% and 50% directed

Table 4.1   Results of the Factorial ANOVA

	Source of Variance	Sum of Squares	Degree of Freedom	Mean Squares	F-Ratio	p-Value
Percentage tardy	(PCS)	4243	1	4243	1796	<0.001
	(RD)	807.2	2	403.6	170.9	<0.001
	(RWL)	218.6	2	109.3	46.28	<0.001
	PCS×RD	30.79	2	15.4	6.518	0.002
	PCS×RWL	2.671	2	1.335	0.5654	0.569
	RD×RWL	7.609	4	1.902	0.8053	0.522
	PCS×RD×RWL	8.423	4	2.106	0.8914	0.469
	Within (error)	1233	522	2.362		
WIP level	(PCS)	303.4	1	303.4	259.6	<0.001
	(RD)	48.92	2	24.46	20.93	<0.001
	(RWL)	97.75	2	48.88	41.82	<0.001
	PCS×RD	277	2	138.5	118.5	<0.001
	PCS×RWL	3.779	2	1.889	1.616	0.200
	RD×RWL	7.195	4	1.789	1.539	0.190
	PCS×RD×RWL	10.49	4	2.623	2.244	0.063
	Within (error)	610.1	522	1.169		
Pre-shop inventory level	(PCS)	5184	1	5184	29,560	<0.001
	(RD)	242.6	2	121.3	691.7	<0.001
	(RWL)	2.262	2	1.131	6.447	0.002
	PCS×RD	242.8	2	121.4	692.2	<0.001
	PCS×RWL	2.27	2	1.135	6.47	0.002
	RD×RWL	12.21	4	3.052	17.4	<0.001
	PCS×RD×RWL	12.24	4	3.059	17.44	<0.001
	Within (error)	91.55	522	0.1754		

(*Continued*)

Table 4.1 (Continued)   Results of the Factorial ANOVA

	Source of Variance	Sum of Squares	Degree of Freedom	Mean Squares	F-Ratio	p-Value
Gross throughput time	(PCS)	1572	1	1572	1712	<0.001
	(RD)	280.1	2	140	152.5	<0.001
	(RWL)	31.32	2	15.66	17.06	<0.001
	PCS×RD	7.795	2	3.897	4.245	0.015
	PCS×RWL	0.3429	2	0.1715	0.1867	0.830
	RD×RWL	1.033	4	0.2581	0.2812	0.890
	PCS×RD×RWL	2.74	4	0.6849	0.7461	0.561
	Within (error)	479.2	522	0.9181		
Shop-floor throughput time	(PCS)	120.2	1	120.2	160.3	<0.001
	(RD)	39.62	2	19.31	25.76	<0.001
	(RWL)	42.98	2	21.49	28.67	<0.001
	PCS×RD	116.2	2	58.12	77.55	<0.001
	PCS×RWL	2.424	2	1.212	1.617	0.199
	RD×RWL	3.013	4	0.7534	1.005	0.404
	PCS×RD×RWL	5.488	4	1.372	1.831	0.122
	Within (error)	391.2	522	0.7494		
Pre-shop time	(PCS)	2561	1	2561	34,310	<0.001
	(RD)	119.8	2	59.89	802.4	<0.001
	(RWL)	1.185	2	0.5923	7.934	<0.001
	PCS×RD	119.9	2	59.94	803	<0.001
	PCS×RWL	1.188	2	0.5942	7.96	<0.001
	RD×RWL	5.972	4	1.493	20	<0.001
	PCS×RD×RWL	5.984	4	1.496	20.04	<0.001
	Within (error)	38.97	522	0.07465		

Table 4.2 Summary of Experimental Results

PCS	RD (%)	RWL (%)	Gross Throughput Time (Time Units)		Shop-floor Throughput Time (Time Units)		Pre-shop Time (Time Units)		Pre-shop Inventory Level		WIP Level		Percentage Tardy (%)	
			Mean	Standard Deviation	Mean	Standard Deviation	Mean	Standard Deviation	Mean	Standard Deviation	Mean	Standard Deviation	Mean	Standard Deviation
KS	0	0	16.063	0.572	16.063	0.572	0.000	0.001	0.001	0.002	15.541	0.944	12.076	1.068
		1	16.290	0.521	16.289	0.520	0.000	0.001	0.001	0.001	15.927	0.869	12.441	1.146
		5	16.788	0.788	16.788	0.788	0.000	0.001	0.000	0.001	16.622	1.299	13.614	1.437
	50	0	15.917	0.454	15.917	0.454	0.000	0.000	0.000	0.000	15.375	0.791	11.976	0.998
		1	16.045	0.582	16.045	0.582	0.000	0.000	0.000	0.001	15.521	0.977	12.201	1.239
		5	16.761	0.671	16.761	0.671	0.000	0.000	0.000	0.001	16.576	1.116	13.635	1.202
	100	0	14.473	0.500	14.473	0.500	0.000	0.001	0.000	0.002	13.397	0.822	9.463	0.730
		1	14.608	0.517	14.608	0.515	0.001	0.003	0.001	0.006	13.609	0.853	9.692	0.823
		5	15.019	0.498	15.018	0.498	0.001	0.002	0.001	0.003	14.161	0.852	10.684	1.029
WLC	0	0	19.285	0.637	14.428	0.290	4.857	0.384	6.910	0.581	13.063	0.537	17.080	1.638
		1	19.366	0.726	14.506	0.308	4.860	0.442	6.924	0.678	13.169	0.562	17.336	1.787
		5	19.864	0.667	15.051	0.342	4.813	0.358	6.848	0.553	13.940	0.592	18.677	1.766
	50	0	19.335	0.622	14.281	0.231	5.054	0.424	7.176	0.646	12.816	0.453	17.491	1.605
		1	19.747	0.833	14.343	0.273	5.404	0.582	7.693	0.888	12.936	0.532	18.445	2.023
		5	20.221	0.818	15.120	0.347	5.101	0.508	7.259	0.783	14.029	0.631	19.872	1.964
	100	0	17.958	0.583	14.413	0.356	3.545	0.245	5.038	0.382	13.262	0.625	15.242	1.405
		1	17.965	0.593	15.277	0.519	2.688	0.088	3.824	0.146	14.602	0.897	15.381	1.398
		5	18.374	0.615	15.492	0.474	2.883	0.172	4.102	0.257	14.866	0.771	16.261	1.469

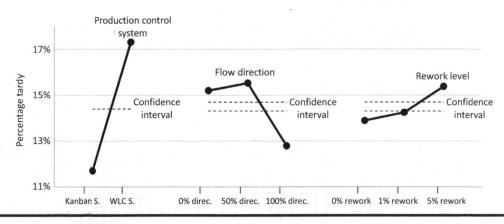

Figure 4.6   ANOM chart for means of tardy jobs.

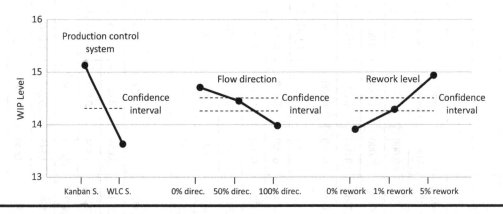

Figure 4.7   ANOM chart for means of WIP level.

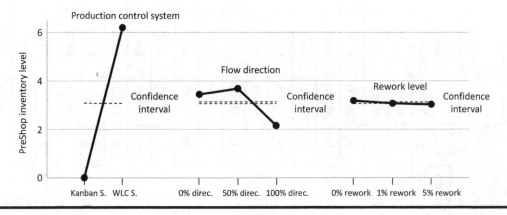

Figure 4.8   ANOM chart for means of pre-shop inventory level.

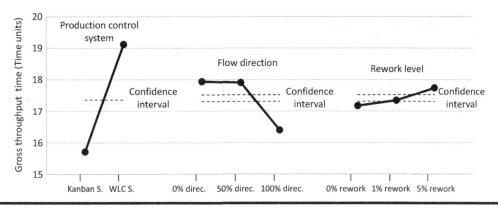

Figure 4.9 ANOM chart for means of gross throughput time.

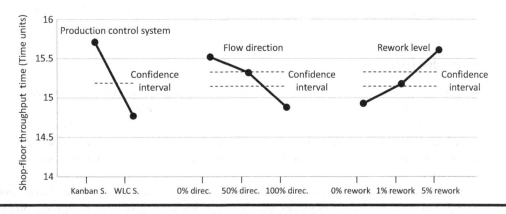

Figure 4.10 ANOM chart for means of shop-floor throughput time.

routing) are almost negligible. Finally, Figure 4.9 shows an increase of the gross throughput time when the rework ratio increases, although the variation range due to this factor is the narrowest.

The WIP level and the shop-floor throughput time are intrinsically related, and for that reason these two indicators respond similarly. The ANOVA results show that the three studied factors have a significant influence on the shop-floor throughput time. Figure 4.10 shows that the shop-floor throughput time achieved by the KS are higher than the WLC levels, because the pre-shop time is practically zero in the KS. Nevertheless, the magnitude of orders of both systems are close. Regarding the influence of the flow direction, Figure 4.10 shows a decrease of the WIP level when the flow direction level increases, and an increase of the WIP level when the rework ratio increases.

Finally, the pre-shop inventory level and the pre-shop time are also intrinsically related, for that reason, the response of these two indicators are similar. The ANOVA results show that the three studied factors exert a significant influence on the pre-shop time. Figure 4.11 shows that the pre-shop times achieved by the KS are practically zero, because the pre-shop inventory levels are practically zero. Although a decrease of the pre-shop time occurs when

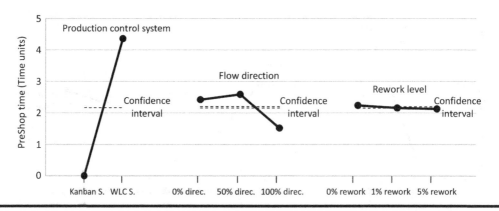

Figure 4.11   ANOM chart for means of pre-shop time.

the rework ratio increases, the variation range due to the rework factor is the narrowest, as can be seen in Figure 4.11 and can be deduced by the lowest F-ratio of the ANOVA results.

4.6 Conclusions

Pull systems have proven to be very easy to use in practice and easy to implement, especially in flow shops and MTS environments. However, they have not been studied, and there are only a few applications in MTO environments, which are usually oriented to a load controlled by the WLC systems. It is known that the system performance depends largely on the context in which it is used: for example, repetitive processes, batch manufacturing, existence of breakdowns, set-ups, or even reprocessing.

The practical interest in this chapter is comparing the WLC systems and KS under the context of consecutive visits in an MTO job-shop, which to our knowledge has not been done previously. The results show that the KS outperforms the WLC implemented, at least on average in the following responses: gross throughput time, the percentage tardy and the pre-shop time, and pre-shop inventory level. This means that the lead time is less in the KS than in the WLC, and a lower percentage of delays is achieved. Furthermore, the limited use of the pre-shop provided an idea of the ease in the orders management by using the KS. However, the KS is worse in the following responses: shop-floor throughput time and WIP level, which is logical since the pre-shop to a lesser extent dampens the variability of orders, as in WLC. However, such damping occurs in a distributed manner among all stations with a suitable configuration of cards.

Concerning the flow direction, a great difference between the performance in a pure flow shop and the rest shop configurations, has been noted. It has been observed that the greatest effect of reworking occurs in the responses at the shopfloor level: percentage of the delays, the WIP level, and shop-floor throughput time.

4.6.1 Managerial Implications

The pull card-based systems are easier to manage than a centralized system such as the WLC. This contrasts with the few studies on the use of KS out of the scope of JIT environments. The practical application of a KS has been demonstrated for an MTO and different types of job-shop environments, and offers the following advantages:

1. Pre-shop management is easier as they are ordered according to the FIFO rule, and it is only necessary to check card availability. This produces a slight increase in the WIP level and shop-floor throughput time, but the difference, although significant, is not very large and could be assumed by the manager.
2. Although there is a slight increase in the average WIP level, it produces a significant reduction in the number of delays.
3. The KS management of each order in the shop is made by transferring cards, without needing to report the current inventory status, or the current pending workload to a centralized system as in the WLC.

4.6.2 Future Research Direction

This study needs to be expanded to extrapolate findings in more complex environments, accounting for other factors affecting the production environment, such as breakdowns, set-ups, and others. Since much of the effect of reworking occurs within the shop floor, it would be interesting to study the influence of the priority rules to be used in the shop floor for the job-shop KS in MTO.

It would also be interesting to study the effect of other WLC approaches (e.g., LUMS, LUMS COR, etc.) regarding our proposed KS.

It is important to note that the biggest drawback of the PCSs is the determination of the appropriate parameters for the correct operation in a particular work environment. This corresponds to a correct card setting in the KS. It would be interesting to study how to dynamically adjust the number of cards in an MTO job-shop KS, as has been previously done in other manufacturing systems such as in flow shops.

There is no doubt that the internet of things will simplify the implementation of such pull systems, where electronic devices will play the role of cards, but allowing global, transparent and immediate access to the Advanced Planning Systems, allowing the natural evolution toward a Cloud Manufacturing. In the same way, the information can be accessible to all the nodes of the Smart Supply Chain which will know at every instant the state of the system, reacting and making decisions according to the shared information.

References

Akturk, M.S.; Erhun, F. (1999). An overview of design and operational issues of kanban systems. *International Journal of Production Research*, 37(17), 3859–3881.

Benton, W.C.; Shin, H. (1998). Manufacturing planning and control: The evolution of MRP and JIT integration. *European Journal of Operational Research*, 110, 411–440.

Bergamaschi, D.; Cigolini, R.; Perona, M.; Portioli, A. (1997). Order review and release strategies in a job-shop environment: A review and a classification. *International Journal of Production Research*, 35, 399–420.

Berkley, B.J. (1992). A review of the kanban production control research literature. *Production and Operations Management*, 1(4), 393–411.

Bertrand, J.W.M.; Van Ooijen, H.P.G. (2002). Workload based order release and productivity: A missing link. *Production Planning and Control*, 13, 665–678.

Ding, F.-Y.; Yuen, M.-N. (1991). A modified MRP for a production system with the coexistence of MRP and Kanbans. *Journal of Operations Management*, 10(2), 267–277.

Duri, C.; Frein, Y.; Lee, H.-S. (2000). Performance evaluation and design of a CONWIP system with inspections. *International Journal of Production Economics*, 64, 219–229.

Gershwin, S.B. (2000). Design and operation of manufacturing systems: The control-point policy. *IIE Transactions*, 32(10), 891–906.

Glover, F.; Kelly, J.P.; Laguna, M. (1996). New advances and applications of combining simulation and optimisation. *Proceeding of the Winter Simulation Conference*, Coronado, California, USA, 144–152.

Gong, Q.; Yang, Y.; Wang, S. (2014). Information and decision-making delays in MRP, KANBAN, and CONWIP. *International Journal of Production Economics*, 156, 208–213.

González-R, P.L.; Framinan, J.M.; Pierreval, H. (2012). Token-based pull production control systems: An introductory overview. *Journal of Intelligent Manufacturing*, 23, 5–22.

González-R, P.L.; Framinan, J.M.; Ruiz-Usano, R. (2013). A methodology for the design and operation of pull-based supply chains. *International Journal of Manufacturing Technology and Management*, 24(3), 307–330.

González-R, P.L.; Molina, J.M.; León, J.M.; Ruiz-Usano, R. (2010). Evaluación del Impacto del Reprocesado en los Sistemas Kanban y CONWIP. *Dirección y Organización*. 42, 46–53.

Gravel, M.; Price, W.L. (1988). Using the kanban in a job-shop environment. *International Journal of Production Research*, 26, 1105–1118.

Harrod, S.; Kanet, J.J. (2013). Applying work flow control in make-to-order job-shops. *International Journal of Production Economics*, 143, 620–626.

Hopp, W.J. (2007). *Supply Chain Science*. New York, New York: McGraw-Hill.

Huang, C.-C.; Andrew Kusiak, A. (1996). Overview of Kanban systems. *International Journal of Computer Integrated Manufacturing*, 9(3), 169–189.

Khojasteh, Y. (2016). *Production Control Systems. A Guide to Enhance Performance of Pull Systems*. Tokyo: Springer.

Khojasteh, Y.; Sato, R. (2015). Selection of a pull production control system in multi-stage production processes. *International Journal of Production Research*, Tokyo 53(14), 4363–4379.

Kingsman, B.G. (2000). Modelling input–output workload control for dynamic capacity planning in production planning systems. *International Journal of Production Economics*, 68, 73–93.

Kumar, C.S.; Panneerselvam, R. (2007). Literature review of JIT-KANBAN system. *International Journal of Advanced Manufacturing Technology*, 32(3), 393–408.

Lage Jr., M.; Godinho Filho, M. (2010). Variations of the Kanban system: Literature review and classification. *International Journal of Production Economics*, 125(1), 13–21.

Land, M.J. (2004). Workload control in job-shops: Grasping the tap. PhD Thesis, University of Groningen, The Netherlands, Labyrinth Publications, Ridderkerk, the Netherlands.

Land, M.J. (2006). Parameters and sensitivity in workload control. *International Journal of Production Economics*, 104(2), 625–638.

Land, M.J.; Gaalman, G. (1996). Workload control concepts in job-shops—A critical assessment. *International Journal of Production Economics*, 46/47, 535–548.

Law, A.M.; Kelton, W.D. (2000). *Simulation Modeling and Analysis* (3rd ed.). Boston, MA: McGraw-Hill.

Lee, Y.-J.; Zipkin, P.H. (1992). Production control in a kanban-like system with defective. *International Journal of Production Economics*, 28, 143–155.

Oosterman, B.; Land, M.J.; Gaalman, G. (2000). The influence of shop characteristics on workload control. *International Journal of Production Economics*, 68(1), 107–119.

Smet, R.; Gelders, L. (1998). Using simulation to evaluate the introduction of a Kanban subsystem within an MRP-controlled manufacturing environment. *International Journal of Production Economics*, 56–57, 111–122.

Spearman, M.L.; Woodruff, D.L.; Hoop, W.J. (1990). Conwip: A pull alternative to Kanban. *International Journal of Production Research*, 28(5), 879–894.

Stevenson, M.; Hendry, L.C.; Kingsman, B.G. (2005). A review of production planning and control: The applicability of key concepts to the make-to-order industry. *International Journal of Production Research*, 43(5), 869–898.

Sugimori, Y.; Kusunoki, K.; Cho, F.; Uchikawa, S. (1977). Toyota production system and kanban system materialization of just-in-time and respect-for-human system. *International Journal of Production Research*, 15(6), 553–564.

Thürer, M.; Silva, C.; Stevenson, M. (2010). Workload control release mechanisms: From practice back to theory building. *International Journal of Production Research*, 48(12), 3593–3617.

Thürer, M.; Silva, C.; Stevenson, M. (2011a). Optimising workload norms: The influence of shop floor characteristics on setting workload norms for the workload control concept. *International Journal of Production Research*, 49(4), 1151–1171.

Thürer, M.; Stevenson, M. (2016). Workload control in job-shops with re-entrant flows: An assessment by simulation. *International Journal of Production Research*, 54(17), 5136–5150.

Thürer, M.; Stevenson, M.; Silva, C. (2011b). Three decades of workload control research: A systematic review of the literature. *International Journal of Production Research*, 49(23), 6905–6935.

Thürer, M.; Stevenson, M.; Silva, C.; Land, M.; Fredendall, L. (2012). Workload control and order release: A lean solution for make-to-order companies. *Production and Operations Management*, 21(5), 939–953.

Uzsoy, R.; Martin-Vega, L.A. (1990). Modelling Kanban-based demand-pull systems: A survey and critique. *Manufacturing Review*, 3(3), 155–160.

Wein, L.M. (1988). Scheduling semiconductor wafer fabrication. *IEEE Transactions on Semiconductor Manufacturing*, 3(1), 115–130.

Xiaobo, Z.; Xu, D.; Zhang, H.; He, Q.M. (2007). Modeling and analysis of a supply-assembly-store chain. *European Journal of Operational Research*, 176, 275–294.

Yan, H.; Stevenson, M.; Hendry, L.; Land, M. (2016). Load-oriented order release (LOOR) revisited: Bringing it back to the state of the art. *Production Planning and Control*, 27(13), 1078–1091.

Chapter 5

Takt Time Grouping: A New Approach to Flow Manufacturing

Mitchell A. Millstein and Joseph S. Martinich

Contents

5.1 Introduction

In a manufacturing flow process, products or parts are made by going through the same set of operations, in the same sequence. When the process is well-balanced with little variation and set-up time, the process can operate like a "synchronized dance." At each operation, a unit is processed for a set amount of time (often the takt time), then all units can move simultaneously to the next operation for the next step of processing. With this "one-piece flow" system, products pass quickly through the process at a constant tempo, with little idle time at any operation, and little or no inventory is needed between operations. This nearly ideal lean system maximizes operation efficiency and minimizes flowtime, with a minimum of WIP inventory. Unfortunately, in practice, many, if not most, manufacturing flow processes are used to produce a set of different products which require possibly long set-ups between different product types. In addition, each product may require different processing times at operations, possibly with considerable random variation. In these cases, a traditional one-piece flow approach can perform poorly: the production tempo is disrupted, resulting in considerable operational idle time and loss of productivity.

Two widely used approaches to deal with these situations are the DBR method (based on Goldratt's Theory of Constraints [Goldratt and Cox 1986]) and CONWIP (Spearman et al. 1990). Both methods process and transfer products among operations in batches, and they use time buffers (DBR) or kanbans (CONWIP) to buffer operations from processing time imbalances and variations, or set-up delays. DBR focuses on the constraint/bottleneck operation and explicitly controls WIP, only in front of that operation. CONWIP is designed to maintain a constant level of WIP throughout the flow process, but allows the amount of WIP (number of kanbans) at any operation to vary over time. These two approaches have proven to do a good job of producing high operational efficiency (resource utilization) while controlling the amount of WIP.

Although effective, when there is a single, stable constraint operation, while trying to implement these methods in an actual manufacturing flow process, we found that their performance degraded when the constraint operation varied from product to product, not a rare situation in practice (Plenert 1993; Ronen and Starr 1990).*

It is easy to see that DBR's WIP will be at the wrong location when the constraint shifts. DBR's timebuffer is fixed at one operation, and therefore, the largest WIP buffer can be in front of a non-constraint operation. CONWIP, while more flexible because it doesn't designate the locations of kanbans, will form WIP queues in front of the constraint operation. When the constraint moves, this WIP queue can take time to move to the new constraint operation and, for a time, the largest WIP queue will be in front of a non-constraint operation. Additionally, neither DBR nor CONWIP allow flow process designers to buffer specific operations from long set-up times.

5.2 Motivation for TTG's Development

Takt Time Grouping (TTG) was created when one of the authors, in the role of a consultant, was working with a mid-size manufacturing company to implement flow manufacturing. This company was suffering from long production flowtime (and therefore long lead times quoted to customers), unacceptably low throughput rates, poor on-time delivery to customers, high reject rates, and excessive WIP inventory.[†] The company used material requirements planning (MRP) to schedule production of components through multiple work-centers and processed in batches equal to order quantities. Order quantities could be in the thousands for the machined components

---

* When the constraint operation is different for different products produced in a flow process or flow cell, this has been called "moving" or "wandering" constraints.

[†] *Flowtime* is the time from when a unit begins processing at the first operation until it completes the last operation.

  Throughput quantity is the number of finished goods completed by the process.

  Throughput rate is throughput quantity per unit of time (such as an hour, day, shift, or week).

  WIP inventory is measured as the total number of units that have completed the first process but have not been completed at the last process.

they produced. The components produced were of the company's own design, which are used in downstream assembly operations.

From classes the company managers had taken, they thought that one-piece flow or DBR might be the solutions to their problems. However, problems with each, for the specific application, were identified. One-piece flow relies on:

1. Well-balanced operations with approximately equal work content at each operation
2. Minimal operation or workstation cycle time variation
3. Very fast set-ups to change from one product to another
4. Short distances (or moving assembly lines) to hand-off products from one operation to the next*

These four requirements enable smooth flow within the process, resulting in very fast flow-times and low WIP inventory levels.

Unfortunately, the production characteristics of the actual process did not adhere to these requirements. The first product to be manufactured in a flow process, brass and Teflon® piston discs of different sizes, required primarily machining operations, with a few assembly operations. (Piston discs are a component in chemical shut-off valves. Figure 5.1 shows the piston discs in a protective tray, which also acted as the kanban bin in this flow process.) We could not break up machining steps into equal time-buckets. Therefore, the process could never be balanced. The machining and assembly steps in the process also exhibited random operation cycle time variation. As stated earlier, variation can disrupt the even flow of product through a one-piece flow cell. Set-up times varied from 15–45 min, which was large enough to idle operations and operators. These long set-up times eliminated the possibility of using mixed-model sequencing of products through the flow process (Boysen et al. 2009), which is a technique to create balance across imbalanced operations.

DBR seemed more appropriate to use. However, it has two significant problems. First, DBR relies on the process having one constraint that can signal the beginning of the flow process to release the next order. In the piston disc product line, different product families had their constraining cycle time at different operations, or "moving constraints." When a process has moving constraints, the DBR signal concept breaks down. Second, DBR does not generally minimize

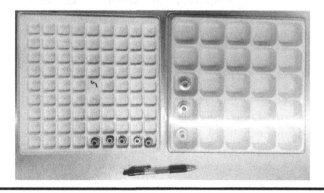

Figure 5.1 Piston discs.

---

* Operation cycle time is defined as the duration of labor and/or machine time at an operation.

WIP inventory or flowtime (Russell and Fry 1997). WIP inventory is controlled at the constraint operation, which can allow greater WIP inventory build-up than with the one-piece flow method. This also translates into longer flowtimes. (Customers wanted reduced lead times and improved responsiveness to emergencies.) The final option was CONWIP. As noted above, we were concerned that the WIP queues, that naturally form at constraint operations in CONWIP, would not adjust quickly enough to changing constraint operations. In addition, CONWIP doesn't designate WIP locations, and we could not depend on natural WIP queues forming in front of operations with longer set-ups. A favorable aspect of kanban-flow manufacturing is that the WIP can be placed strategically to buffer disruptions such as set-up.

These challenges motivated our development of a new method, TTG. TTG was designed especially for flow manufacturing in unbalanced processes with high set-up and processing time variation, and moving constraints. TTG combines the use of kanbans, transfer batch sizing, and Theory of Constraint concepts (Goldratt and Cox 1986) to "size" and distribute kanban bins between operations to protect against production disruptions and random operation cycle time variation. This results in efficient production while controlling WIP. Transfer batches for each product move in kanban bins and are sized (size = the number of units in a bin before it is transferred to the downstream operation) using a formula based on the constraint operation for that product. The sizes of the transfer batches are designed to make the amount of time batches spend at their constraint operations relatively equal. Consequently, the transfer batch sizes for different products are different, depending on the product's cycle time at its constraint. The flow process is then controlled by a kanban pull system, which operates essentially like a one-piece flow system, but where the unit of production, and transfer, is the batch (a subset of the product's order quantity), rather than individual items. The result is that the process becomes better balanced, and the relative processing time variation is reduced for the transfer batches versus one-piece flow. (Because of The Law of Large Numbers, the variation in processing times for batches decreases as batch size increases. This is discussed in more detail in Section 5.3.1.)

5.3 Designing a TTG Flow Process

There are two key aspects for designing a TTG flow process. The first is sizing transfer batches for each product type. (We also call this Takt Time Group sizing.) The second is the placement of kanbans in front of certain operations to buffer the operations from disruptions, such as set-up time, downtime, or large operating time variation.

5.3.1 Takt Time Group Sizing

Splitting large production batches into smaller transfer batches is known to reduce flowtime and flowtime variability, compared to transferring entire production batches at one time (Jacobs and Bragg 1988, Kropp and Smunt 1990). In the development of TTG, we realized that transfer batch sizes do not have to be identical across different products. In fact, due to differences in operation cycle times for different products, we would not want them to be the same. The key idea underlying TTG is to select transfer batch sizes, so as to create better balance and flow through the process. How can this best be done? In creating TTG we borrow the concept of takt time (a German word for tempo) used by one-piece flow cell designers to designate the tempo of the process, or how often one unit of production leaves the process (Costanza 1996). Traditionally, takt time is measured as effective production time divided by customer demand. Instead, in the development of TTG we use this term literally, based on the German definition, to be the time that the transfer batch of a component spends being processed at its constraint operation. This group quantity, also called the transfer batch size, is a subset of the total customer order quantity, or lot size, for each component. The parts in a transfer batch travel as a group and do not wait for the rest of the production lot quantity to be completed at any operation.

The Takt Time Group Quantity (TTGQ) is calculated as follows:

$$TTGQi = \frac{T}{CTCi} \quad \text{for all } i = 1,...,n \tag{5.1}$$

where:

$TTGQi$ is the TTGQ (transfer batch size) of component i

T is the chosen grouping tempo of the flow process (see Figure 5.2 for explanation of how the tempo is determined).

$CTCi$ is defined by

$$CTCi = \text{maximum } CTij \text{ with respect to } j = 1,...,m, \quad \text{for all } i = 1,...,n \tag{5.2}$$

where $CTij$ is the average operation cycle time for component i at operation j; n is the number of different components produced by the flow process; and m is the number of operations in the process. Notice that $CTCi$ is the average operation time for component i at its "slowest" operation—its constraint.

These formulae create transfer batch sizes for the components so that the average amount of time to process a transfer batch of each component at its own constraint operation is approximately equal to the tempo (T). In Figure 5.2, which shows the logic flow for determining the tempo (T), we include a decision, "are group sizes large enough to sufficiently reduce batch time variation relative to the mean?" As discussed at the end of Section 5.2, because of The Law of Large Numbers, the sum of the variation of a large number of an operation's cycles will converge to zero. In other words, the cycle-to-cycle variation of a workstation in a flow process can be very large, but the sum of the variation of a large transfer batch will be greatly reduced because cycle times faster and slower than the average will balance each other out.

As a simple example, suppose we are producing three components in a TTG-controlled flow process with the following operation cycle times at their constraint operations:

- CTC of product 1 = 60 s
- CTC of product 2 = 30 s
- CTC of product 3 = 15 s

If the chosen tempo (T) = 15 min (900 s), then

- TTGQ of product 1 = 900 s/60 s per unit = 15 units
- TTGQ of product 2 = 900 s/30 s per unit = 30 units
- TTGQ of product 3 = 900 s/15 s per unit = 60 units

Component 1 would be processed in transfer batches of 15 units, and Components 2 and 3 would have transfer batches of 30 and 60 units, respectively. At the constraint operation for

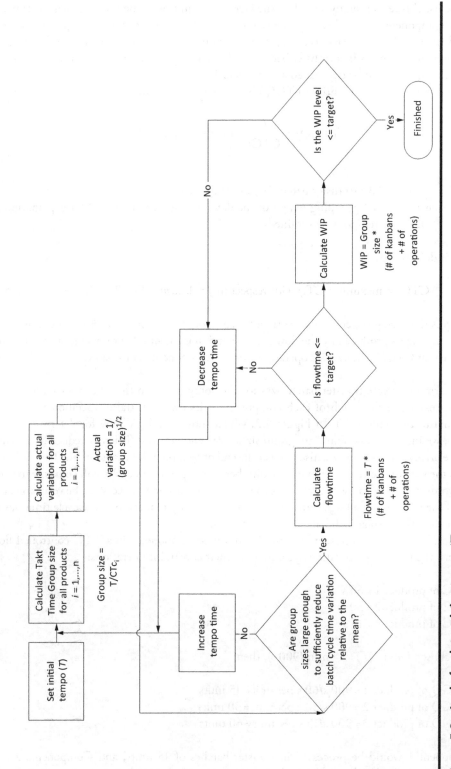

Figure 5.2 Logic for determining tempo (*T*).

each component, a transfer batch would be processed every 15 min on average, regardless of the component type.

To use a more humorous analogy, suppose you were filling a ski gondola with a weight limit of 2000 pounds. If you had a group of 400 pound sumo wrestlers, you could fit 5 on the gondola; 200 pound soccer players, you could fit 10; or 100 pound ballerinas, you could fit 20. In this analogy, the 2000 pound weight limit is like the tempo (T) in the Takt Time Group sizing formula. The weights of the sumo wrestlers, soccer players, and ballerina are like the cycle times at the constraint (CTC) for each product going through the flow process.

Customer and/or stocking orders are broken up into multiple Takt Time Groups (transfer batches) that are scheduled sequentially through the flow process. The last transfer batch of one component is immediately followed by the first transfer batch of the next component on the schedule. The total required quantity of a single component is produced together, as sequential transfer batches, with no extra set-ups (no mix-model sequencing) required. The number of Takt Time Groups (transfer batches) of a component is the demand (or order) quantity for that component divided by the TTGQ (transfer batch size). Total number of Takt Time Groups should be rounded up to multiples of the TTGQs to ensure an integer number of Takt Time Groups are produced. For this reason, TTG works best when the total order quantity relative to the TTG size is large, or for stocking orders where producing a small quantity extra is acceptable.

For example, if the total demand for each of the three hypothetical products shown above is 600 units each, then the number of Takt Time Groups (transfer batches) that flow sequentially through the flow process is equal to:

- Number of Takt Time Groups of product 1 = 600/15 = 40 groups
- Number of Takt Time Groups of product 2 = 600/30 = 20 groups
- Number of Takt Time Groups of product 3 = 600/60 = 10 groups

For operations that are not the constraint, the Takt Time Group will spend less time than the predetermined tempo (T) at these operations. Using the principles of DBR, however, we know that the constraining operation controls the tempo of production. Therefore, we are not concerned that the line is imbalanced. Like the DBR method, we do not try to create a perfectly balanced production line (Cook 1994), but instead focus on creating a constant tempo in the process.

5.3.2 Number and Distribution of Kanban Bins

The Takt Time Group sizing algorithm above creates a smooth and even flow of transfer batches, which are moved in kanban bins through the flow process. In TTG we use kanban bins, not cards, because the Takt Time Groups (or transfer batches) move between two operations in kanban bins (see Figure 5.3). TTG's kanban bins move forward (full) and back (empty) between two operations, buffering disruptions between them. As with any kanban flow process, we can choose how many kanbans to use in the process, and how to distribute them across operations. In this way, TTG is similar to a typical kanban flow process. This is done with some level of experimentation, either on the real flow process (adding or removing kanbans, and observing performance) or using a simulation model. In this section, we provide basic guidelines on distributing kanbans in our TTG flow process and considerations for decisions.

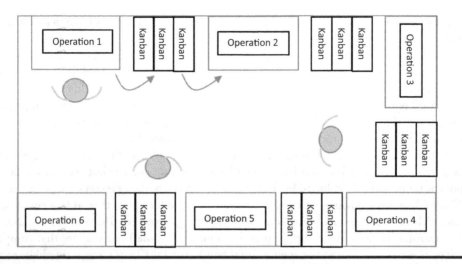

Figure 5.3 Even kanban bin distribution in TTG flow process.

5.3.2.1 Trade-off of Throughput Rate versus WIP and Flowtime

When using kanbans in a flow process, the designer has an important trade-off. More kanbans allow for more WIP to accumulate in the process, which will generally buffer process variation and disruptions (such as, set-up time and unplanned downtime), thereby increasing throughput rate. A higher throughput rate is usually desirable, but more WIP will also create higher inventory carrying costs and longer flowtimes. From Little's Law (Little 1961) and the Theory of Constraints, we know that flowtime is controlled by the amount of WIP in the system and the throughput rate of the bottleneck operation:

$$\text{Max flowtime} = \frac{\text{Max WIP}}{\text{average throughput rate of the bottleneck}} \tag{5.3}$$

For example, if the maximum WIP in the process were 300 units and the average throughput rate of the constraint were 60 units per h (cycle time = 1 min per unit), the maximum flowtime of the process would be 5 h. Depending on the value of the products manufactured in the process, WIP costs may dominate the benefit of higher throughput, or vice versa. In addition, depending on the value of quick response to customer demands, speed (as measured by flowtime) may dominate the value of higher throughput, or vice versa. Given that we know a TTG kanban bin has a varying quantity, but specific amount of time that quantity spends being processed at the constraint (15 min in our example in Section 5.3.1), we can use these formulae to determine how much to "time buffer" individual operations and the entire process, similar to what is done in a DBR process. Figure 5.3 shows three kanban bins between each operation, evenly distributed between all operations, for a total of 15 kanban bins in the process. Using this and other information, we can calculate the flowtime that would result from the WIP in the kanban bins. For example, let us assume that all kanban bins are full (holding an entire Takt Time Group). In addition, if our chosen TTG process tempo (T), which can also be defined as the average time the transfer batch spends at its constraint, was 15 min (0.25 h), then the throughput rate of the constraint (or bottleneck) in terms of kanban bins is 4 per h. Using the flowtime calculation based on Little's Law from above, this process would have WIP equivalent to 3.75 h or 225 min of flowtime.

$$\text{Maximum WIP time} - \text{buffer in the process} = \frac{15 \text{ kanban bins}}{4 \text{ kanban bins per hour}} = 3.75 \text{ h}$$

(Note, it is likely that not all the kanban bins will be full, therefore the actual flowtime should be lower. This was confirmed in our experimentation.)

Based on these calculations, our initial kanban placement may be too much WIP, or too little. We can experiment with this by removing kanban bins. If they can be removed, with no effect on throughput, then they should be removed to reduce WIP inventory carrying costs. If throughput decreases when kanban bins are removed, the flow process designer should consider the tradeoff of throughput versus inventory carrying costs of that WIP, and possibly add them back.

5.3.2.2 Strategic Kanban Distribution

Another strategy is to apply the kanban bins unevenly. This would be similar to the method used in DBR, which uses a time buffer only at the constraint operation. However, because we know constraints can move, TTG allows us to buffer multiple operations with kanban bins. If Operations 3 and 5 are the constraint operations, we could remove some kanban bins from in front of Operation 2 (shown in Figure 5.4). This would reduce WIP inventory carrying costs and probably have no effect on performance. This change would need to be verified.

Another consideration for placing kanban bins is protecting against disruptions due to set-up or downtime. The easiest disruption to consider is set-up, as these times are relatively well known (although subject to variation). If an operation has an average 90 min set-up time, we can place three to four kanban bins in front of, and directly after that operation. The three or four kanban bins in front of that operation allow the upstream operation to continue to fill kanban bins for the duration of the set-up, and not violate kanban discipline (producing quantities greater than the kanban signals). The three or four kanban bins after that operation allow the downstream operation to continue to pull product for the duration of the set-up. Experimentation will find the best combination of buffering operations to maximize throughput, while controlling WIP inventory carrying costs. An example of this design is shown in Figure 5.5, with Operation 4 having the longest set-up, with a duration of 90 min. Also important to point out is that buffering set-up

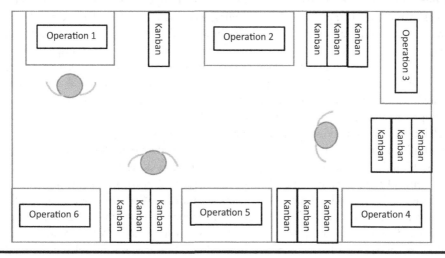

Figure 5.4   Uneven kanban bin distribution in TTG process.

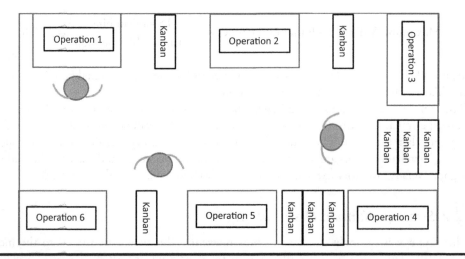

Figure 5.5 Buffering long set-up operations with kanban bins.

downtime with extra kanban bins does not always work. This cannot be done if the operation with the long set-up time also is the constraint operation for that product. If it is the constraint operation, then the downtime due to set-up cannot be regained because downtime at the constraint is lost capacity. In addition, buffering operations with extra kanban bins only works if there is only one or two long set-up operations in the flow process.

5.4 Simulation Models

To test the performance of TTG against one-piece flow, DBR, and CONWIP, we created a discrete event simulation model. This simulation model is based on the characteristics of a functioning TTG flow process at an actual manufacturing facility noted in the Introduction. The process has six operations with set-up required at four of the six operations. The need to compare the differences in methods using simulation modeling was due to the fact that we had limited ability to make comparisons among methodologies in the real flow process. The primary concern of the client's management team was achieving the performance goals of the implementation and meeting customer orders. The TTG flow process implementation was very successful, reducing flowtime from 6 weeks to 1 day, and proportionally reducing WIP inventory, as compared to their MRP-scheduled, batch production process. Once these goals were achieved, management did not want to experiment and make comparison analyses. It should be noted that the simulation model in this chapter was validated using the actual performing TTG flow process.

The simulation model allowed us to compare empirically the performance of TTG to one-piece flow, CONWIP, and DBR. Set-up and operation cycle times were randomized by the model. Details of the probability distributions are discussed in Millstein and Martinich (2014). Performance was measured by three metrics; throughput rate, WIP inventory level, and flowtime. Throughput rate is measured as the number of individual units of finished goods completed in 110 h: a 5 day, 3 shift operation (120 h minus a 10 h warm-up period). WIP inventory is measured as units of production that have completed Operation 1 but have not completed the final operation. WIP is measured hourly and averaged for the entire week, minus the 10 h warm-up period.

Flowtime is measured as the average time individual items spent in the flow process, from the time they entered the first operation until they exited the last operation.

Separate models were created to test TTG, one-piece flow, CONWIP, and DBR. The one-piece flow model utilized two kanbans at each operation. In practice, this can be decreased or increased. We used two kanbans (with a single unit associated with each kanban) to minimize WIP and flowtime. The kanban prevents any new unit from entering the operation directly upstream if that kanban is full. This effectively limits the number of items in the one-piece flow process to 16, or one item in each of the two kanbans in front of Operations 2, 3, 4, 5, and 6, and one item in the workstation at operations 1, 2, 3, 4, 5, and 6. (The first operation pulls in only raw materials and therefore doesn't require a kanban.)

The difference between the TTG and one-piece flow models is the number of kanbans and the number of parts in the kanban. A one-piece flow cell's kanban holds a single unit. A TTG entity has a varying quantity of components based on the group size calculation for that part number. We used a 15-min tempo (T). Based on the operation cycle time at the constraints for each product (see Table 5.1), the Takt Time Group sizes were 45 units for part numbers 1, 2, and 3; 30 units for part numbers 4, 5, and 6; and 15 units for part numbers 7, 8, and 9. In addition, we used three kanbans (each holding a Takt Time Group or transfer batch) in front of Operations 2, 3, 4, 5, and 6 of the TTG flow process, for a total of 15 kanbans in the process. As discussed in Section 5.3.2, experimentation could be used to find the number of kanban bins to buffer operations against disruptions and variation, while controlling inventory carrying costs.

The DBR simulation model has important differences. The DBR model utilizes a hold step, but it holds new orders at the beginning of the flow process, based on a time buffer in front of Operation 5. Operation 5 is the highest overall utilization operation, and therefore is considered the "drum." The "rope" from Operation 5 releases demand into the flow process. Using the formula from Radovilsky (1998), which balances inventory holding cost with the cost of stock-out disruptions in the process, we calculated an optimal time buffer of 2.5 h. (Radovilsky's formula is based on a concave profit curve to determine maximize total profit, similar to an economic-order quantity [EOQ] function.) The number of components in Operation 5's queue, multiplied by the cycle time of these components at Operation 5, determines the actual "time" in front of Operation 5. When this time is greater than 2.5 h, the process stops releasing new orders into the flow process. The demand (order) that flows into the DBR simulation model is a fixed quantity transfer batch. Using the range of Takt Time Group sizes (15–45) as a guide, we follow the methods from Hilmola (2004) and iteratively reduce the transfer batch size to balance improved throughput rate (which generally requires more WIP) versus inventory carrying costs. Our experiments yielded a transfer batch size of 15 units.

The CONWIP model is similar to the DBR model, except the limitation for releasing new entities into the production process is the maximum number of kanbans (or transfer batches) in the process as a whole. Using the same experimentation described in the description of the TTG and DBR model, the maximum number of kanbans for the CONWIP model was set at 30 and the transfer batch size was set at 15 unit.

It was assumed that demand was sufficient so that orders were always available to be "pulled" into the process based on the signals within the process. We used this design to model our case study company. (This company's demand planners aggregated customer orders to create a fixed schedule based on a backlog of orders.) The process pulled orders from the schedule into the first operation based on signals from kanbans (one-piece flow, TTG, or CONWIP) or time buffers (DBR). We initiate production for all the simulation models with the flow process empty. Therefore, a warm-up period of 10 h is used to allow the flow process, for all four methods, to fill up with WIP.

Table 5.1 Operational Data for Piston Discs in Seconds

Part #	Operation 1			Operation 2			Operation 3			Operation 4			Operation 5			Operation 6		
	Machine Time	Labor Time	Set-Up Time	Machine Time	Labor Time	Set-Up Time	Machine Time	Labor Time	Set-Up Time	Machine Time	Labor Time	Set-Up Time	Machine Time	Labor Time	Set-Up Time	Machine Time	Labor Time	Set-Up Time
1	**20**	**20**	2700	0	5	100	12	12	900	0	7	100	19	19	1800	12	12	600
2	**20**	**20**	2700	0	7	100	17	17	900	0	5	100	19	19	1800	12	12	600
3	**20**	**20**	2700	0	12	100	15	15	900	0	7	100	19	19	1800	12	12	600
4	27	27	2700	0	7	100	**30**	**30**	900	0	10	100	19	19	1800	12	12	600
5	27	27	2700	0	9	100	**30**	**30**	900	0	8	100	19	19	1800	12	12	600
6	27	27	2700	0	21	100	**30**	**30**	900	0	9	100	25	25	1800	12	12	600
7	34	34	2700	0	5	100	12	12	900	0	7	100	**60**	**60**	1800	12	12	600
8	34	34	2700	0	8	100	21	21	900	0	5	100	**60**	**60**	1800	12	12	600
9	34	34	2700	0	12	100	15	15	900	0	7	100	**60**	**60**	1800	12	12	600

Note: Constraint operation in **bold** print.

5.5 Performance Comparisons (One-Piece Flow, DBR, CONWIP, TTG)

The simulation results for TTG, one-piece flow, CONWIP, and DBR, for all three performance metrics, are shown in Table 5.2. The results show that for production processes and products similar to the piston discs, TTG produces the highest average throughput rate. During the same period of time (5 day, three shift operation minus a 10 h warm-up), TTG produced an average of 8,887 piston discs, which is 10.2% more than one-piece flow (8,064 piston discs), 2.8% more than CONWIP (8,645 piston discs), and 1.1% more than DBR (8,790 piston discs). While the 1.1% difference between TTG and DBR may not seem large, due to the sample size of 100 simulation replications the difference is statistically significant (p value < 0.001.)

Not surprisingly, in terms of WIP inventory level and flowtime, one-piece flow was the clear winner. One-piece flow completed piston discs, on average, in 7 min, with only an average of 10 units of WIP in the entire flow process. CONWIP, DBR, and TTG were much slower and had greater WIP inventory levels. One-piece flow "allows" only a minimum amount of WIP inventory in the flow process. Our piston-disc one-piece flow process could have, at most, 16 units in the process. (This design was discussed in Section 5.4.) With one-piece flow, items (piston discs) do not have to wait at a given operation for other units to be completed at that operation before they move to the next operation. However, with CONWIP, DBR, and TTG items are processed and transferred in batches, so each unit must wait at an operation until an entire transfer batch has been processed, before moving to the next operation. Although one-piece flow keeps WIP low, it comes at the expense of considerable idle time and lower utilization, as will be explained in Section 5.5.2.

5.5.1 Throughput Rate Comparison

While we evaluate the four methods based on three performance metrics, throughput rate is our primary concern. The results in Table 5.2 show that although one-piece flow has the advantage in flowtime and WIP, one-piece flow is the worst performer for throughput rate. Because one-piece flow processes a single unit at each operation, it is subject to the full variation at each operation. Even the slightest delay at one operation can idle adjacent operations. Individual items pass through the flow cell quickly with one-piece flow, but because of the low amount of WIP "allowed" in the cell, delays and variation frequently leave individual operations, or even the entire cell, idle for periods of time. This can be seen in Figure 5.6, which shows the average WIP level (for all replications) by hour in the one-piece flow cell. (The standard deviation of each operation cycle time in the simulation was set at 50% of the average operation cycle time. This is a relatively high, but realistic, level of variation.) Whenever WIP is below six units, at least one of the flow cell operations is idle. Note, what is not seen, is that for several

Table 5.2 Performance of One-Piece Flow, DBR, CONWIP, and TTG

	One-Piece Flow	*DBR*	*CONWIP*	*TTG*
Average throughput (units)	8064	8790	8645	8887
Average WIP inventory (units)	10	420	372	213
Average flowtime (min)	7	284	215	153

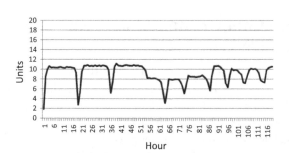

Figure 5.6 One-piece flow average WIP by hour.

replications the one-piece flow cell has zero WIP, which implies that all operations must be idle (zero throughput). Essentially, the one-piece flow cell's design did not provide enough WIP to overcome the gaps of "zero WIP" that result from variation in operation cycle time and when set-up occurs. These gaps created "lost utilization" on constraints, resulting in lost throughput. As opposed to CONWIP, DBR, and TTG, which allow larger amounts of WIP in the flow cell, one-piece flow "starved" itself at various points in time. As shown in Table 5.2 this resulted in one-piece flow having a throughput rate of 10.2% less than TTG, 9% less than DBR, and 7.2% less than CONWIP. While we did not show the WIP in 10 h intervals for CONWIP, DBR, and TTG, it was never close to zero.

The effects of delays and operation idleness are reflected by the variation in flowtimes. Table 5.3 shows the average, standard deviation, and coefficient of variation (COV) of the flowtimes for all four methods. One-piece flow has a flowtime COV of 90%, as compared to 56% for CONWIP, 36% for DBR, and 17% for TTG. Although the average flowtime for the one-piece flow cell was small, the variation was relatively large. In comparison, the larger transfer batches used by TTG reduced the impact of operation cycle time variation due to the Law of Large Numbers. CONWIP and DBR use smaller transfer batch sizes than TTG, and while not as consistent as TTG, they have a lower flowtime COV than one-piece flow.

5.5.2 Overall Comparison of TTG, DBR, and CONWIP

TTG is closer to CONWIP and DBR than it is to one-piece flow. TTG, CONWIP, and DBR all use transfer batches. In the application of producing piston discs, TTG outperformed CONWIP and DBR on all three performance metrics (greater throughput with less WIP and faster flowtime). The superiority of TTG in this case can be attributed to:

1. The nature of the TTG transfer batch sizing
2. Kanban control at every operation when there are moving constraints

The Takt Time Group sizes for this application were either 15, 30, or 45 units depending on the part number (average Takt Time Group size for all products was 30). In contrast, the CONWIP and DBR transfer batch size was fixed at 15 units. Intuitively, it would seem that with CONWIP and DBR, entities would go through the flow process faster and with less average WIP than they would with TTG, because of their smaller average transfer batch sizes. In fact, Table 5.4 shows that TTG is almost 29% faster than CONWIP, and 46% faster than DBR (smaller flowtime),

Table 5.3 Flowtime Coefficient of Variation for One-Piece, CONWIP, DBR and TTG

One-Piece			CONWIP			DBR			TTG		
Average Flowtime (min)	*Standard Deviation*	*COV*	*Average Flowtime (min)*	*Standard Deviation*	*COV*	*Average Flowtime (min)*	*Standard Deviation*	*COV*	*Average Flowtime (min)*	*Standard Deviation*	*COV*
7	6.3	0.901	215	120	0.558	284	104	0.365	153	26	0.172

Table 5.4 Average Flowtime, WIP and Maximum Machine Utilization of CONWIP, DBR and TTG

Measure	CONWIP	DBR	TTG	TTG vs. CONWIP (%)	TTG vs. DBR (%)
Flowtime (min)	215	284	153	−28.8	−46.1
WIP (units)	372	420	213	−42.7	−49.3
Maximum machine utilization	77.3%	78.1%	80.0%	+3.5	+2.4

with 43% less WIP than CONWIP, and 49% less WIP than DBR. (Table 5.4 shows the average flowtime, WIP, and maximum machine utilization results of CONWIP, DBR, and TTG and the % difference. Maximum machine utilization is the highest machine utilization observed across all operations in the flow process. Note: utilization does not include set-up time, which was coded as non-value-added.)

5.5.2.1 DBR

Previous research has shown that DBR can operate well with relatively low WIP, and techniques exist to minimize flowtime. However, that research assumes a stationary constraint, with constant operation cycle times at the constraint. In the piston-disc production process neither of those conditions hold, which substantially decreases the performance of DBR. First, for the piston-disc production process, the operation cycle time at the constraint varies from product to product. Because the DBR transfer batch quantity is fixed at 15 units, the operation cycle times at the constraints vary from 20–60 s (see Table 5.1), so the transfer batches spend substantially different amounts of time (5–15 min) at their constraint. If a "fast" product follows a "slow" product, the slow product can back-up the fast product (idling some operations) while creating queues at operations that are not supposed to be time buffered. This creates excess WIP and increases flowtime. Second, the piston-disc production process has three different constraints depending on the product in the flow process (see Table 5.1). The time buffer was placed in front of Operation 5, because it is overall the highest utilization operation. Operation 5, therefore, sends the signal to release more transfer-batches. However, depending on the product in the DBR production process, the constraint may, in fact, be Operation 1 or 3. When the constraint moves, DBR creates unplanned WIP queues at locations other than Operation 5. The unplanned queues cause inventory to not flow smoothly, resulting in greater levels of WIP inventory, reduced machine utilization and throughput, and longer flowtime as compared to TTG.

5.5.2.2 CONWIP

CONWIP, like DBR, uses a fixed transfer batch size, which results in the same uneven times spent at the constraint by transfer batches and creates delays and reduces machine utilization and throughput just like DBR. Unlike DBR (and TTG), CONWIP does not try to control the location of the WIP. The kanbans in CONWIP are not operation-specific. Instead, there are a fixed number of kanbans, and therefore, transfer batches, "allowed" in the process. The result is that WIP can move as constraints change, but this WIP "movement" takes time, so WIP does not always get where it is needed quickly to facilitate production. The result was that although CONWIP had less average WIP and faster average flowtime than DBR, it had lower machine utilization and throughput than DBR.

5.5.2.3 TTG

TTG, in contrast to CONWIP and DBR, uses varying transfer batch sizes (Takt Time Group sizes) to create a constant tempo. We then use kanbans at every operation in TTG because we don't know which operation may be the constraint at any point in time, but we control the amount and location of the kanbans consciously. In the piston-disc simulations each queue was set at two kanbans (two Takt Time Groups). The combination of constant tempo and kanban control at every operation creates smooth product flow with no unplanned queues. The results (as shown in Tables 5.2 through 5.4) are clear: compared to CONWIP and DBR, TTG not only produces larger throughput and machine utilization using less WIP, it has shorter average and more consistent flowtimes, with a flowtime COV of 17%, versus CONWIP's COV of 56%, and DBR's 36%.

These results demonstrate the benefit of the TTG method in this specific application. While not as responsive as one-piece flow, it produced at a 10.2% greater throughput rate than one-piece flow. This was largely due to the reduction in realized variation in processing time from greater WIP inventory of a TTG flow process. More importantly, these results suggest that when components are produced in an unbalanced, high-variation process where set-up time is a consideration and constraints move, TTG is the superior methodology. Even if the process did not have moving constraints, TTG can be an enabler of DBR and easily incorporated into the DBR methodology. Instead of an iterative process of determining the transfer batch size of a DBR process (Hilmola 2004), TTG provides a quantitative method of calculating transfer batch sizes that is easily implemented in real production systems.

5.6 Conclusions

TTG provides several benefits as a flow process control method. First, TTG accommodates (the not uncommon) situations where constraints can occur at different operations. Second, flow process designers can buffer individual or multiple operations with time buffers to protect them from disruptions, such as set-up or known downtime, and random processing times. Finally, TTG, while unique, would be familiar to kanban-flow practitioners, because of the use of kanbans to create pull between operations, and DBR practitioners, because of the calculation of time buffers and transfer batch sizes based on constraint operation cycle times.

For the piston-disc manufacturing application, TTG outperformed one-piece flow, DBR, and CONWIP. This process had moving constraints, moderate set-up times, moderate variation, and imbalances across operations cycle times that were machine-dependent. However, there are applications where the other methods would likely perform better than TTG. If the operation cycle times are relatively balanced, have low set-up times, and minimal variation, and if the cost of WIP is very high (such as for electronics or auto-parts), then one-piece flow is likely the best choice of flow-control method. DBR may be best when there is a single constraint operation in an unbalanced process. This is, in fact, the application that DBR was designed to optimize. CONWIP, while underperforming TTG in this limited study, has been shown to perform better than DBR, and just as well or slightly better than TTG in other applications. Another benefit of CONWIP is its design simplicity. CONWIP's kanbans move through the system and do not require the same level of kanban discipline. TTG and one-piece flow's kanbans are operation specific-and require a higher level of discipline to ensure they stay at the intended operations. In addition, without moving constraints, CONWIP will find the system's constraints and buffer these naturally with more WIP. Therefore, flow process designers should consider TTG, but depending on the application, they should also consider other flow-control methods as potentially better choices.

Work is currently underway to improve TTG. These efforts include the effect of varying staffing levels (and therefore labor utilization) on the performance of TTG, one-piece flow, DBR, and CONWIP. Some methods may perform better under constrained labor than others. An important parameter in TTG, that can potentially be optimized, is the tempo (T) used in the group sizing formula. Based on the cost of WIP and value of a unit of throughput, it may be possible to optimize this tempo using some of the same methods Radovilsky (1998) used to optimize time buffers in DBR. Lastly, sequencing of products through a TTG process, based on the location of each product's constraint, is likely an area that can improve throughput and reduce WIP.

References

Boysen, N., Fliedner, M., and Scholl, A. 2009. Level scheduling of mixed-model assembly lines under storage constraints. *International Journal of Production Research*, 47(10), 2669–2684.

Cook, D. 1994. A simulation comparison of traditional, JIT, and TOC manufacturing systems in a flow shop with bottlenecks. *Production and Inventory Management Journal*, 35(1), 73–78.

Costanza, J. 1996. *Quantum Leap in Speed to Market: Demand Flow Technology & Business Strategy*, 3rd ed. JCIT, Boulder, CO.

Goldratt, E., and Cox, J. 1986. *The Goal*, revised edition. North River Press, New York.

Hilmola, O. 2004. Transfer batch sizes and the financial performance of manufacturing—Theory of constraints perspective. *International Journal of Manufacturing Technology and Management*, 6(1/2), 125–136.

Jacobs, F.R., and Bragg, D.J. 1988. Repetitive lots: Flowtime reductions through sequencing and dynamic batch sizing. *Decision Sciences*, 19(2), 281–294.

Kropp, D.H., and Smunt, T. L. 1990. Optimal and heuristic models for lot splitting in a flow shop. *Decision Sciences*, 21(4), 691–708.

Little, J.D.C. 1961. A proof for the queuing formula. *Operations Research*, 9(3), 383–387.

Millstein, M.A., and Martinich, J.S. 2014. Takt Time Grouping: Implementing kanban-flow manufacturing in an unbalanced, high variation cycle time process with moving constraints. *International Journal of Production Research*, 52(23), 6863–6877.

Plenert, G. 1993. Optimizing theory of constraints when multiple constrained resources exist. *European Journal of Operational Research*, 70, 126–133.

Radovilsky, Z. 1998. A quantitative approach to estimate the size of the time buffer in the theory of constraints. *International Journal of Production Economics*, 55, 113–119.

Ronen, B., and Starr, M. 1990. Synchronized manufacturing as in OPT: From practice to theory. *Computers and Industrial Engineering*, 18(4), 585–600.

Russell, G.R., and Fry, T.D. 1997. Order review/release and lot splitting in drum-buffer-rope. *International Journal of Production Research*, 35(3), 827–845.

Spearman, M., Woodruff, D., and Hopp, W. 1990. Conwip a pull alternative to kanban. *International Journal of Production Research*, 28(5), 879–894.

Chapter 6

A Framework for Performance Evaluation of Pull Systems

S. Vinodh, R. Ben Ruben, and P. Asokan

Contents

6.1 Introduction

Lean manufacturing is a management philosophy that originated from the Toyota Production System (TPS) for improving overall customer value (Womack et al. 1990). Lean manufacturing is a systematic approach that aims for consistent elimination of waste ("Muda") within a manufacturing system (Liker 1997). Lean also considers the waste that is being created through overburden ("Muri") and through unevenness ("Mura") in workloads. Lean manufacturing focuses on elimination of seven basic types of wastes that prevail in a manufacturing environment (Shah and Ward 2003). The seven Lean wastes include (Abdulmalek and Rajgopal 2007). They are

1. Transportation
2. Motion
3. Inventory
4. Waiting
5. Over processing
6. Over production
7. Defects

Underutilization of skills and environmental wastes are designated as eighth and ninth Lean waste (Kuriger and Chen 2010, Vinodh et al. 2016). For achieving leanness, a set of dedicated tools and techniques are available to systematically guide the Lean implementation process. There are five key Lean principles which help in implementing Lean to achieve continuous improvement (Womack et al. 1990). Five key Lean principles are

1. Identify value from customer's standpoint.
2. Identify all the steps that exist in the value stream and eliminate the steps that do not add any value.
3. Make the value-creating steps to occur in a rigid sequence, such that product will flow smoothly toward the end customer in a stream.
4. As flow is induced, make customers pull the value from the upstream activity.
5. Seek perfection until a perfect value is created without any waste.

As the fourth Lean principle describes establishing a pull system, it becomes an integral part of Lean production and aims at delivering products/services based on customer demand (Kimura and Terada 1981). The main aim of a pull system is to reduce inventory levels and total costs associated with carrying and holding inventories (Gaury et al. 2000). A pull system also helps in creating a flow and avoids waste of overproduction and over processing. The developed pull system performance evaluation framework also is validated with a case study to test its applicability.

6.2 Pull System

The pull system is a Lean manufacturing strategy that is used to reduce wastes that occur during the production process (Kim 1985). It can be defined as a method of controlling resources flow by replacing the materials that have been consumed. Pull systems are frequently designated as just-in-time (JIT) systems as both operate with the common objective to deliver goods based on the need to avoid accumulation of inventory. Pull systems standardize inventory in the production process and help in reducing batch size (Spearman and Zazanis 1992). Pull systems also help in facilitating Lean excellence by transforming a queue and batch type production to a continuous, or single piece flow production (Khojasteh and Sato 2015). The purpose of the pull system is to maintain a measured quantity of materials that includes raw materials, work-in-process, and finished goods that are pulled by the successive processes. After the materials are pulled, a signal is sent to the preceding process to replace the materials that have been consumed. A Kanban system is considered the back bone of a pull system as it is used to identify, withdraw, and replenish materials to the production sequence based on customer orders (Deleersnyder et al. 1989). Kanban basically works on the signal principle as the signal is generated when a part or material needs to be replaced. A pull system that uses Kanban helps in business transition where a batch or queue type process becomes a one piece or continuous flow process by having a hold over inventory. A pull system controls the amount of inventory and focuses on building customer value. It also helps in improving the pace of the process and reduces the lead time.

6.2.1 Push Versus Pull Systems

A push system is a manufacturing strategy based on information flows and projected production plan originating from having management-to-market in the same direction as the materials flow (Olhager and Östlund 1990). In a push system, the production is not based on daily demand. Items are made to stock. It involves forecasting of inventory needs that are required to satisfy customer demand (Puchkova et al. 2016). An effective, predictive strategy is needed for an organization to accurately determine the production quantity need to be manufactured. The main difference between push and pull systems is that in a pull system, the items are made-to-order, whereas in a push system, the items are made-to-stock. Pull production systems are often compared with push production systems where goods are being pushed from one operation station to the next through the organization.

Though Lean philosophy recommends the use of a pull strategy, an organization can choose an appropriate strategy depending upon product sales and customer demand (Jasti and Kodali 2016). Selection of an appropriate strategy should be done carefully such that the inventory forms and costs associated with its carrying and holding are kept at a minimum. The difference between push and pull systems are shown in Table 6.1.

6.2.2 Types of Pull Systems

Pull systems are broadly categorized into four types namely: continuous flow pull, replenishment pull, sequential pull, and mixed push–pull systems. This categorization is mainly based on batch size, replenishment rate, and level of production mix.

6.2.2.1 Continuous Flow Pull System

A continuous flow pull system is suitable when the production pattern is fixed. In this system, product flow is sequential and an inventory of one number is maintained between two work stations. This system is best suited for cellular manufacturing systems and production systems that follow a "U" type manufacturing cells. A continuous flow pull system has the maximum pull, as it maintains a maximum of one piece of inventory in-between the work stations.

Table 6.1 Difference between Push and Pull Systems

Description	Push System	Pull System
Core objective	Minimizes cost	Maximizes service level
Process complexity	High	Low
Resource consumption	Anticipated usage	Actual consumption
Managing inventory	Management by firefighting	Management by sight
Inventory levels	High inventory	Low inventory
Batch size	Large	Small
Orders	Manufacturer oriented	Customer oriented
Demand	Fluctuating	Stable
Planning horizon	Long	Short
Indication/signal	Schedules and plans	Customer signal
Adaptability	Repetitive manufacturing	Non-repetitive manufacturing

6.2.2.2 Replenishment Pull System

This type of pull system is used to eliminate shortages and overstocking in a production system as the system automatically replaces the goods once they are consumed. This type of pull system also is called a supermarket pull system. This type of pull system is usually adopted for goods that have low variability and are repetitive. One of the major disadvantages of this system is traceability. Issues may arise when the number of parts is large. A proper numbering and tracing system must be introduced to avoid parts getting lost and enable ease of tractability.

6.2.2.3 Sequential Pull System

In this type of pull system, goods are essentially "made-to-order" to minimize the overall inventory. To attain this, proper planning must be made considering batch size and product mix. First-in-first-out (FIFO) lanes and Kanban cards are used in implementing a sequential pull system. One of the challenges of implementing this system is that the shop floor must maintain a strong committed planning strategy to avoid shortages or overstocking in crisis situations.

6.2.2.4 Mixed Push–Pull System

The advantages of both push and pull strategies are integrated to create a new system called Mixed Push–Pull system or a Hybrid Push–Pull system. A traditional push system operates, based on forecasted demand, whereas the pull system operates based on the actual demand. The interface that is created between these two strategies is termed as the push–pull boundary or decoupling point (Davis et al. 2014). The working principle of this system is that the order is provided for the preceding point by the succeeding point. The preceding point immediately reacts to the order by replenishing from stock that is rebuilt directly . A Mixed Push–Pull System is usually recommended for products that have high demand uncertainty, while economies of scale also are important in reducing production and/or delivery costs. A system that operates based on the mixed push–pull strategy must follow a proper Material Requirements Planning (MRP) schedule and a pull control system, such as Kanban, to have control over the inventory.

6.2.2.5 Benefits of Pull System

Creating a pull system offers a wide range of operational and financial benefits. It helps manufacturing firms to maintain optimum inventory levels and have control over resources. Establishing a pull system also maintains stock levels aligned with actual demand and creates a smoother production process to satisfy customer needs. The benefits attainable after creating a pull system are

1. Reduces inventory levels and production lead times
2. Creates an organized work place
3. Creates a common system for material movement and tracking
4. Effective decision making during crucial demand variability
5. Satisfies customer needs through visual control
6. Creates ability to manage change
7. Saves floor space and improves cash flow
8. Detects issues pertaining to product quality rapidly
9. Minimizes inventory holding and carrying costs
10. Increased customer satisfaction

6.3 Performance Evaluation of Pull Systems

A performance evaluation tool helps in evaluating current practices and presents the information either as quantitative or qualitative score (Rajak and Vinodh 2015). Performance evaluation of pull systems is performed in order to quantify Lean benefits and to recognize the scope for further improvements. Measured for improvements such as throughput, forecast accuracy, inventory flow, quality, flexibility, and lead times, all are considered critical measures for evaluating the pull system. The performance evaluation of pull systems helps the firm to find its level of pull performance and identifies scope for further development. Based on the score obtained, the firm can plan its improvement activities to enhance its pull performance from the current state. On reviewing the literature, various Lean performance evaluation models are developed by researchers and are being validated in a practical way. To the best knowledge of the authors, a systematic performance model for evaluating the performance of pull systems has not been attempted.

6.3.1 Development of Conceptual Model for Evaluating Performance of Pull System

For evaluating the performance of a pull system, a fuzzy-based two-level, multi-criteria performance evaluation model has been developed. The model consists of 6 enablers and 26 criteria derived from the literature. The enablers and criteria used in this performance evaluation model were derived through an extensive literature review and were ensured they are measurable and in line with strategic objectives that help in establishing a pull system. The selected enablers and criteria are performance indicators proposed by various authors used for evaluating the components of Lean and pull production systems. Enablers and criteria were more appropriate in evaluation of pull systems were selected to develop the conceptual model for evaluating the performance of pull systems. The selected six enablers are

1. Flexible Process
2. Inventory Control
3. Continuous Flow
4. Kanban
5. Maintenance
6. Quality

The selected enablers are considered crucial metrics for establishing a pull system. The criteria associated with each enabler was chosen so that each criterion drives the enabler and is directly related to enhance the enabler. For example, enabler "Kanban" has five criteria:

1. Selection of appropriate Kanban strategy
2. Proper coordination of Kanban signals
3. Optimal release of trigger point
4. Usage of FIFO principle
5. Managing proper Economic Order Quantity (EOQ)

All these five criteria are considered deciding factors and the effect of each is directly proportional to the affect on the enabler. The developed conceptual model for evaluating the performance of pull systems is shown in Table 6.2.

6.3.2 Fuzzy Logic Application

Fuzzy logic is one of the successful mathematical tools for developing sophisticated control systems as it addresses such applications perfectly and resembles human decision making with an ability to generate precise solutions from certain or approximate information. Fuzzy logic is capable of handling ambiguous concepts and provides crisp solutions to problems that possess more complexity. The fuzzy logic approach is preferred for performance evaluation of complex systems as it amalgamates the advantage of both quantitative and qualitative assessment. Also, it provides a quantitative score as the output, using linguistic variables and membership functions. The weights and ratings needed for evaluating the pull system were obtained from experts from the case organization. Considering, that experts make their decision based upon their accumulated knowledge, applying a mathematical heuristic technique is recommended to remove uncertainty and to provide precise results. The methodological basis of other evaluation techniques like Analytical Hierarchy Process (AHP), Analytic Network Process (ANP), Technique for Order of Preference by Similarity to Ideal Solution (TOPSIS), and Preference Ranking Organization Method for Enrichment of Evaluations (PROMETHEE) is based on the formation of hierarchies and the use of peer assessment to make decisions. In contrast, fuzzy logic focuses on the formation of fuzzy sets and rules, using criteria to determine an output result. On applying fuzzy logic, the inputs are collected in terms of linguistic variables and are converted into a logic based numerical

Table 6.2 Conceptual Model for Performance Evaluation of Pull Systems

Enabler	Criteria
Flexible process (Doolen and Hacker 2005)	Small batch size (Abdulmalek and Rajgopal 2007)
	Visual control (Vinodh and Vimal 2012)
	Customer driven orders (Mascolo et al. 1996)
	Proper communication (Shah and Ward 2003)
	Flexibility in delivery (Doolen and Hacker 2005)
Inventory control (Mascolo et al. 1996)	Maintaining low inventory (Mascolo et al. 1996)
	Usage of replenishment based inventory (Karim and Arif-Uz-Zaman 2013)
	Uninterrupted material flow (Benton and Shin 1998)
	Practicing Vendor Managed Inventory (VMI) approach (Marquès et al. 2010)
Continuous flow (Shah and Ward 2003)	Uniform production levels (Doolen and Hacker 2005)
	Existence of facility layout (Vinodh and Balaji 2011)
	High responsiveness (Vinodh and Vimal 2012)
	Maintain proper value stream (Shah and Ward 2003)
Kanban (Mascolo et al. 1996)	Selection of appropriate Kanban strategy (Mascolo et al. 1996)
	Proper coordination of Kanban signals (Mascolo et al. 1996)
	Optimal release of trigger point (Karim and Arif-Uz-Zaman 2013)
	Usage of FIFO principle (Slomp et al. 2009)
	Maintaining proper EOQ (Benton and Shin 1998)
Maintenance (Gibbons and Burgess 2010)	Overall Equipment Effectiveness (OEE) monitoring (Gibbons and Burgess 2010)
	Zero breakdowns (Shah and Ward 2003)
	Adopt preventive maintenance (Gibbons and Burgess 2010)
	Minimal set-up time (Vinodh and Vimal 2012)
Quality (Shah and Ward 2003)	Follow standardized work (Hasle 2014)
	Minimized rework and rejection rates (Gibbons and Burgess 2010)
	Increased customer satisfaction (Shah and Ward 2003)
	Inspection at source (Page 2010)

approach. Compared to other techniques, fuzzy logic is widely accepted as it is used for evaluating human judgment based results as fixed values, within the fuzzy sets with defined intervals, that are provided for each response. Moreover, the mentioned techniques are best suited for ranking of alternatives compared to performance evaluation. Fuzzy logic is preferred over other techniques to demonstrate correctness of a model or algorithm and to achieve quality solutions, even if the model is robust. Based on these insights, the fuzzy logic evaluation method was chosen to evaluate pull system performance. A fuzzy logic approach has been deployed in prior studies for performance evaluation of Lean systems, agile systems, and supplier performance.

6.3.3 Case Study

A study for evaluating pull system performance has been conducted in an automotive part manufacturing organization located in Tamil Nadu, India. The components manufactured in the firm include cylinder heads, cylinder blocks, crank shafts, cam shafts, cam rods, and transmission gears used in automotive transmissions and drive systems. The firm manufactures around 60 varieties of transmission components, and has an annual turnover of USD 1.2 billion. The firm is certified with TS16949 and QS 14001 certification. The firm focuses on improving the customer value and contributes toward Corporate Social Responsibility (CSR) activities. It also has a dedicated team with members rich in Lean and quality system expertise . The firm also is interested in improving its value chain, as well as making manufacturing practices environmentally friendlier. It emphasizes more employee involvement to sustain quality and working skills. The firm operates to a system with pull production and has implemented various Lean strategies. The management of the organization showed interest in evaluating their pull system to determine their pull performance and to identify improvement opportunities to enhance their performance.

The ratings and weights pertaining to each enabler and criteria have been collected from experts of this case organization. Expert opinion technique was used to collect data pertaining to ratings and weights. The linguistics variables as proposed by Lin et al. (2006) were selected to evaluate the performance of the pull system: Excellent (E), Very Good (VG), Good (G), Fair (F), Poor (P), Very Poor (VP), and Worst (W). Similarly, the linguistic variables Very Low (VL), Low (L), Fairly Low (FL), Medium (M), Fairly High (FH), High (H), and Very High (VH) were used for assigning the weights W_i, W for criteria and enabler. Table 6.3 shows the linguistic variable and its corresponding fuzzy number for weights and ratings.

For this study, a panel consisting of four experts was formed for the collection of ratings and weights. The panel was constructed by considering expertise and knowledge of the experts in their respective domains. The experts are heads of various departments of the case organization and have vast experience and knowledge in specialization of Lean manufacturing. The performance ratings and weights for the conceptual model obtained from the experts are shown in Table 6.4. In Table 6.4, R1, R2, R3, and R4 denotes the response obtained from four experts. W_{ij} and W_i denote weights of the criteria and enabler, respectively.

6.3.4 Computation of FLPPI with Fuzzy Ratings with Fuzzy Weights

To obtain a Fuzzy Logic Pull Performance Index (FLPPI), fuzzy ratings and weights must be consolidated to compute the fuzzy weighted average. The fuzzy index of pull performance level is calculated by using Equation 6.1:

Table 6.3   Linguistic Variable and Its Fuzzy Number

Ratings (R1, R2, R3, R4)		Weights (Wi, W)	
Linguistic Variable	*Fuzzy Number*	*Linguistic Variable*	*Fuzzy Number*
Worst (W)	(0, 0.5, 1.5)	Very low (VL)	(0, 0.05, 0.15)
Very poor (VP)	(1, 2, 3)	Low (L)	(0.1, 0.2, 0.3)
Poor (P)	(2, 3.5, 5)	Fairly low (FL)	(0.2, 0.35, 0.5)
Fair (F)	(3, 5, 7)	Medium (M)	(0.3, 0.5, 0.7)
Good (G)	(5, 6.5, 8)	Fairly high (FH)	(0.5, 0.65, 0.8)
Very good (VG)	(7, 8, 9)	High (H)	(0.7, 0.8, 0.9)
Excellent (E)	(8.5, 9.5, 10)	Very high (VH)	(0.85, 0.95, 1.0)

Source: Lin, C.T. et al., *International Journal of Production Economics*, 100(2), 285–299, 2006.

$$\text{FLPPI}_i = \frac{\sum_{j=1}^{n} W_{ij} \times R_{ij}}{\sum_{j=1}^{n} W_{ij}} \quad (i = 1, \ldots, 6) \tag{6.1}$$

where:

   R_{ij}: aggregated fuzzy performance rating
   W_{ij}: importance weight for pull performance.

   R_{ij} is the aggregated fuzzy performance rating which is the average value of all the linguistic terms obtained as inputs for the criteria from experts. For example, the inputs obtained for the criteria small batch size (LP_{11}) are E, VG, F, and G and their corresponding fuzzy values are (8.5, 9.5, 10.0), (7.0, 8.0, 9.0), (3.0, 5.0, 7.0) and (5.0, 6.5, 8.0). The average value of these corresponding fuzzy numbers is computed using Equation 6.2:

$$R_{11} = \frac{(R1 + R2 + R3 + R4)}{4} \tag{6.2}$$

$$R_{11} = \frac{((8.5, 9.5, 10.0) + (7.0, 8.0, 9.0) + (3.0, 5.0, 7.0) + (5.0, 6.5, 8.0))}{4}$$

$$= (5.8, 7.2, 8.5)$$

Similarly, the aggregated fuzzy performance rating for the remaining criteria is computed. Using Equation 6.1, FLPPI for the first enabler ($i = 1$) is calculated as shown below

Table 6.4 Obtained Ratings and Weights

Enabler	Criteria	R1	R2	R3	R4	W_{ij}	W_i
Flexible process (LP$_1$)	Small batch size (LP$_{11}$)	E	VG	F	G	VH	H
	Visual control (LP$_{12}$)	G	F	F	VG	H	
	Customer driven orders (LP$_{13}$)	G	VG	G	F	H	
	Proper communication (LP$_{14}$)	F	G	F	G	H	
	Flexibility in delivery (LP$_{15}$)	F	G	G	F	H	
Inventory control (LP$_2$)	Maintaining low inventory (LP$_{21}$)	VG	G	G	E	VH	VH
	Usage of replenishment based inventory (LP$_{22}$)	G	F	G	F	H	
	Uninterrupted material flow (LP$_{23}$)	G	G	F	VG	H	
	Practicing VMI approach (LP$_{24}$)	VG	G	E	VG	VH	
Continuous flow (LP$_3$)	Uniform production levels (LP$_{31}$)	VG	G	G	VG	VH	VH
	Existence of facility layout (LP$_{32}$)	G	F	G	F	H	
	High responsiveness (LP$_{33}$)	G	G	F	F	H	
	Maintain proper value stream (LP$_{34}$)	VG	G	E	VG	VH	
Kanban (LP$_4$)	Selection of appropriate Kanban strategy (LP$_{41}$)	VG	G	G	F	H	H
	Proper coordination of Kanban signals (LP$_{42}$)	G	G	VG	G	VH	
	Optimal release of trigger point (LP$_{43}$)	G	F	VG	G	H	
	Usage of FIFO principle (LP$_{44}$)	G	F	F	G	H	
	Maintaining proper EOQ (LP$_{45}$)	G	VG	F	G	H	
Maintenance (LP$_5$)	OEE monitoring (LP$_{51}$)	VG	G	G	VG	VH	H
	Zero breakdowns (LP$_{52}$)	F	G	F	G	H	
	Adoptive preventive maintenance (LP$_{53}$)	G	F	G	F	FH	
	Minimal set-up time (LP$_{54}$)	G	VG	G	G	H	
Quality (LP$_6$)	Follow standardized work (LP$_{61}$)	VG	G	G	VG	VH	H
	Minimized rework and rejection rates (LP$_{62}$)	G	F	G	VG	H	
	Increased customer satisfaction (LP$_{63}$)	G	G	F	G	H	
	Inspection at source (LP$_{64}$)	G	VG	F	F	FH	

$$\text{FLPPI}_1 = \frac{\sum\limits_{j=1}^{5} W_{1j} \times R_{1j}}{\sum\limits_{j=1}^{5} W_{1j}}$$

$$= \frac{\begin{array}{l}(0.85, 0.95, 1.0) \times (5.8, 7.2, 8.5) + (0.7, 0.8, 0.9) \times (4.5, 6.1, 7.7) + (0.7, 0.8, 0.9) \\ \times (5.0, 6.5, 8.0) + (0.7, 0.8, 0.9) \times (4.0, 5.7, 7.5) + (0.7, 0.8, 0.9) \times (4.0, 5.7, 7.5)\end{array}}{\left((0.85, 0.95, 1) + (0.7, 0.8, 0.9) + (0.7, 0.8, 0.9) + (0.7, 0.8, 0.9) + (0.7, 0.8, 0.9)\right)}$$

$$= (4.9, 6.4, 7.9)$$

The performance index for other enablers also is computed in a similar way and the computed values are shown below:

$$\text{FLPPI}_2 = (5.6, 7.2, 8.3)$$

$$\text{FLPPI}_3 = (5.3, 6.7, 8.1)$$

$$\text{FLPPI}_4 = (4.9, 6.4, 7.9)$$

$$\text{FLPPI}_5 = (5.0, 6.4, 7.9)$$

$$\text{FLPPI}_6 = (5.3, 6.7, 8.1)$$

After computing FLPPI for the enabler level, FLPPI for the manufacturing organization is computed using Equation 6.3. R_i is the computed FLPPI_i value for the enabler level:

$$\text{FLPPI} = \sum_{i=1}^{n} \frac{W_i \times R_i}{W_i} \tag{6.3}$$

$$= \frac{\left(\begin{array}{l}(0.7, 0.8, 0.9) \times (4.9, 6.4, 7.9) + (0.85, 0.95, 1) \times (5.6, 7.2, 8.3) + (0.85, 0.95, 1) \times (5.3, 6.7, 8.1) \\ + (0.7, 0.8, 0.9) \times (4.9, 6.4, 7.9) + (0.7, 0.8, 0.9) \times (5.0, 6.4, 7.9) + (0.7, 0.8, 0.9) \times (5.3, 6.7, 8.1)\end{array}\right)}{\left((0.7, 0.8, 0.9) + (0.85, 0.95, 1) + (0.85, 0.95, 1) + (0.7, 0.8, 0.9) + (0.7, 0.8, 0.9) + (0.7, 0.8, 0.9)\right)}$$

$$\text{FLPPI} = (5.1, 6.6, 8.1)$$

6.4 Results and Discussions

6.4.1 Matching the Fuzzy-Based Levelness of Pull with Appropriate Level Using Euclidean Distance

After computing FLPPI, the obtained value is fitted with a linguistic label using the Euclidean distance method. Euclidean distance implies geometric distance in multi-dimensional space where

Table 6.5 Level of Pull Performance Corresponding to the Output Crisp Value

Level of Pull Performance	Output Crisp Value Range
Slow level of pull performance (SLP)	(0, 1.5, 3.0)
Fair level of pull performance (FLP)	(1.5, 3, 4.5)
Average level of pull performance (ALP)	(3.5, 5, 6.5)
High level of pull performance (HLP)	(5.5, 7, 8.5)
Very high level of pull performance (VLP)	(7, 8.5, 10)

distance between two entities is not affected by the inclusion of any new objects. The level which has the minimum Euclidean distance reveals the actual level of the case. The membership function is matched with appropriate linguistic terms. The level of pull performance corresponding to the output crisp value is shown in Table 6.5.

From the natural-language set LPi, levels namely Slow Level of Pull (SLP), Fair Level of Pull Performance (FLP), Average Level of Pull Performance (ALP), High Level of Pull Performance (HLP), and Very High Level of Pull Performance (VLP) is selected for labeling. The Euclidean distance from FLPPI is computed by using Equation 6.4 as follows:

$$D(\text{FLPPI}, \text{LP}_i) = \sum \left(\text{fFLPPI}(x) - \text{fLP}_i(x)^2 \right)^{1/2} \tag{6.4}$$

where:

$D(\text{FLPPI}, \text{LP}_i)$	= Euclidean distance between FLPPI and LP_i
FLPPI	= Fuzzy logic pull performance index
LP_i	= Fuzzy number for natural-language expression
fFLPPI (x)	= triangular fuzzy number of FLPPI
$\text{fLP}_i(x)$	= triangular fuzzy number of LP_i

where:

x denotes the lower, middle, and upper triangular numbers.

The model calculation for $D(\text{FLPPI}, \text{VLP})$ is shown as follows:

$$D(\text{FLPPI}, \text{VLP}) = \left\{ (5.1 - 7)^2 + (6.6 - 8.5)^2 + (8.1 - 10)^2 \right\}^{1/2}$$

$$= 3.28$$

Similarly Euclidean distance is computed for all the other natural sets.

$$D(\text{FLPPI}, \text{SLP}) = 26.91$$

$$D(\text{FLPPI}, \text{FLP}) = 13.59$$

$$D(\text{FLPPI}, \text{ALP}) = 2.84$$

$$D(\text{FLPPI}, \text{HLP}) = 0.09$$

$$D(\text{FLPPI}, \text{VLP}) = 3.28$$

By matching minimum Euclidean distance D with linguistic label, the case organization was found to possess High Level of Pull Performance.

6.4.2 Computation of Fuzzy Performance Importance Index (FPII)

By matching the minimum Euclidean distance D with a linguistic label, the level of pull performance of the case organization was identified as "High Level of Pull Performance." To recognize the principal obstacles for enhancing the level of pull performance, FPII has to be computed. FPII combines performance ratings and importance weights of each pull capability and expresses an impact which improves the level of pull system performance. FPII is the product of aggregated fuzzy performance rating (R_{ij}) and the corresponding inversed weight value of the criteria (W_{ij}'). The lower the FPII of a criterion is, the lower is the degree of contribution for that criterion. If W_{ij} is high, then the corresponding transformation $[(1, 1, 1) - R(W_{ij})]$ is low. Similarly, for each capability i, FPII_i, is computed using Equation 6.5:

$$\text{Fuzzy Performance Importance Index } (\text{FPII}_{ij}) = (\text{Aggregated fuzzy}$$

$$\text{performance rating}) \times (W_{ij}') \qquad (6.5)$$

$$\text{FPII}_{ij} = (R_{ij}) \times (W_{ij}')$$

The sample calculation for (FPII_{11}) is shown as follows:

$$W_{ij}' = \left[(1, \ 1, \ 1) - R(W_{ij}) \right]$$

where $R(W_{ij})$ is the reverse value of the Weighted value W_{ij}

$$(W_{11}) = (0.85, 0.95, 1)$$

$$R(W_{11}) = (1, 0.95, 0.85)$$

$$W_{11}' = \left[(1, 1, 1) - (1, 0.95, 0.85) \right]$$

$$= (0, 0.05, 0.15)$$

For computing FPII, aggregated fuzzy performance rating (R_{ij}) is being multiplied by inversed weight value of the criteria (W_{ij}'). (R_{ij}) is already being computed for all the criteria as shown in Equation 6.2. The corresponding R_{ij} value for R_{11} criterion is computed as (5.8, 7.2, 8.5) and W_{11}' value is computed as (0, 0.05, 0.15). FPII_{11} value is computed as shown below:

$$\text{FPII}_{11} = (5.8, 7.2, 8.5) \times (0, 0.05, 0.15)$$

$$\text{FPII}_{11} = (0, 0.36, 1.2)$$

Table 6.6 Calculated FPII for the Criteria

Pull Performance Level Criteria	Aggregated Fuzzy Performance Rating (R_{ij})	$W'_{ij} = \left[(1,1,1) - R(W_{ij}) \right]$	FPII
LP_{11}	(5.8, 7.2, 8.5)	(0, 0.05, 0.15)	(0, 0.36, 1.2)
LP_{12}	(3.1, 4.9, 6.9)	(0.1, 0.2, 0.3)	(0.3, 0.9, 2.0)
LP_{13}	(3.5, 5.2, 7.2)	(0.1, 0.2, 0.3)	(0.35, 1.04, 2.16)
LS_{14}	(2.8, 4.6, 6.7)	(0.1, 0.2, 0.3)	(0.28, 0.92, 2.0)
LP_{15}	(2.8, 4.6, 6.7)	(0.1, 0.2, 0.3)	(0.28, 0.92, 2.0)
LP_{21}	(5.4, 7.2, 8.7)	(0, 0.05, 0.15)	(0, 0.36, 1.8)
LP_{22}	(2.8, 4.6, 6.7)	(0.1, 0.2, 0.3)	(0.28, 0.92, 2.0)
LP_{23}	(3.5, 5.2, 7.2)	(0.1, 0.2, 0.3)	(0.35, 1.04, 2.16)
LP_{24}	(5.8 ,7.6, 9.0)	(0, 0.05, 0.15)	(0, 0.38, 1.9)
LP_{25}	(5.1, 6.8, 7.5)	(0, 0.05, 0.15)	(0, 0.34, 1.2)

Similarly FPII is calculated for all remaining criteria. An expert of the calculated FPII is shown in Table 6.6.

Since the obtained fuzzy number set may not be of an ordered set, it is necessary to rank all FPIIs involved in performance evaluation. Centroid method is used to rank fuzzy numbers with membership function (*a*, *b*, *c*) using Equation 6.6, where *a*, *b*, and *c* indicates lower, middle, and upper number of the obtained triangular fuzzy number, respectively:

$$\text{Ranking score} = \frac{\left(a + 4b + c \right)}{6} \tag{6.6}$$

Ranking score for (LP_{11}) is computed as

$$\text{FPII is } (0, 0.36, 1.2)$$

$$\text{Ranking score for } LP_{11} = \frac{\left(0 + \left(4 \times 0.36 \right) + 1.2 \right)}{6}$$

$$= 0.44$$

6.4.3 *Identification of Weaker Criteria and Proposed Improvements*

For identifying the critical obstacles, a scale of 0.99 was fixed as the management threshold. After calculation, it was inferred that eight capabilities had a performance value lesser than the management threshold. Appropriate improvement actions were proposed to improve the weaker criteria. The score for remaining criteria were computed using the mentioned method and shown for two enablers in Table 6.7.

Improvement actions were initiated considering the present manufacturing practices and the ability of the organization to deploy proposed improvements. Before finalizing and implementing

Table 6.7   Calculated Ranking Score for the Criteria

Pull Performance Level Criteria	Aggregated Fuzzy Performance Rating	W'_{ij}	FPII	Ranking Score
LP_{11}*	(4.9, 6.8, 8.5)	(0, 0.05, 0.15)	(0, 0.34, 1.2)	0.44
LP_{12}	(3.1, 4.9, 6.9)	(0.1, 0.2, 0.3)	(0.3, 0.9, 2.0)	1.05
LP_{13}	(3.5, 5.2, 7.2)	(0.1, 0.2, 0.3)	(0.35, 1.04, 2.16)	1.11
LS_{14}	(2.8, 4.6, 6.7)	(0.1, 0.2, 0.3)	(0.28, 0.92, 2.0)	0.99
LP_{15}	(2.8, 4.6, 6.7)	(0.1, 0.2, 0.3)	(0.28, 0.92, 2.0)	0.99
LP_{21}*	(5.4, 7.2, 8.7)	(0, 0.05, 0.15)	(0, 0.36, 1.8)	0.46
LP_{22}	(2.8, 4.6, 6.7)	(0.1, 0.2, 0.3)	(0.28, 0.92, 2.0)	0.99
LP_{23}	(3.5, 5.2, 7.2)	(0.1, 0.2, 0.3)	(0.35, 1.04, 2.16)	1.11
LP_{24}*	(5.8, 7.6, 9.0)	(0, 0.05, 0.15)	(0, 0.38, 1.9)	0.47
LP_{25}*	(5.1, 6.8, 7.5)	(0, 0.05, 0.15)	(0, 0.34, 1.2)	0.44

* The weaker criteria whose ranking score fall below the fixed management threshold value.

the proposed improvement actions, the applicability of the improvement actions and its possible outcomes were demonstrated to the experts and their suggestions were recorded. The proposed improvement actions for eight capabilities are shown in Table 6.8.

The developed conceptual model for assessing the performance of pull systems helps in determining the current level of pull performance and also helps in identifying and improvising the weaker criteria for enhancing the performance of pull system. On successful implementation of the proposed improvement actions, it would enable the manufacturing firm to improve its level of pull performance and provides scope to substantiate Lean initiatives.

6.5 Conclusions

Creation of a pull system is considered one of the backbones of Lean manufacturing as it focuses on delivering the products and services that are being pulled from the customer end. A pull system controls the amount of inventory throughout the production system by streamlining material flow based on customer orders and by maintaining a build-to-order production system. Pull can be achieved by maintaining a proper flow of materials by adopting Lean techniques like JIT, Kanban, and continuous flow. Performance evaluation of manufacturing systems are performed to monitor and track improvement actions and to locate the vital functional domains that requires immediate attention. Performance evaluation of pull systems is performed to find out its capability in delivering pull and to identify the improvement opportunities to enhance the performance of pull further.

This chapter presents a conceptual performance evaluation model for evaluating the performance of pull systems. The developed performance evaluation model works using a fuzzy logic approach as it is capable of handling vagueness and uncertainty that usually exists in conventional performance evaluation model. The evaluation model comprises of 6 enablers and 26 criteria that

Table 6.8 Proposed Improvement Actions for the Eight Weaker Attributes

Criteria	Proposed Improvement
Small batch size	Smaller batch sizes improve a firm's flexibility and reduces inventory costs. Since variable costs are minimal in small batch sizes, it decreases the firm's overheads and allows achieving a smoother pull with reduced costs. The firm can reduce its batch size by maintaining a uniform palette capacity and by proper production planning.
Maintaining low inventory	Maintaining low inventory helps in reducing the firm's operating costs and also in achieving optimal floor space usage. Low inventory can be maintained by adopting a proper procurement and planning strategy. Economic Order Quantity, safety stock, and delivery schedules must be in line with the customer orders, such that unnecessary pilling up of inventory as overproduction is avoided.
Practicing VMI approach	Vendor Managed Inventory (VMI) approach can be adopted, which helps in reducing the burden of the organization considering raw material inventory. In a VMI approach, the vendor directly has control over inventory where the vendor reviews the customer orders and inventory levels, replenishing inventory when stock levels are low. To practice VMI, the vendor and organization must maintain a good relationship and proper communication must prevail between them. The role of information technology plays a major role in achieving this.
Uniform production levels	The firm must maintain uniform production levels in order to maintain a proper flow in the manufacturing process. It can be achieved by proper understanding of variability that exists on the planning horizon. In a mixed model manufacturing environment, maintaining uniform production levels is a tedious task and this can be achieved by maintaining a synchronized Kanban and following a proper sequencing and scheduling strategy.
Maintain proper value stream	The firm must understand its value stream from a customer point-of-view and continuous flow must be drawn from its upstream process. The production sequence must eliminate waste and facilitate flow by minimizing down times and bottlenecks.
Proper coordination of Kanban signals	Kanban signals must be properly coordinated such that replenishment time is minimal. Factors like number of cards, lead time, demand, container capacity, and safety stocks must be synchronized with customer orders while designing the planning strategy. A strong communication model and highly determined supplier involvement are crucial factors for achieving this.
OEE monitoring	The effectiveness of the equipment must be properly monitored to avoid breakdowns and speed loss, which significantly reduces the pace of pull. This is achieved by following proper maintenance scheduling and by proper usage of technologies to control the OEE metrics of availability, performance, and quality.
Follow standardized work	Documenting the best practices helps the process to operate smoothly and avoids unnecessary waiting that interrupts the pull. Proper training and education on following the standardized work is to be provided for the associated people to effectively operate the process based on standardized work. Techniques like poka yoke and visual management can also be deployed for achieving this.

determine the effective functioning of a pull system. The steps involved in this fuzzy-based evaluation include linguistic assessment of inputs, fuzzification, and computation of FLPPI. The crisp value was found to be 6.6 and when matched with Euclidean distance computation this revealed that the case organization was found to have "High Level of Pull Performance."

Eight further capabilities were found to be weak and subsequent improvement actions were proposed. One of the prerequisites of deploying this model is that the firm where the study is to be conducted must already have adopted Lean concepts. Upon satisfying this requirement, the developed model can be used for evaluating the performance of pull systems holistically. The developed model helps in arriving at accurate evaluations. In the future, the developed performance evaluation model can be enhanced by including more enablers and criteria. Therefore, more studies can be performed to improve the validity of the developed model.

Reference

Abdulmalek, F.A. and Rajgopal, J. 2007. Analyzing the benefits of Lean manufacturing and value stream mapping via simulation: A process sector case study. *International Journal of Production Economics*, 107(1), 223–236.

Benton, W.C. and Shin, H. 1998. Manufacturing planning and control: The evolution of MRP and JIT integration. *European Journal of Operational Research*, 110(3), 411–440.

Davis, A.M., Katok, E. and Santamaría, N. 2014. Push, pull, or both? A behavioral study of how the allocation of inventory risk affects channel efficiency. *Management Science*, 60(11), 2666–2683.

Deleersnyder, J.L., Hodgson, T.J., Muller-Malek, H. and O'Grady, P.J. 1989. Kanban controlled pull systems: An analytic approach. *Management Science*, 35(9), 1079–1091.

Doolen, T.L. and Hacker, M.E. 2005. A review of Lean assessment in organizations: An exploratory study of Lean practices by electronics manufacturers. *Journal of Manufacturing Systems*, 24(1), 55.

Gaury, E.G.A., Pierreval, H. and Kleijnen, J.P. 2000. An evolutionary approach to select a pull system among Kanban, CONWIP and hybrid. *Journal of Intelligent Manufacturing*, 11(2), 157–167.

Gibbons, P.M. and Burgess, S.C. 2010. Introducing OEE as a measure of Lean six sigma capability. *International Journal of Lean Six Sigma*, 1(2), 134–156.

Hasle, P. 2014. Lean production—An evaluation of the possibilities for an employee supportive Lean practice. *Human Factors and Ergonomics in Manufacturing and Service Industries*, 24(1), 40–53.

Jasti, N.V.K. and Kodali, R. 2016. An empirical study for implementation of Lean principles in Indian manufacturing industry. *Benchmarking: An International Journal*, 23(1), 183–207.

Karim, A. and Arif-Uz-Zaman, K. 2013. A methodology for effective implementation of Lean strategies and its performance evaluation in manufacturing organizations. *Business Process Management Journal*, 19(1), 169–196.

Khojasteh, Y. and Sato, R. 2015. Selection of a pull production control system in multi-stage production processes. *International Journal of Production Research*, 53(14), 4363–4379.

Kim, T.M. 1985. Just-in-time manufacturing system: A periodic pull system. *International Journal of Production Research*, 23(3), 553–562.

Kimura, O. and Terada, H. 1981. Design and analysis of pull system, a method of multi-stage production control. *The International Journal of Production Research*, 19(3), 241–253.

Kuriger, G.W. and Chen, F.F. 2010. Lean and green: A current state view. In *Proceedings of the IIE Annual Conference* (p. 1). Institute of Industrial Engineers-Publisher. Norcross, United States.

Liker, J.K. 1997. *Becoming Lean: Inside Stories of US Manufacturers*. Boca Raton, FL: CRC Press. Boca Raton, Florida.

Lin, C.T., Chiu, H. and Chu, P.Y. 2006. Agility index in the supply chain. *International Journal of Production Economics*, 100(2), 285–299.

Marquès, G., Thierry, C., Lamothe, J. and Gourc, D. 2010. A review of vendor managed inventory (VMI): From concept to processes. *Production Planning and Control*, 21(6), 547–561.

Mascolo, M.D., Frein, Y. and Dallery, Y. 1996. An analytical method for performance evaluation of kanban controlled production systems. *Operations Research*, 44(1), 50–64.

Olhager, J. and Östlund, B. 1990. An integrated push–pull manufacturing strategy. *European Journal of Operational Research*, 45(2), 135–142.

Page, T. 2010. Achieving manufacturing excellence by applying LSSF model-A Lean six sigma framework. *i-Manager's Journal on Future Engineering and Technology*, 6(1), 51.

Puchkova, A., Le Romancer, J. and McFarlane, D. 2016. Balancing push and pull strategies within the production system. *IFAC-PapersOnLine*, 49(2), 66–71.

Rajak, S. and Vinodh, S. 2015. Application of fuzzy logic for social sustainability performance evaluation: A case study of an Indian automotive component manufacturing organization. *Journal of Cleaner Production*, 108, 1184–1192.

Shah, R. and Ward, P.T. 2003. Lean manufacturing: Context, practice bundles, and performance. *Journal of Operations Management*, 21(2), 129–149.

Slomp, J., Bokhorst, J.A. and Germs, R. 2009. A Lean production control system for high-variety/low-volume environments: A case study implementation. *Production Planning and Control*, 20(7), 586–595.

Spearman, M.L. and Zazanis, M.A. 1992. Push and pull production systems: Issues and comparisons. *Operations Research*, 40(3), 521–532.

Vinodh, S. and Balaji, S.R. 2011. Fuzzy logic based leanness assessment and its decision support system. *International Journal of Production Research*, 49(13), 4027–4041.

Vinodh, S., Ruben, R.B. and Asokan, P. 2016. Life cycle assessment integrated value stream mapping framework to ensure sustainable manufacturing: A case study. *Clean Technologies and Environmental Policy*, 18(1), 279–295.

Vinodh, S. and Vimal, K.E.K. 2012. Thirty criteria based leanness assessment using fuzzy logic approach. *The International Journal of Advanced Manufacturing Technology*, 60(9–12), 1185–1195.

Womack, J.P., Jones, D.T. and Roos, D. 1990. *Machine that Changed the World*. New York, NY: Simon and Schuster. New York.

REVIEW ON PULL SYSTEMS

Chapter 7

CONWIP and Hybrid CONWIP Production Control Systems: A Literature Review

Mehmet Bulent Durmusoglu and Canan Aglan

Contents

7.1 Introduction

Increasing competition and decreasing profit margins forced companies to find effective ways of providing both services and products offered. Effective ways are realized through the elimination of non-value-added activities from the system. That is what lean philosophy is based upon. One of the best examples of lean philosophy is observed in the Toyota Corporation where this philosophy emerged. The production control mechanism on lean systems is based upon pull logic, instead of push logic. This entails pulling from upstream processes while considering the requirements of the system. However, in push logic, the upstream operations send the processed parts directly to downstream operations, regardless of the requirements. The result of pushing parts to downstream operations is work-in-process (WIP) accumulation in front of stations. This WIP

123

increase would cause lead time increases as Little (1961) proved. At the same time, more importantly, increasing WIP hides the problems. The best way to avoid this WIP increase is to control WIP throughout the system. Sending the right parts, to the right place, and in the right amount improves lead time performance by decreasing WIP. The problems hiding with high WIP can begin to surface. These are opportunities to improve the systems.

Pulling from upstream process is not an easy task. It requires prior activities such as grouping of product types and equipment types to construct group technology cells, production smoothing, set-up time reduction, 5S, which is one of the most well-known methods that concentrates on workplace organization, house-keeping activities and standardization, and others. Before realizing these activities, pull control cannot be applied. The type of control mechanism applied is a decision based upon product type, demand variability, and layout of the production system. The increasing product types and demand variability complicate the application of pure pull control. These require pull and push control mechanisms applied simultaneously, which is called "hybrid production control" throughout this chapter. The advantages of pull control, WIP controlling, and just-in-time (JIT) parts supply are integrated with the advantages of push control, which are demand forecasting and sequencing aspects.

In terms of layout issues, application of pull control to layouts, which are different from cellular layouts, results in transportation waste, since pull control requires small lot production. In cellular layout, raw material is generally inserted in the corresponding cell and exits as a finished product from the system. The distance between production equipment in cellular layout is shorter than the distances between production equipment in functional layout. However, if the layout is functional, where similar types of equipment are placed at the same place, parts or subassemblies would require extra transportation for processing on different types of equipment. This situation would cause traffic congestion, especially if parts are transported in small lots. The advantages of pull control application are not realized on these types of layouts. The same case is also valid in so-called hybrid layouts, where cellular and functional arrangements exist together.

A hybrid production control mechanism, CONWIP combines the advantages of push and pull controls. CONWIP control includes both pull and push principles simultaneously. CONWIP is an easy control mechanism compared to other control mechanisms such as Kanban, workload control (WLC), and paired cell overlapping loops of cards with authorization (POLCA). This practical application advantage increases the popularity of CONWIP control.

The scope of this chapter covers the application of basic control mechanism, design requirements, and other CONWIP-like control mechanisms. CONWIP and other push/pull integrated control policies are also discussed. A literature review for application of basic CONWIP control, design requirements of CONWIP control, control policies that arise from basic CONWIP control such as workload control (WLC), Critical WIP Loops II (CWIPL II), control of balance by card-based navigation (COBACABANA), WIP load control (WIPLCtrl), and combinations of CONWIP control with other control mechanisms are given. A classification for the literature in terms of considered parameters is provided, and future research directions are underlined based on this classification.

7.2 Basic CONWIP Production Control Mechanism

The basic CONWIP production control was proposed by Spearman et al. (1990). In case of demand variability, processing time, and routing variability in a manufacturing system, the performance of Kanban and CONWIP production control differ significantly. For instance, Kanban control performs well in smooth demand and standardized product environments and it requires actual demand information. When there is variability and customized product types, implementation of Kanban control may cause inventory starvation in some workstations and inventory accumulation on remaining workstations. In this kind of manufacturing environment a production control, applying both pull and push principles, to realize lead time performance by limiting WIP and to adapt variability via demand forecasting methods is suggested.

In the basic CONWIP production control, order or backlog lists which show the order of jobs to be processed in the system are derived via material requirements planning (MRP), and total WIP in the system is restricted via CONWIP cards. If a free card exists, the job is released to the system. Figure 7.1 is an activity interaction diagram of CONWIP control mechanism in a four-stage tandem line. Squares (p_i) and ovals (b_i) represent, respectively, processes and buffers, while M and b represents raw material buffer and finished goods buffer, respectively. Queue C represents CONWIP cards buffer. Two conditions, the backlog list is not empty and a CONWIP card is available in the beginning of the line, should be satisfied in CONWIP control for production to be started. The production progresses with a card attached to the semi-finished product until it becomes a final product and is sent to the customer. After demand is satisfied, the card is detached and sent to the beginning of the CONWIP loop to be attached to the next order waiting in the order pool. The cycle continues in this fashion until all orders in the production list are completed. One of the advantages of CONWIP control over Kanban is it has a fewer number of parameter requirements.

The rise of CONWIP control is based on the transition from make to stock (MTS) to make to order (MTO) environments with the diversified needs of customers (Prakash and Chin 2015). In MTS policy the products are standard, so that holding inventory is allowed. However, in MTO policy, the customer can choose from a diversified product portfolio and holding inventory of each type is not an efficient way to satisfy customer needs. The total WIP in the system can be restricted by limiting the total inventory circulating in the system. That's why CONWIP control is suitable in MTO policy (Prakash and Chin 2015).

Thorough implementation of CONWIP control depends on several characteristics of the manufacturing environment. Shop layout, set-up time reduction activities, and quality improvement are some of the characteristics listed in Li (2010). Shop layout in CONWIP control is generally flow shop type, where products are processed based on a route where unidirectional flow exists. Set-up time reduction activities in CONWIP control are also important as manufacturing lot sizes are smaller, when compared to push control. Quality improvement and autonomous maintenance activities should also be considered in a CONWIP controlled line, which has less WIP than an MRP-controlled line.

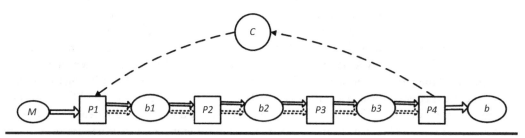

Figure 7.1 CONWIP mechanism (Khojasteh, 2016c).

The design requirements of CONWIP control are to decide the type of cards allocated to part types, card controlling issues, backlog list, lot sizes assigned to each card type, and the number of cards circulating in the CONWIP loop. Huang et al. (2015) investigated the design patterns in a multi-product assembly type production environment. The investigated CONWIP was a multi-loop system in assembly operations. Different policies were investigated and design parameters for multi-loop CONWIP control were determined. The outstanding parameters are layout, facility location, size of facility, proximity of production equipment, and storage type, as well as collaboration between suppliers and material distributors. Each design requirement was discussed in the related literature. In addition, more than one design parameter and their combined effects were discussed. For example, the number of cards calculations and card controlling issues were handled in Enns and Rogers (2008), while backlog list design effect on dispatching rule were investigated in Bahaji and Kuhl (2008). In Section 7.2.1, related design requirements and their combined effects on performance measures are discussed briefly.

7.2.1 CONWIP Card Type Studies

The cards in CONWIP control can be either product type related (dedicated) or line specific (shared). In the dedicated card type, each card represents a typical product type. In shared card types, cards belong to a line instead of product types. Shared card types are typically applied in cases of demand variability and in assembly type manufacturing environments (Onyeocha et al. 2013a). The shared card type allocation responds quickly to changes by switching high demand product types from low demand product types, in case of demand variability (Onyeocha et al. 2013a). Khojasteh-Ghamari (2009) considered an assembly line with three stages where a third stage is fed by two subassembly lines performing final assembly operations. He compared the performance of the shared and dedicated card types, with respect to the average number of products produced per time unit, and the average WIP. Based on the simulation scenarios, card distribution along the line affects the performance of the system. He found that shared card type results in lower WIP than the dedicated card type for a given throughput level. Onyeocha et al. (2013b) showed that shared card type is more robust than dedicated card type in a multi-product variable demand environment, based on simulation experiments. Li (2010) also studied the shared card types in a cellular manufacturing environment.

In a dedicated card type, each product type is assigned a specific card. In addition to deciding the total number of cards in the system, the number of cards allocated to specific product types is decided. Ryan and Vorasayan (2005) proposed a dedicated card type when process requirements of different product types differ significantly. They compared the performance of shared and dedicated card type for lost sales performance measure by performing a sensitivity analysis in case of processing time variability. The investigated system was a multi-product, highly variable environment such that processing time between product types had different mean processing rates, and stations could be visited more than once with different processing time requirements. They concluded that card type design is strongly affected by the difference between capacity and demand rate. Simulation experiments in Framinan et al. (2000) showed that utilizing a dedicated card type gave better performance, in terms of WIP, for a given service level in an MTS flow shop environment. However, the findings of Baynat et al. (2002) did not find a difference between the performances of shared and dedicated card types when different product types are in different queues. Table 7.1 shows the proposed card type, manufacturing environment, and performance measures in CONWIP studies.

Table 7.1 Card Type Related Literature

Study	Aim	Manufacturing Environment	Proposed Card Type
Onyeocha et al. (2013a)	Average total WIP minimization and service level maximization	Multi-product, multi-stage, variable demand profile, subject to machine failures	Shared card type
Khojasteh-Ghamari (2009)	Comparison shared and dedicated card types in terms of throughput rate and WIP	Three stage assembly line producing single part type, demand is unlimited	Shared card type
Li (2010)	Comparison of different control mechanisms in terms of mean and standard deviation of flow time	Multi-product job shop, variable demand, subject to machine failures	Shared card type in simulation experiments for cellular layout
Ryan and Vorasayan (2005)	Lost sales minimization by allocating cards through product types	Multi-product, multi-stage manufacturing environment, backtracking of products exist with different processing time distribution, and bottleneck stations	Dedicated card type
Framinan et al. (2000)	Service level maximization, WIP minimization	Flow shop	Dedicated card type
Baynat et al. (2002)	Throughput maximization	Multi-product, multi-stage	No distinction between shared and dedicated card types

7.2.2 Number of Card Calculation Studies

Studies regarding the number of cards consider other design issues such as card type, backlog list, and card controlling. Card numbers generally are based on finding the WIP level for a given throughput. Ioannidis and Kouikoglu (2008) proposed a model to find the optimal number of CONWIP cards in a MTS single product environment that maximizes profit rate. The system was modeled as a single server with finite queue length. Backlog allowance also was investigated in the developed model.

The simulation model proposed in the study of Onyeocha et al. (2013a) utilized a genetic algorithm to find the optimal number of card types, in addition to a comparison between shared and dedicated card type performance.

Duenyas and Hopp (1993) developed approximations to calculate throughput and the number of jobs in the queue. These values were utilized in capacity allocation, WIP setting, and bottleneck identification. The validity of approximations was tested via simulation with exponential and stochastic distribution of processing times. Ryan et al. (2000) studied the job shop environment with multiple products that have diverse routings. The aim of the study was to calculate the total WIP and allocate them to product types. A heuristic algorithm was proposed for achieving a target customer service level.

In some studies the number of cards calculation is done as secondary work to attain better performance. In a study by Enns and Rogers (2008), the aim was to compare the performance of push and CONWIP control. The inventory level in the system was determined as a parameter in the simulation experiments.

Another design-related issue with the number of cards allocation is card controlling or card setting. In card controlling, the number of cards in the system is changed based on the system load. In the latter case, card number is calculated at the beginning of the planning period and does not change during the entire period. Hopp and Roof (1998) proposed a statistical throughput control to adjust the number of cards circulating in the system. Throughput estimates were performed to adjust the card numbers. When the throughput falls beyond the three sigma limits, a new card is either added or discarded from the system. The proposed methodology was tested under single and multi-product environments and the effectiveness of the methodology was shown under static and dynamic conditions. Framinan et al. (2006) investigated the card controlling issue and proposed a new methodology which is suitable for both MTO and MTS environments. The proposed methodology was compared to the statistical throughput control for throughput and service level performance measures. Results showed the superiority of the developed methodology.

On card setting, Braglia et al. (2011) considered a flow shop with batch processing. Two analytical models for two cases in which the batching processing machine has a bottleneck and does not have a bottleneck were developed to maximize throughput and minimize WIP. The validity of the models was shown in two examples. Table 7.2 shows the related literature for card number calculation studies.

7.2.3 Backlog List Related Studies

In CONWIP control, a backlog list shows the order of products to be produced during the planning period. Herer and Masin (1997) developed a mathematical model that minimizes inventory holding, backorder, and overtime cost. The results of the model are backlog list, regular time, and overtime. Aglan and Durmusoglu (2015) developed a mathematical model to find the sequence of products in a hybrid manufacturing environment. The model minimizes average flow time of jobs under lot splitting and sequence dependent set-up time constraints.

In addition to constructing backlog list, dispatching rules also are important to achieving lead time and due date-related goals. In a simple flow shop environment, with CONWIP control, a first-come first-served (FCFS) dispatching rule is applied. However, for more complex environments, simple dispatching rules are insufficient to realize the mentioned goals. For complex environments, a backlog list is prepared by considering the system's dynamic structure and

Table 7.2   Card Number Studies

Study	Aim	Design Parameters	Card Controlling/ Card Setting	Manufacturing Environment
Ioannidis and Kouikoglu (2008)	Profit maximization	Holding cost, backlog cost, revenue, production capacity, annual demand	Card setting	One type product, random demand
Onyeocha et al. (2013a)	Average total WIP minimization and service level maximization	Quality improvement, set up time	Card setting	Multi-product, multi-stage, variable demand profile, subject to machine failures
Duenyas and Hopp (1993)	Analytical model for throughput and average number of jobs in queue	Processing time, service time	Card setting	Multi-product, subject to bottlenecks assembly line
Ryan et al. (2000)	Service level maximization	Product mix rates between two product types	Card setting	Multi-product, diverse routing job shop
Hopp and Roof (1998)	Average inter-output time, standard deviation of inter-output time and average cycle time	Simple flow line, number of product types, routes in case of shared resources	Card controlling	Single and multi-product environment
Framinan et al. (2006)	Throughput rate maximization for MTO and service level maximization for MTS	Target throughput rate, processing time distribution, mean time between failure and mean time to repair	Card controlling	Single product simple flow shop
Braglia et al. (2011)	Throughput maximization by keeping WIP minimum	Bottleneck source place, number of product types, batch size in batch operation	Card setting	Flow sop with batch processing machine

performance measures. Bahaji and Kuhl (2008) compared simple dispatching rules and proposed a new composite dispatching that aims to minimize mean and standard deviation of flow time in a low-variety high-volume CONWIP-controlled manufacturing environment. The comparison results show that the FCFS dispatching rule is superior with respect to the previously mentioned objectives. Ryan and Vorasayan (2005) also utilized the FCFS dispatching rule after finding the number of dedicated cards for each product type.

The majority of studies focus on job release decisions, considering the dynamic nature of demand profile. Instead of sequencing and scheduling jobs, rules for releasing jobs to the system are determined. The combination of different control mechanisms is done to prevent starving and blocking, as well as to handle variability. Huang et al. (2013) combined and applied Kanban and CONWIP control mechanisms in an assembly line. Three different combinations of CONWIP and Kanban were proposed. The difference between combinations is the control mechanisms applied to a bottleneck, before and after the bottleneck resource. In the first combination, a bottleneck resource was controlled via Kanban, while the remaining resources were controlled via CONWIP. In the second combination, resources before the bottleneck were controlled via CONWIP, while resources after bottleneck were controlled via Kanban, and in third combination it was vice versa. The effect of bottleneck resource location on system performance was evaluated via simulation experiments. Performance of Kanban, CONWIP, and hybrid polices were compared with respect to the throughput rate, WIP, and number of cards. The results of the simulation experiments showed that in the majority of scenarios CONWIP outperforms Kanban and hybrid policies, whereas hybrid policies are more robust than Kanban and CONWIP. Additionally, performance of the hybrid polices were affected by the location of bottleneck resource. If the first station was a bottleneck, then controlling the bottleneck via Kanban and remaining resources via CONWIP had a better performance. It was the opposite if the bottleneck resource was the last station. Finally, controlling the line via CONWIP before the bottleneck resource and controlling the line via Kanban after the bottleneck, performed well in terms of WIP performance measure.

Bonvik and Gershwin (1996) proposed a release mechanism, which is based on Kanban and CONWIP principles, to avoid machine blocking. Inventory accumulation in front of machines was prevented via Kanban, and total WIP in the system was controlled via CONWIP. Chong et al. (2013) investigated a multi-stage, unbalanced, high product mix environment. Based on simulation scenarios, Kanban control for a stable and high demand pattern. and CONWIP control for variable and low demand pattern, generated scheduling smoothness and a WIP reduction.

Dong et al. (2016) proposed a dynamic job release policy in CONWIP controlled assembly process. The policy was applied for a ship building outfitting process. Gastermann et al. (2012) constructed a diverse backlog policy for a plastics sanitary manufacturing firm. In the proposed policy, standard subassemblies, based on a demand forecast, were produced via a backlog list, while due date-related dispatching rules applied for the products that had actual demand data. A summary of backlog list and dispatching rules proposed is given in Table 7.3.

7.2.4 CONWIP Lot Size Related Studies

In general, each CONWIP card is assigned to a job which may consist of different lot sizes. This approach does not prevent variability inside the system, if job lot sizes differ significantly. By considering this problem, some studies calculated the workload for each job and assigned cards to standard workloads (Cao and Chen 2005, Zhang and Chen 2001).

Cao and Chen (2005) developed a mixed integer, nonlinear mathematical model for simultaneously finding the sequence and lot sizes in a CONWIP controlled assembly line. The aim of the

Table 7.3   Literature for Backlog List Studies

Study	Aim	Dispatching Rule	Proposed Methodology
Herer and Masin (1997)	Inventory holding, backorder, and overtime minimization	FCFS	Mathematical model in simple flow shop that finds mean effective processing time
Aglan and Durmusoglu (2015)	Average flow time minimization	FCFS	Mathematical model under lot splitting and hybrid production environment subject to sequence dependent set-up
Bahaji and Kuhl (2008)	Minimization mean and standard deviation of flow time	Different single dispatching rules and a novel dispatching rule which is based on priority index and dynamic scaling parameter	Simulation considering different dispatching rules and push control experimental settings
Ajorlou and Shams (2013)	Makespan minimization	FCFS	Mathematical model and artificial bee colony optimization
Cao and Chen (2005)	Workload difference minimization	FCFS	Mathematical model that considers assembly operations
Alfieri and Matta (2012)	Makespan minimization	FCFS	Mathematical model that considers flow shop environment
Dong et al. (2016)	Product cost and completion time minimization	Static and dynamic scheduling comparison	Mean value analysis recursive functions
Gastermann et al. (2012)	WIP reduction, throughput and flexibility increase	Due date-related rules	Planning structure

developed model was to minimize the total set-up time and the load differences between fabrication lines. Zhang and Chen (2001) developed a similar mathematical model for single flow shop manufacturing system that minimizes set-up time and workload differences to find the production lot sizes and the backlog list. Aglan and Durmusoglu (2015) proposed a lot splitting model in which the lot size of an order is divided into smaller sized lots in a CONWIP controlled hybrid manufacturing system. The experiments showed the superiority of lot sizing technique in terms of average lead time.

The study by Muhammad et al. (2015) considered the batching of jobs in the backorder list to gain the set-up time advantage for similar type of products. Simulation experiments were performed to understand if batching is superior to a non-batching system. The performance measures were throughput, mean and standard deviation of flow time, average waiting time, workstation utilization, and total critical output. In designing the experiment, the number of CONWIP cards, ratio of order distribution, and set-up time were considered as factors. The results showed that batching of orders is always superior to non-batching, regardless of design factors.

7.3 CONWIP Performance Comparison Studies

In addition to the design of CONWIP control, there are studies comparing the performance of CONWIP control with other pull and/or push-based control mechanisms. As mentioned in previous sections, Enns and Rogers (2008) compared the performance of CONWIP control with workload control in a balanced flow shop type manufacturing environment. Simulation experiments were performed for comparison. Performance measures were throughput and inventory. The effect of performance measures on inter-arrival time and processing time variability was investigated via simulation scenarios. They found that the performance of CONWIP control outperforms when inter-arrival times are highly variable. However, the constant release mechanism in workload control performed better than CONWIP control in several scenarios.

Farnoush and Wiktorsson (2013) compared multiple CONWIP (M-CONWIP) control with three different versions of POLCA control. In POLCA control, the machines are virtually connected to each other with a card. Paired machines are determined via the routing information for products. A central planning department schedules the production and products go through the machine pairs when cards are available in front of the first machine in the pair. This control mechanism is generally applied to one-of-a-kind production, such as mold. M-CONWIP was proposed for multiple stages production systems by Germs and Riezebos (2010). Simulation experiments showed that M-CONWIP is superior to all types of POLCA control in terms of throughput rate, throughput time, and WIP. Kabadurmus (2009) compared the performance of CONWIP and POLCA in terms of inter-arrival times, coefficient of variation in processing times, batch size, and product mix parameters. The simulation experiments showed that CONWIP performs worse than POLCA for all values of parameters. However, the performance difference between CONWIP and POLCA was reduced for low machine failure time, large batch size values, and low demand values.

Gilland (2002) compared CONWIP, drum-buffer-rope (DBR), and pull from bottleneck control policies in a microprocessor assembling plant. The system was a flow shop cell. Comparisons were done under single and multi-bottleneck scenarios. The marginal value of output and cost of additional output were performance measures. In a single bottleneck case, DBR, which manages the bottleneck source, outperformed other control methods. In multi-bottleneck case, pull from bottleneck, as the name implies a pull policy, controls WIP near the bottlenecks outperformed CONWIP and DBR controls.

Jodlbauer and Huber (2008) investigated the performance of MRP, Kanban, DBR, and CONWIP in a multi-product, multi-level, MTS flow shop environment via simulation, with respect to the service level and WIP measures. The results showed that CONWIP has superior performance under static conditions. The parameters are important in service level performance, that is, a small deviation from optimal operating parameters would deteriorate the service level performance. MRP was found to have the highest stability. A similar comparison was done in Lee and Seo (2016). A max-plus algebra based solution was developed to make comparisons between DBR, Kanban, and CONWIP. DBR and CONWIP outperformed Kanban in terms of required buffer capacity and WIP level. Between DBR and CONWIP, DBR was found to need less buffer capacity, whereas larger WIP was needed. CONWIP was found to be superior to DBR under a given service quality level.

In a study by Pettersen and Segerstedt (2009), CONWIP was compared with Kanban under production environment where operation times are stochastic. The simulation experiments showed that when the amount of WIP is equal in Kanban and CONWIP policies, throughput rate of CONWIP policy is higher than the Kanban policy. A similar result was found by Yang (2000) in a multi-product single line flow shop environment. Policy variables, affecting the performance of each system, were also investigated. Performance measures were average customer waiting time, total WIP, number of upstream and downstream trips, and total number of trips. CONWIP control was superior to Kanban in terms of mean customer waiting time and total WIP. Another finding showed that, in terms of number of trips between stations, CONWIP is not always superior to Kanban, and that CONWIP requires larger storage area.

A different approach comparing the information content of MRP, Kanban, and CONWIP was studied by Gong et al. (2014). The delay for decision making was investigated in terms of information content. Information content of each control was calculated via information entropy. The findings showed that CONWIP control has less information content than Kanban, and Kanban has less information content than MRP.

Khojasteh (2016a,b) investigated Kanban, CONWIP, and base-stock performance in flow shop and assembly environments via theory of token transaction systems. The findings for flow shop and assembly environments revealed that the superiority of one approach to another is dependent on the total card number. The performance measure was WIP that attain the desired number throughout. A control system is then superior to another if, and only if, it reaches the same throughput level with less WIP. Table 7.4 represents comparison studies, performance measures, experimental factors and manufacturing environment.

The results of comparison studies show that CONWIP control is not suitable for every manufacturing environment. For instance, the existence of variable manufacturing batch sizes of product types, bottleneck resources, complex routings, and multiple stages in production processes adversely affects the performance of CONWIP control. In a CONWIP controlled line, the cause of inventory accumulation and starvation is the existence of bottleneck resources, which would eventually increase variability and lead time in the system (Bonvik and Gershwin 1996). To cope with variability, Parvin et al. (2012) developed a fixed task zone chain algorithm, which is about the cross training of employees, in a U-shaped CONWIP controlled line. The developed algorithm applied to the case where the number of workers is less than the number of machines. The aim of the proposed algorithm was to maximize throughput by balancing the line and decreasing the variability in the system.

The existence of shifting bottlenecks, that is, bottlenecks that change overtime due to different product types and breakdowns, makes CONWIP application difficult (Nahavandi 2014). CONWIP application also requires set-up time reduction activities since batch sizes are smaller than the batch sizes in push control policies. An information delay in intermediate stages may result since demand information is sent to only first and last stages in CONWIP control (Onyeocha et al. 2013a).

Table 7.4   CONWIP and Other Control Mechanisms Comparison Studies

Study	Compared Control Mechanisms	Performance Measures	System Specifications	Result
Enns and Rogers (2008)	WLC	Throughput, inventory	Balanced flow shop subject to processing time and inter-arrival time variability	CONWIP outperforms in variability cases
Farnoush and Wiktorsson (2013)	POLCA	Throughput, throughput time, WIP	Multi stage, processing time variability, different batch size and product mix parameters exist	CONWIP outperforms in all cases
Kabadurmus (2009)	POLCA	Lead time, WIP	System is subject to machine failures, processing time, and demand variability, batch size, product mix parameters exist	POLCA outperforms in all scenarios
Gilland (2002)	DBR, pull from bottleneck	Value and cost of output	Assembly line subject to multiple and single bottlenecks	DBR outperforms in single bottleneck case, pull from bottleneck outperforms in multi-bottleneck case
Jodlbauer and Huber (2008)	MRP, Kanban, DBR	Service level and WIP	Multi-product, multi-stage	MRP is superior to other in terms of stability
Lee and Seo (2016)	DBR, Kanban	Service level and WIP	Flow shop subject to variability	DBR and CONWIP outperforms Kanban
Pettersen and Segerstedt (2009)	Kanban	Throughput, WIP	Flow shop and processing times are stochastic	CONWIP is superior to Kanban

7.4 CONWIP-like Production Control Mechanisms

To cope with the limitations of basic CONWIP control and adopting it to complex environments, extensions of CONWIP control were developed. Prakash and Chin (2015) classified the extensions of basic CONWIP control and listed 15 modified versions. Their classification scheme was based upon the order release mechanism, workload measure that determines WIP, card type (shared or dedicated), system state evaluation (physical or virtual signal) for order release, static or dynamic card calculation, and dispatching rules. The results of the classification scheme showed that modified systems emerged with the needs of demand variability reduction, starving/blocking reduction, and local WIP accumulation prevention in front of a bottleneck resource.

Nahavandi (2014) compared the DBR, shared CONWIP, dedicated CONWIP, and critical WIP loop II (CWIPL II) proposed by Sepehri and Nahavandi (2007) in a job shop environment with respect to average throughput, average lead time, average tardiness, and percent tardy. Two sets of simulation experiments, multi-bottleneck and single bottleneck, were performed. CWIPL II controls the WIP in front of the critical machine and release decisions are based upon the critical machine for the unbalanced flow lines. The simulation experiment results for the multi-bottleneck case showed that CWIPL II was better than DBR, with respect to the lead time and throughput measures, while CWIPL II had better or the same performance in terms of tardiness and percent tardy. DBR was better than dedicated CONWIP control for all performance measures and dedicated CONWIP was better than shared CONWIP for average throughput and tardiness measures. For single bottleneck case DBR was superior to CWIPL II, dedicated CONWIP and shared CONWIP with respect to lead time.

Qi and Sivakumar (2006) compared the performance of CONWIP, WIPLCtrl, and workload regulating (WR) in a semiconductor wafer fabrication environment. In WIPLCtrl, the system workload was measured based upon their remaining processing times. In a WR control mechanism, the release of an incoming order to the system was performed based on a bottleneck resource. If the workload in a bottleneck was below a specified limit, then new orders were accepted to the system. To assess the performance of each control mechanism, simulation experiments were performed considering routing complexity, machine unreliability, processing time variability, part type mix, and congestion level parameters. The results of all simulation experiments showed that WIPLCtrl outperforms CONWIP, and WR control mechanisms in terms of mean and standard deviation of cycle time. The performance difference between CONWIP and WIPLCtrl was higher than the performance difference between WR and WIPLCtrl in all scenarios.

A similar control mechanism, which was proposed by Rose (1999), is named as constant load (CONLOAD) in a wafer fabrication environment. CONLOAD decides the releasing of a lot to the system based on the workload in a single or a group of machines. Based on the comparisons, CONLOAD was found to reduce the variability in cycle time and has a superior performance in product mix change scenarios. Rose (2001) evaluated the CONWIP, M-CONWIP (named layerwise CONWIP in this study), CONLOAD, and total cycle Time (CT). In total CT mechanism, each lot average cycle time was calculated and allowed to enter the system if incoming lot cycle time was less than the remaining total CT in the system. Simulation experiments were utilized to make comparisons and based upon the results, all mechanisms were effective in reducing variability. In terms of WIP measure M-CONWIP was worst performing and total CT was the best performing control mechanism.

Thürer et al. (2016) proposed COBACABANA control mechanism to cope with the disadvantage of CONWIP-like control mechanisms in high-mix low-volume environments and due date estimation. In COBACABANA, each order is first assigned a planned release date and then it is released to the system based on the assigned date. Each job has an operation card that shows the route of job and a release card. The release card shows the workload of the specific operation for the job. The jobs are processed by the machines considering the release card. If the operation workload of the specific job does not increase the workload of the station above 100%, then the order is processed by that station; otherwise the job waits in the job pool. The performance of the proposed control mechanism was evaluated via simulation experiments with respect to the mean throughput time, percentage of tardy jobs, and mean tardiness. The results showed the superiority of COBACABANA to immediate release and simple dispatching rules. Table 7.5 lists the CONWIP-like control mechanisms and their specifications.

In addition to the mentioned the modifications of CONWIP control, hybrid mechanisms that combine CONWIP and pull/push control have been discussed in the related literature. Section 7.5 describes the hybrid CONWIP control mechanisms and discusses the application environment.

Table 7.5 CONWIP-like Control Mechanisms Suitable for Diverse Manufacturing Environments

Study	Proposed Control Mechanism	System Specifications	Job Release Condition	Focused Objectives
Nahavandi (2014)	CWIPL II	Unbalanced flow line, bottleneck sources exist	Bottleneck station work load is observed	Tardiness and percent tardy
Qi and Sivakumar (2006)	WIPLCtrl	Flow shop with bottlenecks and unreliable machines subject to processing time and product mix variability	Target workload is observed in the bottleneck source	Mean and standard deviation of cycle time
Rose (1999)	CONLOAD	Flow shop subject to processing time and product mix variability	Based on the single or a group of machines workload	Variability reduction in cycle time
Rose (2001)	Total CT	Multi stage flow shop environment	Average cycle time of an order is calculated and compared with the allowed CT in the system	WIP reduction
Thürer et al. (2016)	COBACABANA	Job shop subject to part type variability and low volume	Based on due date and workload content of order on a specific machine on its route	Due date adherence

7.5 Hybrid CONWIP Control Studies

Bonvik and Gershwin (1996) proposed a CONWIP-Kanban hybrid control mechanism to avoid inventory accumulation in front of bottleneck sources in a serially arranged six machine and stochastic demand environment. Machines were unreliable and subject to operation variability. Simulation experiments were performed to understand the effectiveness of the proposed control mechanism. Fill rate, average backlog length, WIP, and waiting time were the performance measures. Based on the simulation results, CONWIP control was found to have better performance than Kanban control with respect to the average inventory. Additionally, CONWIP-Kanban hybrid policy had better results with respect to the inventory level, when capacity is close to upper limit.

Onyeocha et al. (2013a) proposed base-stock Kanban-CONWIP (BK-CONWIP) control mechanism to maintain volume flexibility, in case of variable demand, and minimize backlogged inventory levels. A proposed hybrid mechanism was evaluated via simulation experiments in a real case that had four product types. The proposed policy was compared with Kanban and CONWIP control mechanisms. Results showed that BK-CONWIP policy had better performance than Kanban and CONWIP control. The reason for this superior performance was explained as base-stock control policy's eliminating information delay, CONWIP control's restricting the total WIP, and Kanban control's restricting local WIP in front of production sources.

Onyeocha et al. (2013b) investigated the performance of BK-CONWIP control mechanism in a four product, five-stage real case under variable demand profile. The card types were shared in the proposed BK-CONWIP scenario. The system was compared via Kanban control mechanisms. A genetic algorithm was utilized to find the values of operating parameters, and simulation experiments were performed to compare the performances of each control mechanism. The best volume flexibility was observed in shared card type BK-CONWIP policy that maximizes service level and minimizes WIP. A general decline in the performance of each system was observed in case of volume shift between product types. Generally, all shared card type policies outperformed dedicated card type policies in terms of service level performance. A similar comparison-based study was done by Onyeocha et al. (2015), in a four product five-stage assembly line subject to sequence dependent set-up times. The findings were similar to those of Onyeocha et al. (2013b).

7.6 Conclusions

CONWIP design issues such as card type, number of cards, backlog list, and lot size were discussed throughout this chapter. Based on the reviewed literature the findings for each design issue are as follows:

- In card type design studies, the choice between the shared and dedicated card type depends on the aim. For example, if the aim is about service level and profit-related issues then dedicated card types are preferred. However, if the aim is system related measures, such as flow time and throughput rate, the shared card types are preferred based on analytical comparisons. The number of cards circulating in the system is generally considered as static (card setting), rather than dynamic (card controlling). The number of cards in the system is found via heuristic algorithms and analytical approximation methods.

■ Backlog list related studies generally consider mathematical models with the aim of makespan and flow time minimization. For dynamic environments different dispatching rules are also proposed.

■ Lot size is considered a parameter rather than a decision variable.

Studies about CONWIP control generally are applied to flow shop environment, and mainly rely on throughput time and WIP reduction. The majority of studies are based on performance comparison with other push/pull-based control mechanisms. Although there are control mechanisms which have better performance, CONWIP is generally superior to other control mechanisms in comparison studies.

To cope with the disadvantages of pure CONWIP control, CONWIP integrated control mechanisms have also been studied. The most popular among these control mechanisms is base-stock Kanban-CONWIP. The aim of this control mechanism is to utilize the bottleneck source effectively, minimizing the information delay, and controlling the WIP in the system.

For future research directions, CONWIP lot size related issues can further be investigated, in addition to current studies in the literature. Although there are studies suggesting which control mechanism should be applied in specific environments, a thorough classification of these control mechanisms suitable for diverse manufacturing environments is missing in the literature. The application of CONWIP control in real cases also is limited in the related literature. The application of basic CONWIP control and its extensions for different manufacturing environments can be future directions research.

References

Aglan, C and Durmusoglu, MB, 2015, Lot-splitting approach of a hybrid manufacturing system under CONWIP production control: A mathematical model, *International Journal of Production Research*, 53(5), 1561–1583.

Ajorlou, S and Shams, I, 2013, Artificial bee colony algorithm for CONWIP production control system in a multi-product multi-machine manufacturing environment, *Journal of Intelligent Manufacturing*, 24(6), 1145–1156.

Alfieri, A and Matta, A, 2012, Mathematical programming representation of pull controlled single-product serial manufacturing systems, *Journal of Intelligent Manufacturing*, 23(1), 23–35.

Bahaji, N and Kuhl, ME, 2008, A simulation study of new multi-objective composite dispatching rules, CONWIP, and push lot release in semiconductor fabrication, *International Journal of Production Research*, 46(14), 3801–3824.

Baynat, B, Buzacott, JA and Dallery, Y, 2002, Multiproduct Kanban-like control systems, *International Journal of Production Research*, 40(16), 4225–4255.

Bonvik, AM and Gershwin, SB, 1996, Beyond Kanban: Creating and analyzing lean shop floor control policies, In *Manufacturing and Service Operations Management Conference Proceeding*, pp. 46–51. Hannover, New Hampshire.

Braglia, M, Frosolini, M, Gabbrielli, R and Zammori, F, 2011, CONWIP card setting in a flow-shop system with a batch production machine, *International Journal of Industrial Engineering Computations*, 2(1), 1–18.

Cao, D and Chen, M, 2005, A mixed integer programming model for a two line CONWIP-based production and assembly system, *International Journal of Production Economics*, 95(3), 317–326.

Chong, MY, Prakash, J, Ng, SL, Ramli, R and Chin, JF, 2013, Parallel Kanban-CONWIP system for batch production in electronics assembly, *International Journal of Industrial Engineering*, 20(7/8), 468–486.

Dong, F, Deglise-Hawkinson, JR, Van Oyen, MP and Singer, DJ, 2016, Dynamic control of a closed two-stage queueing network for outfitting process in shipbuilding, *Computers and Operations Research*, 72, 1–11.

Duenyas, I and Hopp, WJ, 1993, Estimating the throughput of an exponential CONWIP assembly system, *Queueing Systems*, 14(1–2), 135–157.

Enns, ST and Rogers, P, 2008, Clarifying CONWIP versus push system behavior using simulation, In *Proceedings of the 40th Conference on Winter Simulation*, pp. 1867–1872.

Farnoush, A and Wiktorsson, M, 2013, POLCA and CONWIP performance in a divergent production line: An automotive case study, *Journal of Management Control*, 24(2), 159–186.

Framinan, JM, Gonzalez, PL and Ruiz-Usano, R, 2006, Dynamic card controlling in a Conwip system, *International Journal of Production Economics*, 99(1), 102–116.

Framinan, JM, Ruiz-Usano, R and Leisten, R, 2000, Input control and dispatching rules in a dynamic CONWIP flow-shop, *International Journal of Production Research*, 38(18), 4589–4598.

Gastermann, BC, Stopper, M and Katalinic, B, 2012, Adapting CONWIP characteristics for conventional production planning, In B. Katalinic (Ed.), *DAAAM International Scientific Book*, Published by DAAAM International, Vienna, Austria, pp. 553–565.

Germs, R and Riezebos, J, 2010, Workload balancing capability of pull systems in MTO production, *International Journal of Production Research*, 48(8), 2345–2360.

Gilland, WG, 2002, A simulation study comparing performance of CONWIP and bottleneck-based release rules, *Production Planning and Control*, 13(2), 211–219.

Gong, Q, Yang, Y and Wang, S, 2014, Information and decision-making delays in MRP, KANBAN, and CONWIP, *International Journal of Production Economics*, 156, 208–213.

Herer, YT and Masin, M, 1997, Mathematical programming formulation of CONWIP based production lines; and relationships to MRP, *International Journal of Production Research*, 35(4), 1067–1076.

Hopp, WJ and Roof, ML, 1998. Setting WIP levels with statistical throughput control (STC) in CONWIP production lines, *International Journal of Production Research*, 36(4), 867–882.

Huang, G, Chen, J, Wang, X and Shi, Y, 2015, A simulation study of CONWIP assembly with multi-loop in mass production, multi-products and low volume and OKP environments, *International Journal of Production Research*, 53(14), 4160–4175.

Huang, Y, Kuriger, G and Chen, FF, 2013, Simulation studies of hybrid pull systems of Kanban and conwip in an assembly line, In *Advances in Sustainable and Competitive Manufacturing Systems,* Springer International Publishing, Heidelberg, Germany. pp. 1553–1563.

Ioannidis, S and Kouikoglou, VS, 2008, Revenue management in single-stage CONWIP production systems, *International Journal of Production Research*, 46(22), 6513–6532.

Jodlbauer, H and Huber, A, 2008, Service-level performance of MRP, Kanban, CONWIP and DBR due to parameter stability and environmental robustness, *International Journal of Production Research*, 46(8), 2179–2195.

Kabadurmus, O, 2009, A comparative study of POLCA and generic CONWIP production control systems in erratic demand conditions, In *IIE Annual Conference Proceedings*, Institute of Industrial Engineers, Miami, FL. p. 1197.

Khojasteh, Y, 2016a, Analysis of control systems in assembly production processes, In *Production Control Systems*, Springer, Tokyo, pp. 63–98.

Khojasteh, Y, 2016b, Analysis of control systems in serial production lines, In *Production Control Systems*, Springer, Tokyo, pp. 37–61.

Khojasteh, Y, 2016c. Unified view of pull production systems, In *Production Control Systems*, Springer, Tokyo, pp. 25–30.

Khojasteh-Ghamari, Y, 2009, A performance comparison between Kanban and CONWIP controlled assembly systems, *Journal of Intelligent Manufacturing*, 20(6), 751–760.

Lee, H and Seo, DW, 2016, Performance evaluation of WIP-controlled line production systems with constant processing times, *Computers and Industrial Engineering*, 94, 138–146.

Li, JW, 2010, Simulation study of coordinating layout change and quality improvement for adapting job shop manufacturing to CONWIP control, *International Journal of Production Research*, 48(3), 879–900.

Little, JD, 1961, A proof for the queuing formula: L=λ W, *Operations Research*, 9(3), 383–387.

Muhammad, NA, Chin, JF, Kamarrudin, S, Chik, MA and Prakash, J, 2015, Fundamental simulation studies of CONWIP in front-end wafer fabrication, *Journal of Industrial and Production Engineering*, 32(4), 232–246.

Nahavandi, N, 2014, Comparison of SCONWIP, DCONWIP, TOC and CWIPL II in job shop, *Universal Journal of Industrial and Business Management*, 2(3), 61–68.

Onyeocha, CE, Khoury, J and Geraghty, J, 2013a, A comparison of Kanban-like control strategies in a multi-product manufacturing system under erratic demand, In *Proceedings of the Winter Simulation Conference: Simulation: Making Decisions in a Complex World*, IEEE Press, Washington, DC, pp. 2730–2741.

Onyeocha, CE, Khoury, J and Geraghty, J, 2013b, Evaluation of the effect of erratic demand on a multi-product Basestock Kanban-CONWIP control strategy, In *Proceedings of the 9th Conference on Stochastic Models of Manufacturing and Service Operations*, May, Kloster Seeon, Germany.

Onyeocha, CE, Khoury, J and Geraghty, J, 2015, Evaluation of pull control strategies and production authorisation card policies recovery period in a multi-product system, In *Enhancing Synergies in a Collaborative Environment*, Springer International Publishing, Springer, Cham. pp. 19–28.

Parvin, H, Van Oyen, MP, Pandelis, DG., Williams, DP and Lee, J, 2012, Fixed task zone chaining: Worker coordination and zone design for inexpensive cross-training in serial CONWIP lines, *IIE Transactions*, 44(10), 894–914.

Pettersen, JA and Segerstedt, A, 2009, Restricted work-in-process: A study of differences between Kanban and CONWIP, *International Journal of Production Economics*, 118(1), 199–207.

Prakash, J and Chin, JF, 2015, Modified CONWIP systems: A review and classification, *Production Planning and Control*, 26(4), 296–307.

Qi, C and Sivakumar, AI, 2006, Job release based on WIPLOAD control in semiconductor wafer fabrication, In *8th Electronics Packaging Technology Conference*, IEEE, Singapore, Singapore, pp. 665–670.

Rose, O, 1999, CONLOAD—a new lot release rule for semiconductor wafer fabs, In *Proceedings of the 31st Conference on Winter Simulation: Simulation—A Bridge to the Future*, ACM, Phoenix, AZ, vol. 1, pp. 850–855.

Rose, O, 2001, CONWIP-like lot release for a wafer fabrication facility with dynamic load changes, *Proceedings of the SMOMS*, Phoenix, AZ, USA. 1, 41–46.

Ryan, SM, Baynat, B and Choobineh, FF, 2000, Determining inventory levels in a CONWIP controlled job shop, *IIE Transactions*, 32(2), 105–114.

Ryan, SM and Vorasayan, J, 2005, Allocating work in process in a multiple-product CONWIP system with lost sales, *International Journal of Production Research*, 43(2), 223–246.

Sepehri, MM and Nahavandi, N, 2007, Critical WIP loops: A mechanism for material flow control in flow lines, *International Journal of Production Research*, 45(12), 2759–2773.

Spearman, ML, Woodruff, DL and Hopp, WJ, 1990, CONWIP: A pull alternative to Kanban, *The International Journal of Production Research*, 28(5), 879–894.

Thürer, M, Land, MJ, Stevenson, M and Fredendall, LD, 2016, Card-based delivery date promising in high-variety manufacturing with order release control, *International Journal of Production Economics*, 172, 19–30.

Yang, KK, 2000, Managing a flow line with single-Kanban, dual-Kanban or CONWIP, *Production and Operations Management*, 9(4), 349–366.

Zhang, W and Chen, M, 2001, A mathematical programming model for production planning using CONWIP, *International Journal of Production Research*, 39(12), 2723–2734.

PULL SYSTEMS IMPLEMENTATION – CASE STUDIES

Chapter 8

Making CONWIP Scheme in One-of-a-Kind Production: A Case Study

Guodong Huang and Jie Chen

Contents

8.1 CONWIP and OKP Shop Floor Control

Many researchers have studied CONWIP since Spearman et al. (1990) proposed it. Many studies show that CONWIP has better (or acceptable) performance in short cycle time, by improving throughput and decreasing work-in-process (WIP). Some researchers notice that there are few CONWIP practices due to lack of guidance on CONWIP implementation (Framinan et al. 2003, Pettersen and Segerstedt 2009), but they do not provide a specific solution. Hence, in this chapter, we focus on employing CONWIP in an OKP environment. OKP is a production mode that produces customized products within a product domain (Tu and Dean 2011). In an OKP environment, the customized product that is produced is rarely repeated, although some processes in the production of similar kinds of products can be repeated (Wortmann et al. 1997, Li et al. 2011).

The characteristics of OKP can be briefly summarized as, high customization, great uncertainties in production control, complicated and dynamic supply chains, and dynamic production systems (Tu and Dean 2011). Therefore, how to develop a suitable production planning and control system is the issue to be solved for OKP enterprises. From a practice perspective, we conclude that the advantages of choosing CONWIP for OKP shop floor control are as follows:

1. CONWIP has a simple control structure, which implies that there is no need to develop special hardware and software technologies to implement the CONWIP systems for OKP shop floor control. In other words, the existing technologies are adequate. For example, RFID (radio-frequency identification devices) and bar code scanning can be used to collect CONWIP signal (or card), and PLC (programmable logic controller) and Andon system can be used to trigger or response CONWIP control.
2. CONWIP can be used in complex production and supply chain environments. According to production process, OKP shop floor will show some features of different production organization, for example, hybrid flow shop (HFS), job shop, and assembly flow shop (AFS).
3. CONWIP is suitable for make-to-order (MTO) production (Prakash and Chin 2015). Generally, OKP enterprise belongs to MTO production.
4. CONWIP is suitable for mixed production. Generally, OKP is a mixed production in the context of personalized products.
5. CONWIP pull mechanism can be extended to non-production phase. Due to the response delay between designing and production in OKP environment, the product design changes will disturb the production arrangement strongly. The response delay may be reduced, if the design phase is controlled by CONWIP loop.

The main issues with CONWIP implementation in OKP are

1. CONWIP lacks implementation guidelines that are not simple opinions or notes. The guidelines should be a systematic approach, procedure, or schemes. OKP shop floor needs a feasible blueprint of CONWIP control before developing a CONWIP system. The blueprint should point out some important parameters, which are needed for CONWIP development, including, the triggering position of CONWIP pull, WIP limit setting, and others. We argue that this issue cannot be skipped when people want to develop a CONWIP system.
2. The study of CONWIP loop structure is not adequate. As the system performance depends upon the structure itself, the optimum loop structure can improve the ability to deliver on time under heavy workload in OKP shop floor. Generally, the CONWIP loop structure

includes single and multiple loops. Different CONWIP loop structures achieve different performances in the same production environment (Huang et al. 2015).

3. The approach of WIP limit setting is still worthy of study. For example, setting a WIP limit for each loop in multiple CONWIP loops will affect the overall performance of the CONWIP system, which may be regarded as a combinatorial optimization problem. Therefore, it is necessary to develop an effective search algorithm to solve optimal WIP for OKP shop floor with multiple CONWIP loops.

The remainder of this chapter is organized as follows: Section 8.2 gives a brief literature review. Section 8.3 introduces a CONWIP design framework (CDF). In Section 8.4, we employ the CDF to make CONWIP scheme for a specific equipment manufacturer. Section 8.5 covers conclusions.

8.2 Literature Review

Many researchers pay attention to extracting practical methods, design principles, or insights from theoretical study. Dar-El et al. (1999) introduced the concept of a virtual bottleneck machine to investigate a CONWIP production system. They obtained insights into the system design and modification. Hopp et al. (2009) presented a design and control of manufacturing cells with a mix of manual and automated equipment under a CONWIP pull protocol. Sato and Khojasteh-Ghamari (2012) proposed a novel design discipline for card-based control of production processes, by developing a framework of token transaction systems. Khojasteh and Sato (2015) analyzed the three pull production control policies, Kanban, CONWIP, and base-stock in a deterministic environment, and provided guidelines for selecting an appropriate control policy for multi-stage production processes.

To meet the actual production requirement, another approach is to design or modify the pull control systems based on the existing theories. To design pull production control systems, Gaury et al. (2001) discussed the issue of customized pull systems, and proposed a design concept of decomposing production line. Similarly, Huang et al. (2015) proposed a loop design pattern to implement CONWIP in different production environments. Prakash and Chin (2015) also concluded that the translation of design issues into practice will render CONWIP applicable to various manufacturing scenarios.

In addition, some researchers focused on supporting technology that makes theory transform into practice. Gastermann et al. (2014) presented the concept, design, and implementation of a software prototype for production planning that incorporates aspects of the CONWIP manufacturing system. Wan and Chen (2008) developed an entirely web-based Kanban system. Gastermann and Stopper (2012) reported that the lack of actual implementation is due to the absence of both interface in existing enterprise resource planning (ERP) systems and management functionality to execute CONWIP. Engelhardt and Reinhart (2012) described an approach that enhances for a systematical configuration and a situation-dependent execution of an radio-frequency identification (RFID)-based situational shop floor control. Tu and Dean (2011) developed an OKP management and control software system.

In general, the previously mentioned works do not consider the situation of combined OKP shop floor control with CONWIP. The case studied in this chapter can provide insights into CONWIP implementation.

8.3 CONWIP Design Framework

Generally, a project needs a feasible scheme that selects from some alternatives in order to guide it in the early stage of implementation. The feasible scheme is an important basis for deciding the follow-up, for example, shift arrangement, purchase, installation, debugging, delivery time, and so on. Therefore, a feasible CONWIP scheme can guide CONWIP implementation to ensure success and enhance the enterprise's confidence.

From the loop structure view, we propose a systematic approach, named CONWIP design framework (CDF), as shown in Figure 8.1.

In Figure 8.1, the CDF consists of three major components: the upstream, midstream, and downstream (UMD) identification, the loop design pattern (or loop pattern), and the pattern refinement. First, the different production organization (e.g., flow line, cellular production, network, etc.) is divided into segments or areas (this will be discussed in Section 8.3.1). Second, these segments will be considered to combine with CONWIP mechanism (discussed in Section 8.3.2). Third, the segments linked by CONWIP mechanism will be refined with reality constraints (see Section 8.3.3). Finally, a feasible CONWIP scheme is determined by assessment from the refined loop policies.

The CDF procedure related to the CONWIP scheme development is shown in Figure 8.4. CDF can be generalized as a basic idea that a production organization is breaking down into several elementary units that are controlled by CONWIP. These units are the base of the CONWIP loop structure that can be regard as an important parameter to make a feasible CONWIP scheme. In short, we can obtain CONWIP alternative loop structures through CDF, and these loop structures have inter-group heterogeneity and intra-group homogeneity.

We argue that CONWIP loop structure is the foundation for other CONWIP parameter settings, for example, WIP limit setting, CONWIP card types, dispatching rules, and others.

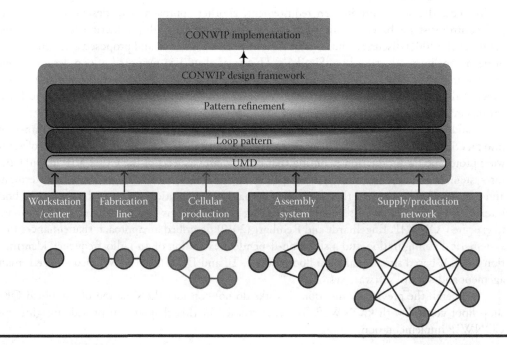

Figure 8.1 CONWIP design framework (CFD).

Therefore, we also refer to the loop structure as the CONWIP loop policy, unless other CONWIP parameters need to be emphasized.

8.3.1 UMD Identification

The UMD identification is a high-level abstraction of the objects controlled by CONWIP. Upstream, midstream, and downstream are considered abstract classes. These rough abstract classes will be refined into one or more UMD subclasses of increasing sophistication and complexity. UMD identification is a process through which production resources (e.g., machine, manpower, department, etc.) are divided into upstream, midstream, and downstream. CDF can be applied in situations where the production system can be divided into upstream, midstream, and downstream, for example, supply network, flow shop, and even cellular production. As the actual production environment needs to be considered in the process of UMD identification, we suggest that a CONWIP developer and enterprise manager should work together to identify UMD.

A CONWIP loop indicates coverage of the CONWIP card (or signal) from sending position to receiving position. Therefore, a CONWIP loop should have the property of a closed-circle. CONWIP pull will not work, if the closed-circle is broken. UMD identification and CONWIP loop division are different concepts. CONWIP loop dividing determines whether the coverage of a CONWIP card contains upstream, midstream, and/or downstream. UMD identification determines whether production resources belong to upstream, midstream, or downstream. For example, there are two departments with relationships of precedence between businesses. These two departments can be identified as upstream and downstream, which is UMD identification. Each department must use one CONWIP loop to control its own business volume, which is CONWIP loop division. It is also worthy of consideration that two departments share the same loop, when the top management integrates business or administrative authority between departments.

8.3.2 Loop Design Pattern

Loop design pattern describes the basic logical dependencies between the abstract class of the UMD and CONWIP loop. The abstract UMD class is the elementary unit controlled by CONWIP. According to loop design pattern, CONWIP loop structure is designed further. We use the symbols below to represent the basic logical dependencies.

- ■ / indicates demarcation point for multiple loops or push–pull interface.
- ■ ∧ indicates that multiple CONWIP loops are merged into a single CONWIP loop.
- ■ ∨ indicates an inverse process of merging (∧).
- ■ ¬ indicates that the loop is cancelled. It also means push control.

Based on these symbols, the basic loop design patterns are shown in Figure 8.2 and the dotted line denotes a CONWIP loop.

Figure 8.2a is the classical pattern of CONWIP, where upstream, midstream, and downstream are controlled by a single loop. For complex types, U∧M/¬M/D implies that CONWIP is cancelled in the part of midstream, and downstream is controlled by another loop (see Figure 8.3). The composite symbol /¬ means there exists a push–pull interface. $U/ \bigvee_{i=1}^{n} M^{(i)} /D$ shows that the midstream is controlled by n loops. CONWIP policy can be grouped by loop design patterns.

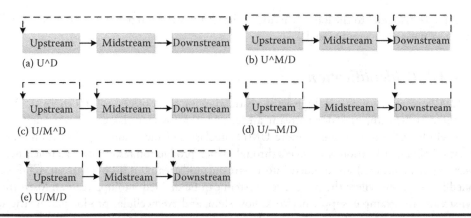

Figure 8.2   Loop design pattern.

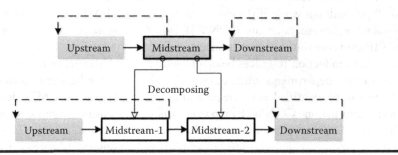

Figure 8.3   U^M/¬M/D pattern.

8.3.3 *Pattern Refinement*

Pattern refinement includes CONWIP loop structure adjustment and other parameter settings (e.g., WIP limit). Specifically, because of real-world constraints (see below), production resources, and loop structure need to be adjusted further in UMD.

- Facility location/geographic position
- Size of workshop
- Requirement of process and quality
- Setting push–pull interface for business requirement
- Flow shop/job shop production
- Importance and role of storage
- Management amplitude/permissions of workshop manager
- Boundary between departments
- Collaboration level of material distribution
- Collaboration level of raw material suppliers
- Bottleneck drift restriction/fluctuation degree
- Workload balancing
- Process analysis

8.3.4 Procedure of CONWIP Scheme Making

Huang et al. (2016) proposed a general procedure to design a CONWIP scheme. We provide an improved version of the general procedure which uses CDF (see Figure 8.4).

WIP limits and dispatching rules are referenced in many studies. The different function of a CONWIP card is collectively called the CONWIP card type. For example, the shared card buffer and the dedicated card buffer (Khojasteh-Ghamari 2009), which respectively involve setting a single card count for all job types and setting individual card counts of each job type (Framinan et al. 2000), and so forth.

8.4 CONWIP Scheme Making in OKP: A Case Study

Here, a wire-rope equipment manufacturer is presented as a case study. This manufacturer is an OKP enterprise in the city of Wuxi, Jiangsu province, China. The range of stranders manufactured by this manufacturer covers different types and sizes of machinery (see Figure 8.5). For convenience, parts and components of the strander are called jobs, and the job processor (e.g., work station, equipment, processing center, etc.) is called the machine in the rest of this chapter.

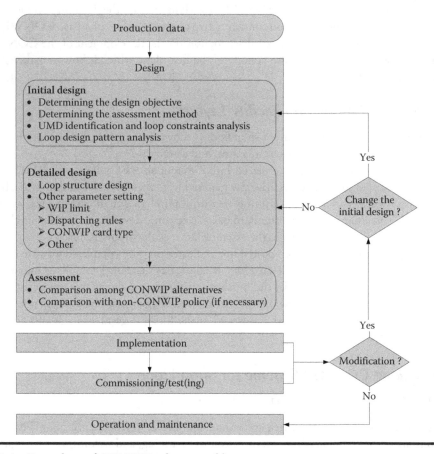

Figure 8.4   Procedure of CONWIP scheme making.

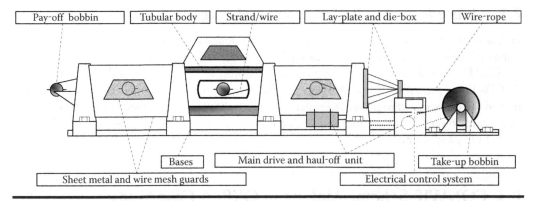

Figure 8.5   Illustration of stranding machine.

A few standard parts, the raw materials, and the electrical control system specified by the customer are supplied by providers. Customers with professional knowledge of wire-rope get involved in product design and production. The quantity of product customized in one order is very small. The quantity of order accepted, however, is large. In addition, the tardiness penalty for a customer order is high (about 1.8–10% of revenues).

The manufacturer intends to implement CONWIP to increase the flexibility on shop floor and shorten tardiness. The implementation consists of two phases. The first phase is a CONWIP scheme making and assessment, while the next phase focuses on the development of the CONWIP system. This section introduces the main content of the first phase which is how to make CONWIP scheme based on CDF.

8.4.1 Process Routing and Facility Layout

A basic overview of this manufacturer's shop floor is shown in Figure 8.6. The shop floor consists of rough machining area, finish machining area, and assembly area.

Raw materials and other jobs are placed into different sizes of pallets with RFID. The WIP inventory is measured in pallet units. The raw material (e.g., sheet metal, tubular goods, bar stock, etc.) is transported to the rough machining area from purchased item storage area, as shown by the black solid line. Some jobs (e.g., standard parts, electronic devices, etc.) in the purchased item storage area are directly transported to the assembly area, as shown by the black dotted line *M1*. In the rough machining area, the green dotted line indicates that the completed jobs are transported to finish machining, and the black dotted line *M2* indicates that some completed jobs are directly transported to the assembly area. In the finish machining area, the purple dotted line indicates that the jobs after machining operations are transported to the assembly area. Finally, the stranders (or finished goods) are assembled and stored in the finished goods storage and dispatch area (see the blue dotted line).

8.4.2 Making CONWIP Scheme for Shop Floor

8.4.2.1 UMD Identification in Shop Floor

We must analyze every production area in the shop floor before UMD identification. First, the main operations include cutting/shearing, grinding, coiling/stamping, and welding in the rough machining area. As shown in Figure 8.7, the rough machining has obvious features of an HFS production.

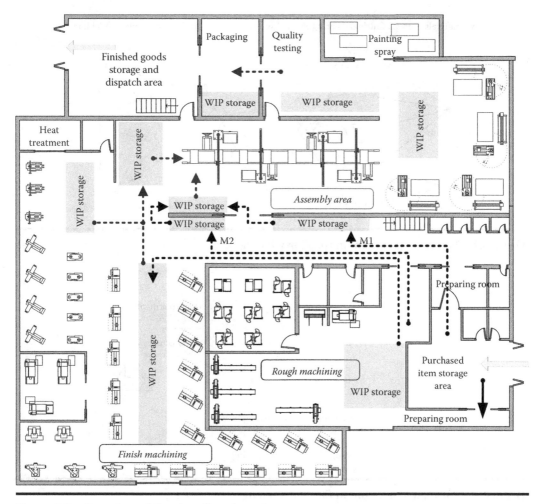

Figure 8.6 Overview of the shop floor layout.

Figure 8.7 also shows the production resources as follows:

- The tubular goods and the bar stock are cut by cutting machines *1–1*, *1–2*, and *1–3*, while shearing machine *1–5* can only process sheet metal. The numerical control (NC) cutter *1–4* can process tubular goods, bar stock, and sheet metal.
- There are four grinding machines, that is, machines *2–1*, *2–2*, *2–3*, and *2–4*.
- There are three work units, that is, machines *3–1*, *3–2*, and *3–3*, which provide the operations of coiling and stamping, but these two operations can be only chosen one at a time.
- There are 15 welding machines, which provide service not only in the rough machining area, but also in other areas of the shop floor.

Second, the finish machining has the features of a job shop production (see Figure 8.8). Figure 8.8 shows the production resources as follows:

- The lathe unit has 20 ordinary machines and 3 NC machines.
- The drilling unit has 5 machines.

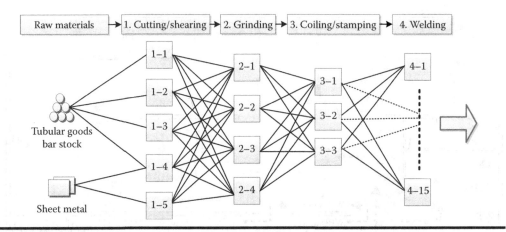

Figure 8.7 The main operations in rough machining.

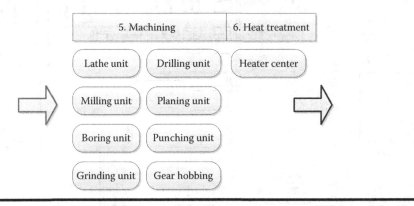

Figure 8.8 The main operations in finish machining.

- The milling unit has 4 machines.
- The planning unit has 3 machines.
- The boring unit has 3 machines.
- The punching unit has 2 machines.
- The grinding unit has 2 machines.
- The gear hobbing unit has 2 machines.
- The heater center has 4 furnaces.

Finally, after the finish machining the jobs are sent to assemble the strander. As shown in Figure 8.9, the assembly area has nine work stations (WS) and it has the features of an AFS production.

To sum up, the rough machining area, the finish machining area, and the assembly area present different production features (i.e., HFS, job shop and AFS). Based on their precedence relationship, these areas are preliminarily identified as upstream, midstream, and downstream.

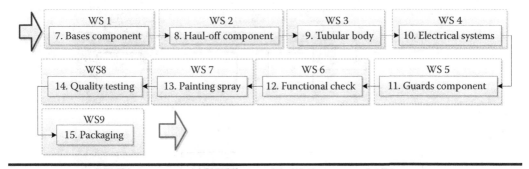

Figure 8.9   The main assembly operations.

8.4.2.2 Loop Design Pattern and Refinement

Every abstract class of the UMD can generate the sophisticated subclasses, which means that the rough machining as upstream can be refined according to the features of HFS production, if necessary.

The stage is viewed as an elementary cell in HFS. In Figure 8.7, the cutting/shearing stage (S1) is upstream. The welding stage (S4) is downstream. The grinding stage (S2) and the coiling/ stamping stage (S3) are identified as midstream. Considering that the welding resource is available to other areas, S4 needs to be controlled by a separate CONWIP loop to avoid breaking the closed-circle property and provide service quickly. Therefore, the loop design pattern only considers U/M/D, U^M/D, U/¬M/D, and their complex types in this case. There is no reason to break the CONWIP loop between S2 and S3 in midstream, and we must remove U/¬M/D. In addition, the machine capacity is unbalanced in S1, which means that the loop refinement needs to be considered further in the upstream.

As to the analysis above, we propose six CONWIP loop policies, which are ρ_{HFS}^1, ρ_{HFS}^2, ρ_{HFS}^3, ρ_{HFS}^4, ρ_{HFS}^5, and ρ_{HFS}^6 (see Figure 8.10a–f). ρ_{HFS}^6 is the classical pattern (U^D), it also considered for further analysis.

U^D pattern is considered in the job shop production, since jobs have one or more repeated processes to do in routing. Based on U^D pattern, we adopt a loop policy (i.e., ρ_{JS}^1), as shown in Figure 8.11.

In AFS production, the assembly interface (AI), which is a work station that needs job coming from components supply line (CSL) to assemble product, is largely affected by CSL's fluctuation. AI should be controlled by CONWIP loop individually to avoid transferring the effect of CSL's fluctuation to AI's upstream and downstream. Therefore, AI is identified as midstream. The work stations in front of AI are identified as upstream. The work stations behind AI are identified as downstream. CONWIP loop policies (i.e., ρ_{AFS}^1 and ρ_{AFS}^2) are shown in Figure 8.12, where ρ_{AFS}^1 belongs to U/M/D pattern and ρ_{AFS}^2 belongs to U^D pattern.

8.4.2.3 Dispatching Rule and WIP Limit

Dispatching rule can enhance the workload balancing capacity of CONWIP. However, we observed that the more complex the dispatching rule, the harder it is to obey in production practice. For example, according to the shortest processing time (SPT) rule, jobs with high priority are first released to the day shift, and other jobs with low priority must be completed on the afternoon

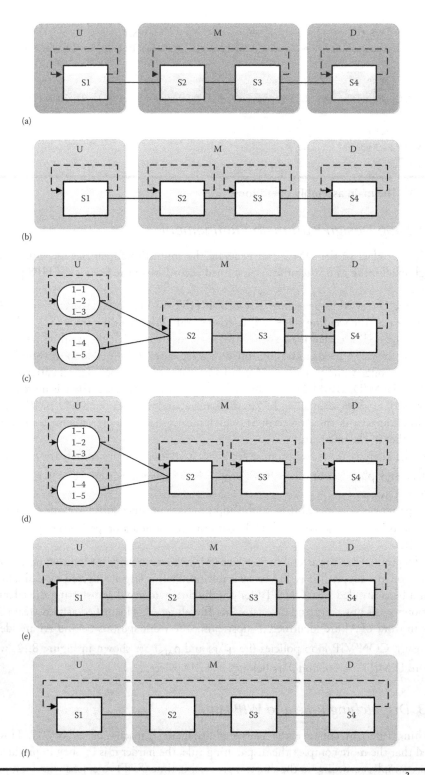

Figure 8.10 CONWIP loop policies for HFS. (a) ρ_{HFS}^1 (U / M / D). (b) ρ_{HFS}^2 (U / $\overset{2}{\underset{m=1}{\vee}} M^{(m)}$ / D). (c) ρ_{HFS}^3 ($\overset{2}{\underset{u=1}{\vee}} U^{(u)}$ /M/D). (d) ρ_{HFS}^4 ($\overset{2}{\underset{u=1}{\vee}} U^{(u)}$ / $\overset{2}{\underset{m=1}{\vee}} M^{(m)}$ /D). (e) ρ_{HFS}^5 (U ∧ M/D). (f) ρ_{HFS}^6 (U ∧ D).

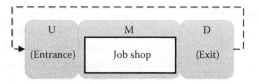

Figure 8.11   CONWIP loop policy for job shop.

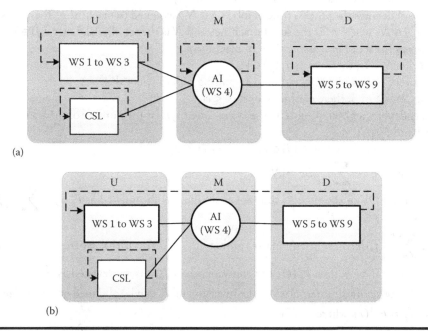

Figure 8.12   CONWIP loop policy for AFS. (a) ρ_{AFS}^1 **(U/M/D or** $\overset{2}{\underset{u=1}{\vee}} U^{(u)}/M/D$**). (b)** ρ_{AFS}^2 **(U ∧ D or** $\overset{2}{\underset{u=1}{\vee}} U^{(u)} \wedge D$**).**

shift or night shift. Obviously, many workers want to work on the day shift. Worker disputes caused by unfair work allocation and the passive enforcement of dispatching rule often occur on the shop floor, if there are no corresponding regulations of workshop management. Furthermore, some dispatching rules with better performance in theory need more information to assist implementation. In our case, the first-come, first-served rule is selected, since the more simply a rule can be described, the more likely it is that it will work well in an actual environment.

In multiple CONWIP loops, a large amount of computation time is spent on searching for the optimal combination of WIP limit. In this case, we focus on the result of the search, rather than the computation efficiency.

8.4.3 Simulation Assessment

8.4.3.1 Methodology

A production system and its elements cannot be observed by a mathematical optimization model. The scheme validation in an actual environment will disturb production running. Thus, we must choose a simulation assessment.

In the OKP, a product belongs to a certain product family in which similar jobs are assigned to the same machine to process. The process time changes in all machines based on the present status of the production system. A method that forms the empirical distribution function (EDF) of process time for each machine to simulate the actual production status is described below.

Step 1. Collect historical data of the process time $t_p(j)$.

Note: $t_p(j)$ denotes the process time of job j ($j \in N$) assigned to machine p. There exist $p \in M$ and $j \in N$, where M is the set of machines and N is the set of jobs. Let $t_p(j) \in T_p$, where T_p denotes the set of processing time in machine p.

Step 2. Let $V_p = T_p$, there exists $t_p(j) \in V_p$.

Note: Every element in V_p is sorted in ascending order by its value.

Step 3. Let $c_h \geq t_p(j)$, there exists $c_1 < c_2 < \cdots < c_l$.

Note: c_h denotes a given boundary of process time $t_p(j)$. l is the number of the boundaries specified and $l \leq |N|$.

Step 4. Let B_h be the set of $t_p(j) \in V_p$, where $t_p(j) \leq c_h$.

Note: There exists $\sum_{h=1}^{l} |B_h| = |N|$.

Step 5. The EDF of the process time for machine p is formulated as $\hat{F}_p^h(t) = \sum_{k=1}^{h} f_k$, where $\max B_{h-1} < t \leq \max B_h$.

Note: $\sum_{k=1}^{h} f_k$ denotes the cumulative probability, and $f_k = |B_k|/n$ where n is sample size, that is, $n = |N|$. If $h = n$, then $\hat{F}_p^h(t)$. For convenience, $\hat{F}_p^h(t)$ is abbreviated as $\hat{F}$.

Step 6. Based on linear interpolation, the inversion of $\hat{F}$ can be obtained or symbolized by $\hat{F}^{-1}$. Let $\hat{t}_p = \hat{F}^{-1}(r)$, where $r \sim U(0,1)$.

Note: $\hat{t}_p$ denotes the simulative process time in machine p, and $\hat{t}_p \sim \hat{F}$.

Step 7. Let π^* be the optimum CONWIP scheme. According to the objective function maximization or minimization, we have $\pi^* = \arg\max_{\pi \in \Pi}\{S(\hat{t}_p, \pi)|\forall p \in M\}$, or $\pi^* = \arg\min_{\pi \in \Pi}\{S(\hat{t}_p, \pi)|\forall p \in M\}$.

Note: π denotes the alternative set of CONWIP policies. $S(\xi_1, \xi_2)$ denotes the performance indicator, where the parameter ξ_1 is a process time in a certain machine and the parameter ξ_2 is a certain loop policy of CONWIP.

Obviously, $\hat{t}_p \sim \hat{F}$ simulates the approximate fluctuation in the actual environment. Since $\hat{F}$ has great effects on simulation assessment, it should be updated regularly. $t_p(j)$ is the basis that generates $\hat{F}$. Therefore, $t_p(j)$ needs to be collected from the historical data of product and the existing orders. In this case, $t_p(j)$ is obtained from the delivered products in the last 2 years and the existing orders in the last 6 months.

8.4.3.2 Performance Indicator

Delivery on time is important for the OKP enterprise. Inventory cost will be increased when the order is completed in advance, and tardiness penalty will be generated when delivery is delayed. In order to describe the performance indicators, we define the following notations.

n: Total number of elements in completed job set *J*.

C_j: Completion time of job *j*.

λ_j: Revenue of job *j*.

w_j: Weighted tardy penalty of job *j*.

d_j: Due date of job *j*.

L_j: Lateness of job *j*, let $L_j = C_j - d_j$.

T_j: Tardiness of job *j*, let $T_j = \max \{L_j, 0\}$.

τ_j: Storage time of job *j*, let $\tau_j = -\min \{L_j, 0\}$.

q: Unit cost of storage per day.

The average net revenue (ANR) and the standard deviation of lateness (SDL) are used to evaluate performance. The SDL applied to the tardiness problem (Gee and Smith 1993, Cheng and Jiang 1998, Vinod and Sridharan 2011)

$$ANR = \frac{1}{n} \sum\nolimits_{j=1}^{n} \left(\lambda_j - \omega_j T_j - \tau_j q \lambda_j \right) \tag{8.1}$$

$$SDL = \sqrt{\frac{\sum\nolimits_{j=1}^{n} \left(L_j - \bar{L} \right)^2}{n-1}} \tag{8.2}$$

where $\bar{L}$ is the average lateness.

In this case, the average cost of storekeeper per day and the lead time of each job are regarded as *q* and d_j, respectively. λ_j is obtained from the bills of material (BOM) cost. w_j denotes the value that an order pricing of 10% is shared to each job in the same one order.

8.4.3.3 Evaluation Result

The model is built using Plant Simulation (www.siemens.com). A full factorial experiment is used to get the optimal WIP limit when lateness time is the shortest in alternative policy. An observation repeats 20 times with different random number generation and the confidence level of 95%. We chose a warm-up period of 200 jobs and collected statistics for a run length of 800 jobs. The evaluation results are shown in Table 8.1.

No.13 in Table 8.1 is regarded as the performance reference point, as shown in Figure 8.13.

In the top left corner of the reference point, the performances of No.9 and No.7 are better than others with respect to the SDL and ANR. Thus, these two policies and the corresponding parameters can be regarded as feasible scheme for our case. However, No.9 and No.7 have higher total WIP volume than others except for No.4 and No.11. In other words, these two policies may not be the optimal choices, if the stock-holding cost of WIP is very sensitive. No.1, No.3, and No.5 have good performance in shorten lateness, but they do not increase revenue. The main reason is that many jobs finished ahead of schedule make high stock-holding cost. No.4 and No.11 performed poorly in SDL and ANR, even poorer than the reference point. It is very similar to the total WIP volume for some policies (i.e., No.1, No.3, No.5, No.6, No.8, and No.10) performed well in different indicators, which implies that the performance of the CONWIP system can be affected by the loop structure.

Table 8.1 **Evaluation Result**

No.	Loop Policy	SDL (95% Confidence Interval)	ANR (95% Confidence Interval	Total WIP (TW)
1	$(\rho^1_{HFS}, \rho^1_{JS}, \rho^1_{AFS})$	432.602 ± 9.757	36.385 ± 0.102	81
2	$(\rho^1_{HFS}, \rho^1_{JS}, \rho^2_{AFS})$	535.357 ± 12.112	36.796 ± 0.135	71
3	$(\rho^2_{HFS}, \rho^1_{JS}, \rho^1_{AFS})$	438.918 ± 9.399	45.614 ± 0.271	78
4	$(\rho^2_{HFS}, \rho^1_{JS}, \rho^2_{AFS})$	556.687 ± 11.959	31.572 ± 0.231	112
5	$(\rho^3_{HFS}, \rho^1_{JS}, \rho^1_{AFS})$	459.984 ± 10.250	52.182 ± 0.145	80
6	$(\rho^3_{HFS}, \rho^1_{JS}, \rho^2_{AFS})$	522.538 ± 12.305	67.891 ± 0.229	83
7	$(\rho^4_{HFS}, \rho^1_{JS}, \rho^1_{AFS})$	477.001 ± 9.601	72.439 ± 0.175	101
8	$(\rho^4_{HFS}, \rho^1_{JS}, \rho^2_{AFS})$	546.835 ± 15.447	55.127 ± 0.156	79
9	$(\rho^5_{HFS}, \rho^1_{JS}, \rho^1_{AFS})$	473.903 ± 7.663	75.002 ± 0.236	95
10	$(\rho^5_{HFS}, \rho^1_{JS}, \rho^2_{AFS})$	527.891 ± 11.169	65.849 ± 0.291	85
11	$(\rho^6_{HFS}, \rho^1_{JS}, \rho^1_{AFS})$	571.489 ± 12.341	35.678 ± 0.320	123
12	$(\rho^6_{HFS}, \rho^1_{JS}, \rho^2_{AFS})$	529.750 ± 12.963	46.455 ± 0.234	74
13	Classical CONWIP	537.206 ± 14.197	43.521 ± 0.349	72

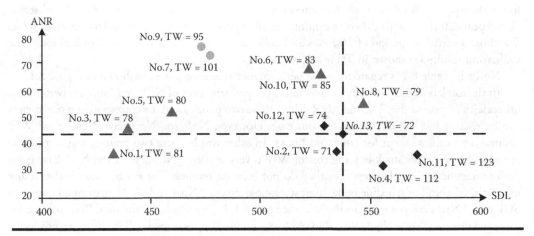

Figure 8.13 **Performance reference point—No.13.**

Based on the case study, the findings are summarized below.

1. Making CONWIP scheme may be regarded as a combination optimization between loop structure and the WIP limit.
2. The CONWIP loop structure is the premise for other CONWIP parameters setting.
3. It is very important to design a suitable CONWIP loop structure, since the multiple CONWIP loop is not always better than the single CONWIP loop.
4. CONWIP loop policy with high robustness serves as CONWIP scheme is a reasonable choice.
5. Once the production environment changes, it is necessary to consider correcting CONWIP loop policy, including loop structure and the WIP limit.

8.5 Conclusions

This chapter demonstrates how to make CONWIP scheme within a case study. CONWIP implementation guidelines should be a systematic design approach to help CONWIP developers execute CONWIP schemes. A feasible CONWIP scheme can effectively guide the CONWIP implementation to success. Hence, a systematic design approach CDF, is proposed to make CONWIP scheme in the OKP environment. The understanding of the loop structure also contributes to rethink a CONWIP pull mechanism itself.

Moreover, the simulation assessment method that we propose needs to update the EDF. If there are no major changes in process routing between the past orders and the new orders, the CONWIP scheme that has already been put into action does not need reassessment. Otherwise, managers should update the EDF at once and then the CONWIP scheme will be reassessed. In practice, the corresponding management system in shop floor controlled by CONWIP is indispensable.

Pull production systems provide a wide range of benefits. The benefits can be easily seen and felt in a best practice operation (Khojasteh 2016). Hence, extending CONWIP to OKP environment is worth further study. We believe that the process mining for pull system will be a valuable exploration in the future.

References

Cheng, T. C. E., and Jiang, J. (1998). Job shop scheduling for missed due-date performance. *Computers and Industrial Engineering*, 34(2), 297–307.

Dar-El, E. M., Herer, Y. T., and Masin, M. (1999). CONWIP-based production lines with multiple bottlenecks: Performance and design implications. *IIE Transactions*, 31(2), 99–111.

Engelhardt, P., and Reinhart, G. (2012). Approach for an RFID-based situational shop floor control. *IEEE International Conference on Industrial Engineering and Engineering Management* Hong Kong, China (pp. 444–448). IEEE.

Framinan, J. M., González, P. L., and Ruiz-Usano, R. (2003). The CONWIP production control system: Review and research issues. *Production Planning and Control*, 14(3), 255–265.

Framinan, J. M., Ruiz-Usano, R., and Leisten, R. (2000). Input control and dispatching rules in a dynamic conwip flow-shop. *International Journal of Production Research*, 38(18), 4589–4598.

Gastermann, B., and Stopper, M. (2012). Conceptual prototype of a planning software for the CONWIP production control system. *Proceedings of the International MultiConference of Engineers and Computer Scientists (IMECS)* (pp. 1–6), Hong Kong.

Gastermann, B., Stopper, M., Luftensteiner, F., and Katalinic, B. (2014). Implementation of a software prototype with conwip characteristics for production planning and stock management. *Procedia Engineering*, 69(5), 423–432.

Gaury, E. G. A., Kleijnen, J. P. C., and Pierreval, H. (2001). A methodology to customize pull control systems. *Journal of the Operational Research Society*, 52(7), 789–799.

Gee, E. S., and Smith, C. H. (1993). Selecting allowance policies for improved job shop performance. *International Journal of Production Research*, 31(8), 1839–1852.

Hopp, W. J., Iravani, S. M. R., Shou, B., and Lien, R. (2009). Design and control of agile automated CONWIP production lines. *Naval Research Logistics*, 56(1), 42–56.

Huang, G., Chen, J., Wang, X., and Shi, Y. (2015). A simulation study of CONWIP assembly with multi-loop in mass production, multi-products and low volume and OKP environments. *International Journal of Production Research*, 53(14), 4160–4175.

Huang, G., Chen, J., Wang, X., and Shi, Y. (2016). An approach of designing CONWIP loop for assembly system in one-of-a-kind production environment. *International Journal of Computer Integrated Manufacturing*, 29(7), 805–820.

Khojasteh, Y. (2016). *Production Control Systems, a Guide to Enhance Performance of Pull Systems*. Springer: Tokyo.

Khojasteh, Y., and Sato, R. (2015). Selection of a pull production control system in multi-stage production processes. *International Journal of Production Research*, 53(14), 1–17.

Khojasteh-Ghamari, Y. (2009). A performance comparison between Kanban and CONWIP controlled assembly systems. *Journal of Intelligent Manufacturing*, 20(6), 751–760.

Li, W., Nault, B. R., Xue, D., and Tu, Y. (2011). An efficient heuristic for adaptive production scheduling and control in one-of-a-kind production. *Computers and Operations Research*, 38(1), 267–276.

Pettersen, J., and Segerstedt, A. (2009). Restricted work-in-process: A study of differences between Kanban and CONWIP. *International Journal of Production Economics*, 118(1), 199–207.

Prakash, J., and Chin, J. F. (2015). Modified CONWIP systems: A review and classification. *Production Planning and Control*, 26(4), 296–307.

Sato, R., and Khojasteh-Ghamari, Y. (2012). An integrated framework for card-based production control systems. *Journal of Intelligent Manufacturing*, 23(3), 717–731.

Spearman, M. L., Woodruff, D. L., and Hopp, W. J. (1990). CONWIP: A pull alternative to Kanban. *International Journal of Production Research*, 28(5), 879–894.

Tu, Y., and Dean, P. (2011). *One-of-a-Kind Production*. Springer: London.

Vinod, V., and Sridharan, R. (2011). Simulation modeling and analysis of due-date assignment methods and scheduling decision rules in a dynamic job shop production system. *International Journal of Production Economics* 129(1), 127–146.

Wan, H. D., and Chen, F. F. (2008). A web-based Kanban system for job dispatching, tracking, and performance monitoring. *The International Journal of Advanced Manufacturing Technology*, 38(9), 995–1005.

Wortmann, J. C., Muntslag, D. R., and Timmermans, P. J. M. (1997). *Customer-Driven Manufacturing*. London: Chapman & Hall.

Chapter 9

Setting Push–Pull Boundaries: A Case of Textile Manufacturer

MD Sarder, Mohsen Hosseini, and Mohammad Marufuzzaman

Contents

9.1 Introduction

Responsiveness of the supply chain is a dominant factor for today's competitive market. Responsiveness is directly related to cost efficiency, and the role of inventory is very evident on the total supply chain cost. In today's world of technology and e-commerce, customers are more demanding and are very sensitive toward price and service level. Many companies are offering guaranteed delivery time and same day shipping, along with the traditional concept of bricks and mortar. These strategic changes come along with high price tags, especially in terms of inventory cost. In a multi-stage supply chain network, defining the push–pull boundaries and what-where-how much to stock are some of the most important strategic decisions that lead toward minimizing the overall inventory cost. Inventories are required to meet certain service levels, however such adjustments will increase product price. This is why it is very important for companies to decide on the correct push–pull strategy in order to reduce operational and transportation costs and maximize profitability. The supply chain which follows the pull strategy is designed to produce and distribute products based on actual customer demand and hence requires no inventory.

The supply chain which follows push strategy is designed to produce and distribute products based on long-term forecast and therefore requires inventory. Thus, pull-based supply chain is significantly more efficient than push-based supply chain in terms of inventory. However, in the case of international sourcing where lead time is too long, it often becomes infeasible to implement the pull-based strategy. It also is difficult to get an economy of scale for manufacturing in pull-based supply chain, and it becomes apparent that it is not necessarily true that a supply chain has to be based on purely pull or push strategy. A combined (push–pull) supply chain strategy is therefore a more feasible option in cases of long and complex multi-stage supply chains. The interface between push and pull is known as push–pull boundary (Simchi-Levi et al. 2008). It indicates the phase when a firm switches from managing the supply chain using one strategy (typically push) to another strategy (typically pull). This push–pull boundary should dictate the supply chain model to provide the lowest possible operational and transportation cost for the system (Harrison et al. 2003).

In a combined push–pull strategy, defining the safety stock, locating of safety stock, and reordering point all play important roles on the cost structure. Customer demand, variation in demand, seasonality, Lead Time (LT), and service level construct the level of safety stock and reordering point, which could inherently vary based on the inventory policy. In continuous review policy, an order is placed when a subjected inventory drops to a particular level. In periodic review policy, an order is placed after a certain period in pursuance of certain base-stock level (Mahadevan et al. 2003). In this chapter, we discuss a case study to define the push–pull boundary for both continuous and periodic review policies. We also compare the cost for push-based supply chain and combined (push–pull)-based supply chain strategy.

9.2 Literature Review

In a push inventory system, producers or resellers keep their inventory at a level that minimizes stock-outs and maximizes the benefit of economy production. Producers or resellers would make enough goods or order enough inventory to meet projected demand, which is mostly poor projection. There are benefits associated with pull systems such as lower risk of stock-outs and shorter lead time to meet customer demand (Krajewski et al. 1987). There are some disadvantages associated with pull systems. Material requirements planning (MRP), including high inventory cost and bull-whip effect on upstream of supply chain (Lee 1989). Push is commonly used in businesses where demand is more predictable.

On the other hand, a pull inventory system is more reactive. A pull system is related to the just-in-time (JIT) approach of inventory management that minimizes stock on hand, focusing on last-second deliveries. Producers or resellers would not make any goods or order any inventory unless there is a real demand from the customer. The major benefits of a pull inventory system include lower inventory cost and ability to adjust inventory levels as time goes on (Deleersnyder et al. 1992). The drawbacks of a pull system, such as Kanban controlled JIT, includes higher chances of stock-outs and higher shipping cost (Spearman and Zazanis 1992).

In reality, every supply chain strategy is a hybrid between push and pull systems. Supply chain strategies that combine push and pull are commonly termed hybrid or hybrid push/pull strategy. As mentioned above, a pull system can handle inventory cost and service level better under undisrupted demand scenarios, but how well it can handle unexpected disruptions was analyzed in Ozbayrak et al. (2004), where a simulation model was proposed to investigate machine and material handling breakdown problems in a pull system. In comparison of push and pull systems, approaches under machine breakdown scenario also are presented in Prakash and Feng (2011). Other authors considered this problem under uneven demand conditions (Gaury et al. 2001, Cochran and Kim 1998, Geraghty and Heavey 2004, Ghrayeb et al. 2009).

A hybrid push–pull strategy that incorporates additional stock points after the push–pull boundary as the pulling points in a serial supply chain was presented in Kim et al. (2012). This strategy can mitigate the risks and improve the robustness of the push–pull strategy. There is limited research in the literature that discuss detailed approaches of setting push–pull boundaries (Simchi-Levi et al. 2008). This research focuses on how to set push–pull boundaries to benefit from both the push and pull systems with a case of a textile manufacturer.

9.3 Methodology of Setting Push–Pull Boundary

The inventory carrying cost can be calculated based on the average inventory that are within a system of policies as discussed above. However, the level of inventory is an important strategic decision driven by holding cost, LT, and economy of scale in manufacturing. In a multi-stage supply chain scenario, the point beyond which a firm decides to go with a make-to-order strategy instead of a make-to-stock strategy can be adequately defined as the push–pull boundary. Considering the whole supply chain as a time line, material procurement is defined as the starting point and customer delivery is defined as the end point along the progression of the event. Thus, the push–pull boundary is a point in the time line, where the manufacturer switches from one strategy (typically push) to another strategy (typically pull).

In case of a multiple-product handling supply chain system where resources like raw materials are being routinely shared, the gradual shift of the supply chain toward downstream triggers more variability within the process. Hence, the semi-finished products would increasingly lose their ability to address the diversity of the products' demand. This inherently makes the value-added products less cost efficient, if the system decides to keep them in stock. For this reason, a typical supply chain starts with the push strategy with the intent to make-to-stock and ends with pull strategy with the objective of make-to-order.

If the demand of the product is very uncertain, then the supply chain should be designed on a pull-based strategy in order to avoid the dead stock, which cannot be sold due to sudden change in demand (Stock and Lambert 2001). On the other hand, if the demand is less variable, then the supply chain should be based on long-term forecast, leading toward the push strategy (Corniani 2008). Also, the economy of scale plays an important role while deciding on the extent of push–pull boundary. If the economy of scale in manufacturing is significant enough to surplus the inventory cost of the stock, then the push strategy is deemed more feasible than the pull strategy (Simchi-Levi et al. 2008).

The other two major factors for defining the push–pull boundary are holding cost and LT identified in and between different stages of the supply chain. For example, after receiving batches of semi-finished parts from certain manufacturing plants, if the committed LT to the customer is long enough and at the same time sustainable by the assembly units, then the ideal situation would normally employ a pull-based strategy. Yet in reality, the LT is one of the competitive factors that does not allow most of the manufacturers to quote a lengthy time interval. Therefore, they would essentially need to place the inventories somewhere within the supply chain system, in order to meet the committed shorter LT. Consequently, the inventory carrying cost of the total structure significantly reduces the efficiency of the globally optimized (combined push–pull) supply chain system. In the following sections, we demonstrate the concept of setting push–pull boundaries and their outcome through the means of analytical examples.

9.4 Inventory Policies

The most ideal and desirable position of a supply chain is to not carry any inventory, which in practicality is a rarely possible scenario. To meet the customer demand, the existing inventory becomes an integral part of the supply chain structure. However, reducing the inventory level is one of the main focuses of supply chain strategy. Therefore, the portion of a multi-stage supply chain where the LT between two stages are long enough, conventionally tends to carry more inventory than any other part of the supply chain.

A few important reasons for carrying inventory are

- To satisfy demand occurrences happening at lead times, inventory must be on hand to meet customer demand, which took place during the time of placing an order and arrival of the order.
- To protect against demand uncertainty.
- To balance annual inventory holding cost and annual fixed order cost. More frequent orders may result in a lower inventory cost, but they eventually lead to a higher annual fixed ordering cost.
- To allow flexibility in production scheduling.
- To provide a safeguard for variation in raw material delivery time.
- To take advantage of economic purchase-order size.

Sometimes there could be a greater need of inventory in-hand; and to manage such inventory, two inventory review policies are discussed below.

9.4.1 Continuous Review Policy

Continuous review policy is driven by the amount of inventory level. In this policy, the inventory is reviewed continuously, and an order is placed when the inventory reaches a particular level, or reorder point. This kind of policy is more appropriate when inventory can be continuously reviewed, for instance a point of sale (POS) system (Setyaningsih and Basri 2013).

To explain the continuous review policy as shown in Figure 9.1 the assumptions are as below:

- Daily demand is random and follows a normal distribution.
- Every time the distributor places an order from the manufacturer, the distributor pays a fixed cost, F, plus an amount proportional to the quantity of the order.
- Inventory holding cost is charged as item per unit time.
- Inventory level is continuously reviewed in order to make sure that if an order is placed, the order arrives after the appropriate lead time.
- If an order arrives when there is no inventory on hand, the order is lost.
- The distributor specifies a service level. The service level is a function of probability of not stocking out during the lead time.

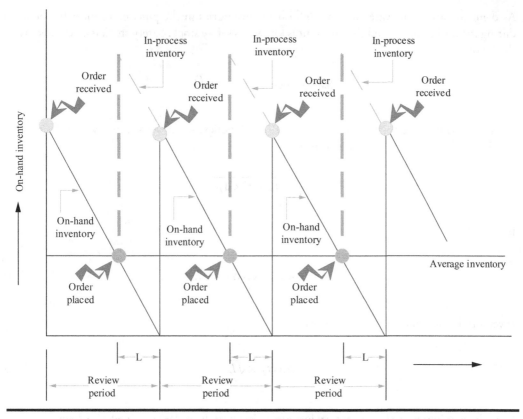

Figure 9.1 Continuous review policy (Setyaningsih and Basri, 2013).

9.4.2 Inventory Position

The inventory position at any point in time is the actual inventory at the warehouse, plus the items ordered by the distributor that have not yet arrived, minus the items that are backordered.

Before the formula we need to know the following:

■ μ_D = average daily demand faced by the distributor
■ σ_D = standard deviation of daily demand faced by the distributor
■ L = replenishment lead time from the supplier to the distributor in days
■ h = cost of holding one unit of the product for one day at the distributor
■ $1 - \alpha$ = service level. This implies that the probability of stocking out is α
■ k = service level factor (for 95% service level, k-value is 1.645)
■ F = fixed cost when each order is placed

Average demand during lead time:

$$L \times \mu_D \tag{9.1}$$

As demand varies, the warehouse needs to have inventories in the pipeline to meet the demand during the lead time (L), and that amount is known as safety stock. Safety stock is calculated using the following:

$$\text{Safety stock} = k \times \sigma_D \times \sqrt{L} \tag{9.2}$$

For the continuous review model known as a (Q, R) policy, whenever inventory level falls to the reorder level R, an order of Q units is placed:

$$Q = \sqrt{\frac{2 \times F \times \mu_D}{h}} \tag{9.3}$$

Reorder level:

$$R = L \times \mu_D + k \times \sigma_D \times \sqrt{L} \tag{9.4}$$

Inventory level before receiving an order:

$$k \times \sigma_D \times \sqrt{L} \tag{9.5}$$

Now the maximum level of inventory just after receiving the order is defined as below:

$$I_{\max} = Q + k \times \sigma_D \times \sqrt{L} \tag{9.6}$$

Average inventory:

$$\frac{\text{Safety stock} + I_{\max}}{2} = \frac{Q}{2} + k \times \sigma_D \times \sqrt{L} \tag{9.7}$$

k is chosen from Standard Normal Table 9.1 to ensure that the probability of stock-outs during lead time is exactly α.

9.4.3 Sample Problem

- A distributor of laptops that orders from a manufacturer and sells to retailers
- Fixed ordering cost = $9900
- Cost of a laptop to the distributor = $150
- Monthly demand of a sample product is shown in Table 9.2
- Annual inventory holding cost = 12% of product cost
- Replenishment lead time = 3 weeks
- Expected service level = 99%
- Average monthly demand = 2259.59

Table 9.1   Standard Normal for Service Levels

Service Level	90%	91%	92%	93%	94%	95%	96%	97%	98%	99%	99.9%
k	1.29	1.34	1.41	1.48	1.56	1.65	1.75	1.88	2.05	2.33	3.08

Table 9.2   Monthly Demand

Jan	Feb	Mar	Apr	May	June	July	Aug	Sept	Oct	Nov	Dec
1500	1300	1800	1400	2500	2050	1200	2400	4000	2450	3015	3500

Table 9.3   Snapshot of Summary Calculations of Sample Problem

Parameter	Average Weekly Demand	Standard Deviation of Weekly Demand	Average Demand During Lead Time	Safety Stock	Reorder Point
Value	525.48	432.96	1576.45	1747.29	3323.74

- Standard deviation of monthly demand = 897.8
- Average weekly demand = average monthly demand/4.3
- Standard deviation of weekly demand = monthly standard deviation/$\sqrt{4.3}$

Summary calculations of the sample problem are shown in Table 9.3.

- Weekly holding cost $= \dfrac{0.12 \times 150}{52} = 0.346$

- Optimal order quantity $= Q = \sqrt{\dfrac{2 \times 9900 \times 525.48}{0.346}} = 5483.68$

- Average inventory level $= \dfrac{5483.68}{2} + 1747.29 = 4489.13$

9.4.4 Periodic Review Policy

In periodic review policy, the inventory is reviewed on a routine basis. In this scenario, fixed ordering cost does not play a role and is considered a sunk cost, and the inventory strategy is driven by the base-stock level. In each inventory review period, the warehouse places enough order to raise the inventory up to the base-stock level (Setyaningsih and Basri 2013).

In Figure 9.2, the periodic review policy can be explained with two distinctive cases:

1. Short intervals (e.g., daily)
   - Define two inventory levels *s* and *S*.
   - During each inventory review, if the inventory position falls below s, order enough to raise the inventory position to S.
   - (s, S) policy.

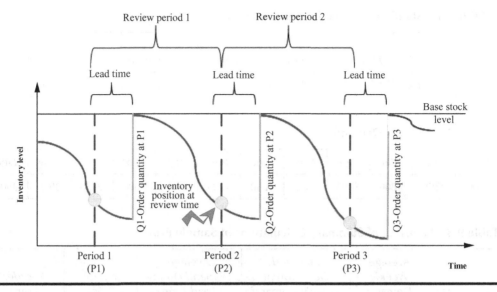

Figure 9.2 Periodic review policy.

2. Longer intervals (e.g., weekly or monthly)
   ■ May make sense to always order after reviewing the inventory level
   ■ Determine a target inventory level, the base-stock level
   ■ During each review period, the inventory position is reviewed
   ■ Order enough to raise the inventory position to the base-stock level
   ■ Base-stock level policy

We assume:

■ q = quantity to be ordered
■ σ_D = standard deviation of this daily demand
■ T = number of days between reviews
■ L = lead time
■ d = forecast avg. daily demand
■ k = k-value for a specified service level
■ I = current inventory level
■ μ_D = average daily demand faced by the distributor

Average demand during an interval of r, is given by

$$r + L \text{ days} = (r + L) \times \mu_D \tag{9.8}$$

For r days of review period and L days of lead time warehouse needs to keep the safety stock that covers the demand of $(r+L)$ days. Therefore, safety stock is calculated as below:

$$\text{Safety stock} = k \times \sigma_D \times \sqrt{(r+L)} \tag{9.9}$$

Expected (maximum) level of inventory just after receiving the order is defined as

$$I_{max} = r \times \mu_D + k \times \sigma_D \times \sqrt{(r+L)} \qquad (9.10)$$

Average inventory is given as

$$\frac{r \times \mu_D}{2} + k \times \sigma_D \times \sqrt{(r+L)} \qquad (9.11)$$

Quantity of order is defined as

$$q = d \times (T+L) + k \times \sigma \qquad (9.12)$$

9.4.5 Sample Problem

From the previous example given for continuous review policy, assume:

■ Distributor places an order for laptops every 4 weeks (i.e., $r = 4$)
■ Lead time is 3 weeks
■ Base-stock level needs to cover 7 weeks
■ Average demand per 7-week = $525.48 \times (4+3) = 3678.36$
■ Safety stock = $2.33 \times 432.96 \times \sqrt{(4+3)} = 2669.02$
■ Base-stock level = $3678.36 + 2.33 \times 432.96 \times \sqrt{(4+3)} = 6347.38$
■ Average inventory level = $\dfrac{4 \times 525.48}{2} + 2.33 \times 432.96 \times \sqrt{(4+3)} = 3719.98$
■ Distributor keeps = 7.07 (=3719.98/525.48) weeks of supply

9.5 Identifying Appropriate Supply Chain Strategy

What is the perfect strategy for a particular product? Should the company use a push-based supply chain strategy, or a pull base strategy or a combined push–pull strategy? Figure 9.3 provides a framework to aid the decision making on strategies for different supply chain scenarios.

In the figure, the vertical axis provides information on uncertainty of customer demand, while horizontal axis represents the importance of economies of scale.

While everything else remains same and equal, higher demand uncertainty leads to preference for managing the supply chain based on demand realization, a pull strategy. On the other hand, smaller demand uncertainty leads to a preference for managing supply the chain based on long-term forecasting, a push strategy.

Similarly, when reducing cost through the means of economies of scale is prioritized, accumulating demand is more valued, and therefore managing the supply chain based on long-term forecast, a push-based strategy, becomes a suitable and favorable option. If economies of scale are

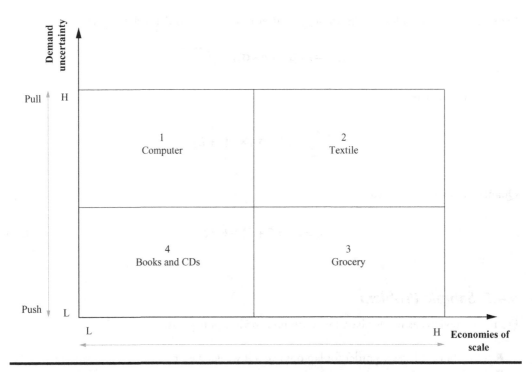

Figure 9.3   Push–pull strategy: Demand uncertainty versus economies of scale.

of a lesser priority, aggregation does not result in a reduced cost, and therefore the supply chain seeks to implement a pull-based strategy.

In Figure 9.3, according to the definition of push-pull, we partition the region spanned by these two dimensions into four boxes. Box 1 represents industries that are characterized by high uncertainty and therefore the economies of scale for production or distribution is of lesser importance. Definition and framework suggest that pull-based supply chain is more appropriate for this kind of product.

Box 3 represents products that have low demand uncertainty and high economies of scale. Products that are needed for daily consumption belong to this category. Demand for this kind of product is more stable than the products belonging to the other groups, and this allows in reducing transportation cost, a critical component of the supply chain, by shipping fully loaded trucks. A pull strategy is not a good idea for this case, rather a push-based retail strategy is more appropriate. It is due to the notion that managing inventories based on long-term forecast does not increase the inventory holding cost, and at the same time reduces delivery cost by leveraging economies of scale.

Boxes 1 and 3 represent the scenario in which a comparatively easy solution of an efficient supply chain strategy can be found. In the remaining two boxes, there is a mismatch between the strategies, represented by the two attributes, demand uncertainty and economies of scales. In one box, uncertainty pulls the supply chain toward one strategy while economies of scales push the supply chain in a different way.

Box 2 represents products and industries for which demand uncertainty, as well as economies of scale, is significantly high and therefore signaling an effort to reduce production and demand delivery costs. The textile and apparel industries are excellent examples of this situation. In fact, a typical textile retailer offers large number of similar products with distinguishable shape, color, and fabric, resulting in a high demand uncertainty. Many high-volume textile and apparel retailers would fall within this category. In this type of case, a more careful analysis is required, and depending on the specific cost and uncertainties, either a traditional push strategy or a more innovative push–pull strategy may be appropriate. For these reasons, there is a need to differentiate between the production and the distribution strategies. It is indicative that the production plan has to follow a push-based strategy, since it is imperative that the decisions are based on long-term forecasts. The initial shipment should also follow the push strategy as it requires a longer lead time to reach the distribution center (DC). On the other hand, the distribution strategy needs to take advantage of economies of scale in order to reduce the overall transportation cost. This is the same strategy that has been employed by many retailers who decide to keep limited or zero stock in their inventory. When stock reaches a certain level it is pulled out from DC, which also delivers the items for other retailers on the same zone. It is shipped to retail stores using truckload carriers, typically along with many other products in a combined shipment. Therefore, to reduce transportation cost due to economies of scale, manufacturers prefer a combined delivery of all products and strictly follow a fixed delivery schedule. Box 4 represents products with low demand uncertainty and low economy of scales, indicating a push-based supply chain and a pull-based supply chain strategy, respectively.

In most of the real-life scenarios, both push and pull systems are present to maximize the benefits of both systems while minimize the pitfalls of both systems. In a low value, generic product supply chain environment, most of the beginning stages follow push systems and final stage(s) follow pull systems.

Figure 9.4 depicts the stages that are involved in the push–pull scenario, where products are generic and customers typically do not wait for a long period in case of stock-out situation. In this case, the company must follow push strategies in most of the stages starting from the beginning and follow pull strategies in the final few stages. Figure 9.4 shows a typical scenario with the raw materials being channeled through different stages of manufacturing and industrial operations. The final stage is the DC, from where the product is being sent out to different retail stores all around the region.

9.6 Case Study

For the particular case of fashion garment production, it is commonly observed to have shorter selling seasons with no opportunity to reorder the product based on continuing customer demand. To study this specific phenomenon, a multinational textile manufacturer and distributor is being considered, where the manufacturing plant cannot instantly fulfill orders, since it involves a fixed lead time for delivery. Therefore, the demand is random and requires the DC to hold inventory, even though there is no fixed set-up cost in place for ordering the products. With raw material sourcing from India and China, the textile manufacturer has manufacturing plants in Bangladesh, a DC in Singapore, and a consumer market in North America and Europe.

In Figure 9.5, it can be seen that the textile manufacturer has a committed LT of about 21 days and assembling/processing time of 7 days. Therefore, within this supply chain, if a plant has a total manufacturing LT (Processing + Delivery) of more than 14 ($21 - 7 = 14$) days, they would be required to keep/hold the inventory. The inventory may be kept at the assembly plant or in the plant where the rest of the parts are being manufactured.

It is observed that a portion of inventory cost is reduced, if the manufacturer keeps the stock at the upstream of the supply chain which results in an optimized combined (push–pull) supply

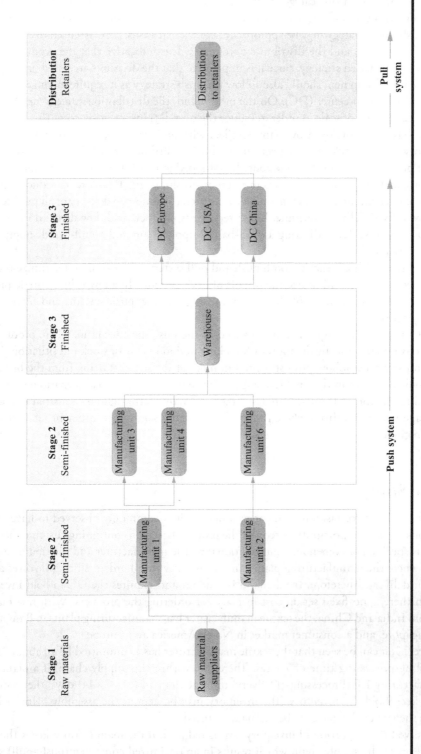

Figure 9.4 All the stages that are involved in the push–pull scenario.

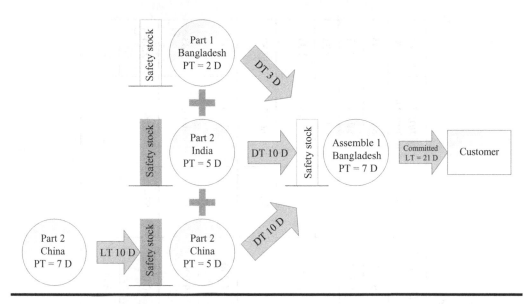

Figure 9.5 Part of the supply chain of textile manufacturer, where DT = delivery time and PT = processing time.

chain. Here, in this chapter we will compare the cost between supply chains that either follow a push strategy or a combined (push–pull) strategy.

For the case study of the textile manufacturer, four types of curtain are considered and denoted as curtain I, II, III, and IV. These curtains are manufactured in two processing plants located in Bangladesh and are stored in the DCs located in Singapore. The North American and European market demands are then satisfied from the DC located in Singapore.

The related LT, demand, standard deviation of demand, processing time (PT), consumption (units require to complete the next process) and the cost is given in Table 9.4. Here the cost of inventory will be compared in light of the continuous review policy and push–pull policy.

Here the agreed LT with customer is set at 25-day period. Therefore, if a product supply chain is less than or equal to 25 days, it can then be considered as a potential product for pull system. The upstream supply chain is able to absorb the demand fluctuations, since there is more variability added to the product in the next (consecutive) steps. In the case of a downstream supply chain, the ability of adding variability is gradually diminished. For example, keeping inventory of a finished product becomes riskier than keeping the raw materials, in this case the fabrics. It is because different design can be produced from the fabrics, but once the final product is manufactured, it cannot be altered/changed. With the risk of reducing demand, the item may not be sold at all resulting in a high inventory holding cost. Due to this reason, the textile supply chain, specifically the upstream supply chain, should maintain a push strategy and the downstream supply chain should be acquiring a pull strategy. Considering different factors of the involved costs, the supply chain can be converted from push to pull system at the DC. Even though the products might have longer LT than the agreed LT with the customer, the system cannot work in a push strategy and are therefore needed to keep stocks in the supply chain system.

In Figure 9.6, we laid out the case in traditional format to show the customer agreed lead time and the demand of each product. Based on our research and analysis, we created a push-pull boundary and calculated the lead time as shown in Figure 9.7. As seen in Figure 9.7, curtains II and III can therefore be converted to a pull system, and this process can take place at the

Table 9.4 Curtain from Raw Materials to Final Product-Ordering and Holding Costs

InventoryType	Source	Receiver	Consumption	LT (DT+PT)	Avg. Daily Demand	Demand Std. Dev	Ordering Cost	Holding Cost (unit/year)	Service Level
Fabrics I	China	Pr Unit-I	1.2	23	630,000	9,371	$4	$0.10	2.33
Fabrics II	BD	Pr Unit-I	1.2	5	1,620,000	8,593	$2	$0.10	2.33
Fabrics III	India	Pr Unit-I	1.2	19	990,000	10,909	$3	$0.10	2.33
Fin Fab I	Pr Unit-I	Pr Unit-II	5	9	525,000	7,810	$0	$0.15	2.33
Fin Fab II	Pr Unit-I	Pr Unit-II	5	5	825,000	9,091	$0	$0.15	2.33
Curtain I	Pr Unit-II	Dist. Cntr.	1	10	25,000	4,000	$5	$0.40	2.33
Curtain II	Pr Unit-II	Dist. Cntr.	1	10	80,000	9,000	$5	$0.60	2.33
Curtain III	Pr Unit-II	Dist. Cntr.	1	10	90,000	10,000	$5	$0.60	2.33
Curtain IV	Pr Unit-II	Dist. Cntr.	1	10	75,000	8,000	$5	$0.60	2.33

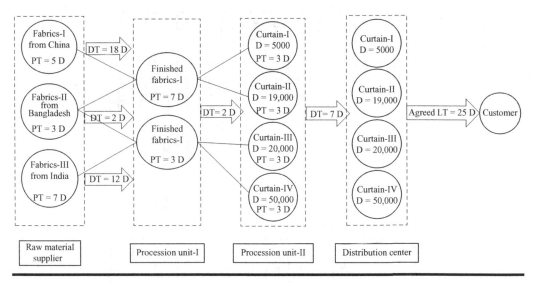

Figure 9.6   Lead times of raw materials to final product to customer.

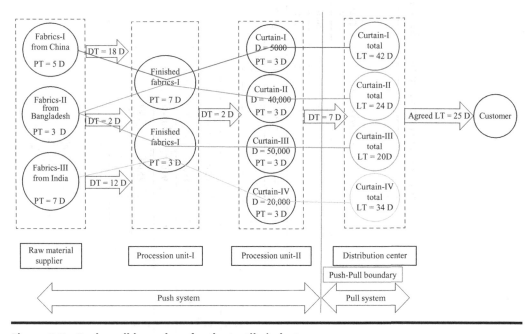

Figure 9.7   Push–pull boundary for the textile industry.

designated DC. The green line shows that the LT is shorter than the agreed upon LT and hence can be converted as pull system while blue line shows that the LT is little longer than the agreed upon LT.

As per the formula of continuous review policy, Table 9.5 shows the cost comparison in cases where curtains II and III converted from push to pull, immediately after processing unit-II. It is to be noted that the DC will not keep any stock of these two finished products, and information regarding the actual sales will eventually be shared/exchanged regularly and which would allow the manufacturing plant to prepare accordingly.

Table 9.5 Implementation of Continuous Review Policy—Curtain Manufacturing and Distribution

Inventory Type	Source	Receiver	Consumption	LT (DT+PT)	Avg. Daily Demand	Demand Std Dev	Order Cost	Holding Cost (unit/year)	Service Level	Order Quantity	Average Inventory	Total Holding Cost Traditional	Total Holding Cost Pull
Fabrics I	China	Pr Unit-I	1.2	23	630,000	9,371	$4	$0.10	2.33	135,632	172,535	$17,253	$17,253
Fabrics II	BD	Pr Unit-I	1.2	5	1620,000	8,593	$2	$0.10	2.33	153,792	121,664	$12,166	$12,166
Fabrics III	India	Pr Unit-I	1.2	19	990,000	10,909	$3	$0.10	2.33	147,245	184,418	$18,442	$18,442
Fin Fab I	Pr Unit-I	Pr Unit-II	5	9	525,000	7,810	$0	$0.15	2.33	0	54,589	$8188	$8188
Fin Fab II	Pr Unit-I	Pr Unit-II	5	5	825,000	9,091	$0	$0.15	2.33	0	47,364	$7105	$7105
Curtain I	Pr Unit-II	Dist Cntr	1	10	25,000	4,000	$5	$0.40	2.33	15,104	37,024	$14,810	$14,810
Curtain II	Pr Unit-II	Dist Cntr	1	10	80,000	9,000	$5	$0.60	2.33	22,061	77,343	$46,406	0
Curtain III	Pr Unit-II	Dist Cntr	1	10	90,000	10,000	$5	$0.60	2.33	23,399	85,380	$51,228	0
Curtain IV	Pr Unit-II	Dist Cntr	1	10	75,000	8,000	$5	$0.60	2.33	21,360	69,625	$41,775	$41,775
											Total	$217,373	$119,739

Based on our calculations, we found that the raw materials and work-in-process (WIP) costs are very similar in both traditional and push–pull systems. We also found that finished goods (FG) cost substantially higher in the traditional system compared to the push–pull system, and hence the same conclusion is applicable to total cost. Figure 9.8 shows the detail cost comparison between traditional and push–pull systems.

9.7 Results and Conclusions

It is observed that a combined push–pull strategy has proven to be more inventory cost efficient than the sole push strategy or other traditional supply chain methods. Through the comparison of the continuous review policy and push-policy, it is seen that a combined push–pull strategy works out better in all four cases, that is, Curtain I through Curtain IV. With products that have longer raw material or manufacturing LT than customer LT, the essence is to implement a combined push–pull strategy to avoid possible stock-out. In the cases of Curtain II and III, the DC will not hold any curtains since the LT for the customer is higher than the supplier/manufacturer, and the implementation of continuous review policy indicated that stocking up these categories would incur higher holding cost within the supply chain. The same formulation initiates the scenario where Curtain I and Curtain IV become a pull strategy, because it was found to have a longer LT (LT = 42 days and LT = 34 days) respectively, than the customer LT (LT = 25 days) and therefore holding cost at the DC is considerably lower. Ideally, the combined push–pull strategy saves approximately 30%–50% of holding cost, as seen in the cost comparison chart (see Figure 9.8), and therefore could become a significant contribution to the cost saving of the entire supply chain model. There are still certain uncertainties, coupled with varying demand scenarios, in the textile case study, but in order to reduce the risk of an increasing holding cost, the push–pull method has been found effective.

It is always a major challenge to match supply with demand. We identified that forecast demand is always wrong. The longer the forecast horizon, the less accurate the forecast. We also

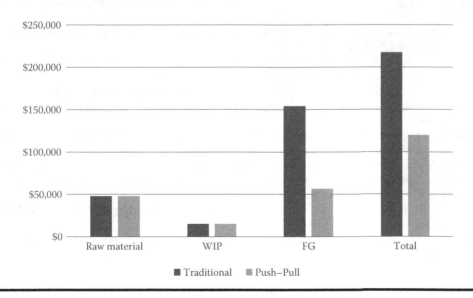

Figure 9.8 Cost comparison: Traditional versus push–pull.

have found from our study that aggregate demand more accurate than disaggregated demand. Inventory management need the most appropriate technique, as well as the most appropriate inventory policy. The other critical component is setting boundaries between push and pull systems. In this research, we found that if a product is a low cost and generic product, the push–pull boundary is much closer to the final stages of supply chain. This finding makes sense as the customer will not wait for a generic product in the case of a stock-out situation. Setting push–pull boundaries at the later stage of supply chain also reduces cost of inventory.

References

Cochran, J.K., and Kim, S.S. (1998). Optimum junction point location and inventory levels in serial hybrid push/pull production systems. *International Journal of Production Research*, 36(4), 1141–1155.

Corniani, M. (2008). Push and pull policy in market-driven management. In: I.-U. Bicocca, ed. *Emerging Issues in Management*. Retrieved from https://www.unimib.it/upload/gestioneFiles/Symphonya/2008,issue1/cornianieng12008.pdf

Deleersnyder, J. Hodgson, T., King, R., O'Grady, P., and Savva, A. (1992). Integrating kanban type pull systems and MRP type push systems: Insights from a Markovian model. *IEE Transactions*, 24(3), 43–56.

Gaury, E.G.A., Kleijnen, J.P.C., and Pierreval, H. (2001). A methodology to customize pull control systems. *Journal of the Operational Research Society*, 52(7), 789–799.

Geraghty, J., and Heavey, C. (2004). A comparison of hybrid push/pull and CONWIP/pull production inventory control policies. *International Journal of Production Economics*, 91(1), 75–90.

Ghrayeb, O., Phojanamongkolkij, N., and Tan, B.A. (2009). A hybrid push/pull system in assemble-toorder manufacturing environment. *Journal of Intelligent Manufacturing*, 20(4), 379–387.

Harrison, T.P., Lee, H.L., and Neale, J.J. (2003). *The Practice of Supply Chain Management: Where Theory and Application Converge*. Springer: New York.

Kim, S.H., Fowler, J.W., Shunk, D.L., and Pfund, M.E. (2012). Improving the pushpull strategy in a serial supply chain by a hybrid pushpull control with multiple pulling points. *International Journal of Production Research*, 50(19), 5651–5668.

Krajewski, L., King, B., Ritzman, L., and Wong, D. (1987). Kanban, MRP, and shaping the manufacturing environment. *Management Science*, 33(1), 39–57.

Lee, L. (1989). A comparative study of the push and pull productions systems. *International Journal of Operations and Production Management*, 9(4), 5–18.

Mahadevan, B., Pyke, D., and Fleischmann, M. (2003). Periodic review, push inventory policies for remanufacturing. *European Journal of Operational Research*, 151(3), 536–551.

Ozbayrak, M., Cagil, G., and Kubat, C. (2004). How successfully does JIT handle machine breakdowns in an automated manufacturing system? *Journal of Manufacturing Technology Management*, 15(6), 479–494.

Prakash, J., and Feng, C. (2011). A comparison of push and pull production controls under machine breakdown. *International Journal of Business Science and Applied Management*, 6(3), 58–70.

Setyaningsih, S., and Basri, M.H. (2013). Comparison continuous and periodic review policy inventory management system formula and enteral food supply in public hospital Bandung. *International Journal of Innovation, Management and Technology*, 2(2), 253–258.

Simchi-Levi, D., Philip, K., and Edith, S.-L. (2008). *Designing and Managing the Supply Chain: Concepts, Strategies, and Case Studies*. McGraw-Hill/Irwin: New York.

Stock, J.R., and Lambert, D.M. (2001). *Strategic Logistics Management* (3rd ed.). The McGraw-Hill: New York.

Chapter 10

Balancing Flexibility and Lean in Manufacturing Environments

Gwendolyn Holowecky and Ratna Babu Chinnam

Contents

10.1 Introduction

Literature on manufacturing flexibility has developed a consensus on the need for an effective framework for determining a firm's flexibility competency, and the necessary methods for converting those competencies into flexibility capabilities. The end goal of these efforts is to provide the proper fit between competencies, capabilities, and internal/external uncertainties with no cost, quality, or delivery (time) penalty. However, most of this research has taken place in non-Lean production environments. The rigidly scripted and highly "routinized" nature of Lean production was seen as a barrier to a firm's flexibility abilities and in fact, to overcome that barrier would reduce Lean's efficiencies. Recently, this efficiency/flexibility trade-off has been questioned by some research that suggest Lean's formalization is a necessary trait to improving a firm's flexibility effectiveness and performance. More specifically, the literature has begun to look at how Lean firms can approach flexibility through solutions in strategy, organization, and operational leadership. By customizing Lean's strengths in iterative operational routines and cumulative learning processes/worker knowledge, a company can be strong in both efficiency and flexibility. This chapter aims to shed more light on the efficiency/flexibility trade-offs and offers a framework for balancing the two in manufacturing environments.

10.1.1 What Is Lean?

Toyota's Production System (TPS), the most famous Lean system, works by "making the factory operate for the company just like the human body operates for an individual. We should have a system in a factory that automatically responds when problems occur" (Ohno 1988). The TPS House as shown in Figure 10.1 is a visual interpretation of such a system. The base of the house is a strong foundation of standardization and stability. The pillars of the house, just-in-time (JIT), and quality-built-in (QBI), ensure that the right high-quality parts, in the right quantity, are available at the right time. Tying the two pillars together is a strong organization culture that is rooted in respect for a firm's employees and suppliers. The glue that holds the house together is a set of tacit rule-sets (Spear and Bowen 1999) that makes TPS difficult to duplicate:

1. All work is highly specified in its content, sequence, timing, and outcome.
2. Each worker knows who provides what to him/her, and when.
3. Every product and service flows along a simple, specified path.
4. Any improvement to processes, worker/machine connections, or flow path must be made through the scientific method, under a teacher's guidance, and at the lowest possible organizational level.

Finally, the entire house is driven by the need for business success through continuous improvement of customer satisfaction related to cost, quality, and delivery.

10.1.2 What Is Flexibility?

Even a Lean manufacturing organization must be aware of the eventual need for flexibility in their company to stay relevant. "Plans change very easily. Worldly affairs do not always go according to plan and orders must change rapidly in response to circumstances. If one sticks to the idea that, once set, a plan should not be changed, a business cannot exist for long" (Ohno 1988). In the literature, there seems to be a general consensus on the definition of flexibility. Flexibility speaks

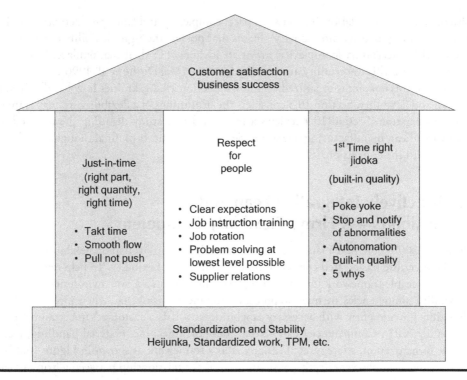

Figure 10.1 Toyota production system "house" (Ohno 1988).

to the capabilities of surprise and speed to deal with uncertain and volatile environments, whether the environmental source is internal or external to a company (Anand and Ward 2004). Flexibility capabilities should have the "ability to change or react with little penalty in time, effort, cost or performance" (Upton 1994) while flexibility competencies can be tangible (e.g., multi-function machines) and intangible (e.g., organizational characteristics), multi-level and multi-discipline (Cannon and St John 2004).

10.1.3 What Is Uncertainty/Volatility?

Volatility is the rate of change and uncertainty is the unpredictability of change (Anand and Ward 2004). Uncertainty can result from both external and internal sources (Beach et al. 2000). Examples of external uncertainty include competitors, consumers, technology, macroeconomic policies, product market and demand, social/political uncertainty (Chang 2011). Examples of internal uncertainty sources include machine breakdowns, manpower changes, material shortage, poor departmental coordination, supply chain uncertainty (Chang 2011). A study by MacDuffie et al. (1996) shows how uncertainty can affect performance (labor productivity and quality in this case) in automotive original equipment manufacturer (OEM) plants. In this study, uncertainty is defined as being made up of fundamental variety (i.e., demand uncertainty for different product models and their mix), intermediate variety (i.e., demand uncertainty for different parts that makeup the final products), and peripheral variety (i.e., demand uncertainty for optional content that go into final products). The results found no statistically significant effect of their various measures of product variety (complexity) on product quality. However, the study did find a consistent and negative relationship between parts complexity and labor productivity (e.g., higher complexity leading to lower productivity). Firms that possess the right flexibility competencies to counteract this uncertainty (complexity) are at an advantage in their marketplace. Firms that do nothing to address this uncertainty are at a disadvantage (MacDuffie et al. 1996).

The rest of this chapter is organized as follows: Section 10.2 examines how to effectively integrate Lean and flexibility. Section 10.3 considers the beginnings of a flexibility strategy framework for a Lean operation. Section 10.4 reviews a real-world case study detailing the targeted use of flexibility in a Lean manufacturing operation. Section 10.5 reflects on final thoughts, and Section 10.6 closes with the conclusion.

10.2 Effectively Integrating Lean and Flexibility—A Firm's Flexibility Competency

Zhang et al. (2003) note that a lack of consensus and significant overlap on flexibility descriptions within the literature has created confusion on the concepts of flexibility. To help reduce this confusion, an agreeable framework for integrating flexibility within a Lean environment is necessary.

Flexibility competencies are internal processes and mechanisms that, when applied in the right combination, provide a firm with necessary capabilities to satisfy a customer's uncertainty/volatility (Zhang et al. 2003). Competencies can be both tangible (machine, material handling, etc.) and intangible (organization, strategy, etc.). Zhang et al.'s framework as shown in Figure 10.2 is used here to provide a simple, yet effective, visualization of the relationship between a firm's flexibility competence, capability, and customer satisfaction.

Competencies in of themselves are not perceived important to the customer. Rather, the customer values the product of the competencies: the capabilities of a firm to provide the exact product, quantity and delivery timing. To help further define flexibility competency, three distinct classifications have been proposed that cover all industries (Upton 1995b):

1. Range/variety: "the ability to make a small number of products that are very different from one another, or a large number of products that are slightly different from one another" or somewhere in between. (Upton 1995b). "Managers interested in offering a wide range of products need inbuilt capabilities to produce diverse products in reaction to fast-paced changes in the environment" (Anand and Ward 2004).

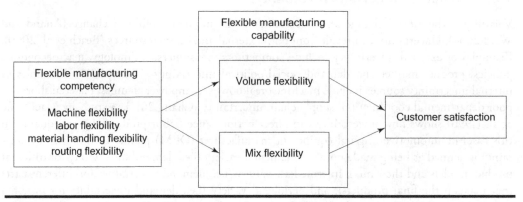

Figure 10.2 Framework for flexible manufacturing: Competencies, capabilities, and customer satisfaction.

2. Mobility: The ability to quickly change from one product to the next in order to minimize run size and inventory slack (Upton 1995b). Another definition speaks of mobility's capabilities to quickly switch between products (mix) and/or respond to changes in volume (Anand and Ward 2004).
3. Uniformity: Refers to the need to maintain cost, quality, delivery (customer satisfaction) across the entire range of flexibility. In terms of cost uniformity, "a cost curve that is U-shaped with a long flat bottom, it is viewed as flexible because there is a wide range of production volumes with little difference in costs" (Zhang et al. 2003).

Zhang et al.'s (2003) "value chain flexibility" considers several flexibility competency categories for an entire company operation: product development, manufacturing flexibility, and logistics flexibility. Each of these categories can include several sub-category competency dimensions within the next level down. For example, manufacturing flexibility can include machine flexibility, routing flexibility, labor flexibility, material handling flexibility, slack flexibility, organizational flexibility, and others. Upton's (1995b) three classifications are applicable for each of these competencies. Figure 10.3 is provided to visually show an example of competency categories, dimensions, and classifications based on an expanded "value chain flexibility" by Zhang et al. (2003).

Despite the many types of competencies reviewed and studied in the literature, there is no definitive list of those that are necessary to improve flexibility capabilities in Lean manufacturing environments. To help remedy this shortfall, this review attempts to find flexibility literature with strong empirical studies, in non-Lean contexts, logically link those results with the literature on Lean manufacturing practices, and conclude with a case study as confirmation. The findings can be categorized into the following competencies: organizational, human resources, slack, and supply chain (to a lesser degree).

10.2.1 Organizational Competency

Based on contingency theory, the literature has spoken of a Lean/flexibility paradox: while efficiency requires a highly rule-structured bureaucratic organization, a flexible organization should be more organic in nature (Adler et al. 1999). Adler et al. (1999) pointed out that the older literature, built around organizational theory, states companies "must choose between organization

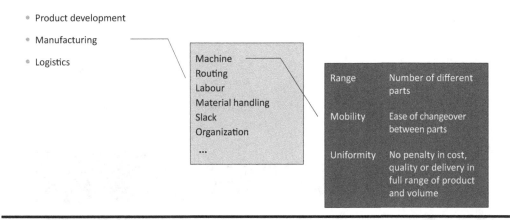

Figure 10.3 **"Value chain flexibility" of flexibility competencies.**

designs suited to routine, repetitive tasks and those suited to non-routine, innovative tasks." More recent literature considers organizational structures that facilitate both the efficiency (e.g., Lean) and flexibility concurrently, show that companies which manage both within their organization have performance advantages. Narasimhan's study (2004) suggests that companies with high flexibility competencies have already resolved organizational and technical issues (see Figure 10.4 for visualization).

MacDuffie et al. (1996) argues that Lean production plants have a "distinctive organizational logic" allowing them greater flexibility to overcome uncertainties. This is supported by his results which show for a Japanese auto OEM that both North American and Japanese plants can effectively absorb higher levels of option variability due to high model mix (product range/variability), with no loss of productivity. In contrast, their US OEM counterparts, with the same higher levels complexity, lead to lower productivity (MacDuffie et al. 1996). What is organizationally different in companies that seem to have overcome this efficiency/flexibility paradox?

First, organizational competencies that promote flexibility in non-Lean contexts will be reviewed. Narasimhan et al. (2004) suggested that organizational flexibility competence may be a factor in how an organization creates, collects, and shares knowledge. Patel et al. (2012) approached the question of flexibility competence from two organizational learning contingencies. He found that an organizations' operational absorptive capacity and organizational ambidexterity are strong moderators of a company's flexibility capability (machine, labor, material handling, product mix, and new products) and ultimately a company's performance. Where this study differs from past research is in the operational level context. In Patel et al.'s (2012) study, absorptive capacity is defined as the ability of an organization at the operational level to rapidly gather, understand, and transform/exploit manufacturing environmental knowledge into flexibility capabilities necessary to overcome uncertainty. This supports the earlier statement of Narasimhan et al. (2004). The other contingency, operational ambidexterity, is defined as the ability of an organization to pursue both exploration and exploitation in the right mix, or balance, necessary for the environmental uncertainty at that time. "Operational ambidexterity helps channel learning efforts to maintain continuity with prior routines while incorporating novel processes" (Patel et al. 2012).

Next, Lean applications/practices that support these studies are considered. Patel et al. (2012) and Narasimhan's (2004) ideas for organizational mechanisms that promote flexibility competency are supported in Adler's (1999) case study of New United Motor Manufacturing, Inc. (NUMMI). NUMMI was an automobile manufacturing company in Fremont, California, jointly

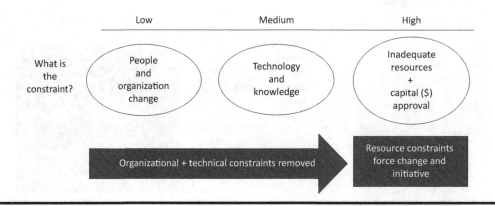

Figure 10.4   Firm's overall flexibility competence and roadblocks (Narasimhan et al. 2004).

owned by General Motors and Toyota that successfully utilized TPS. Through TPS, NUMMI leveraged existing specialized process knowledge for exploitation at the operational level, and created new knowledge through exploration in temporary cross-functional teams. This was accomplished using four organizational mechanisms: meta-routines, job enrichment, switching, and partitioning (ambidexterity). To help overcome the Lean/flexibility paradox, these mechanisms allow for non-routine and routine tasks to be carried out in parallel without reducing the effectiveness of day-to-day Lean operations (Adler et al. 1999).

As one moves from meta-routines to partitioning, the mechanisms progressively give more freedom to the process owners for stepping outside of their routine. Since routine is seen as a hindrance to the creativity necessary for exploration, Toyota uses "three forces of expansion" to bring about exploration type change: impossible goals, experimentation, and local customization (Adler et al. 2009). The three forces are part of creating value-added improvements using "a mix of exploit and explore without making this distinction" (Adler et al. 2009). The experimentation phase is followed up with a standardization phase, where the newly improved processes are made routine. Each of these iterations in improvement is attempting to close a gap between the current state and some clearly defined ideal target that ultimately satisfies some customer/market demand or some unique company goal (Adler et al. 2009). The problem solving of the experimental phase is framed as a learning opportunity (Adler et al. 2009) and the new knowledge and lessons learnt are documented in a reflection-review "hansei" process (Adler et al. 1999). Over time and many iterations of experimentation, this knowledge accumulates and becomes "organizational memory" providing a valuable feedback loop for the organization at each subsequent iteration (Adler et al. 1999). This is in line with Patel et al.'s (2012) observation of the past literature findings that absorptive capacity "tend(s) to develop cumulatively" in both individuals and organizations. A visual representation of these iterative and cumulative processes of absorptive capacity are shown in Figure 10.5.

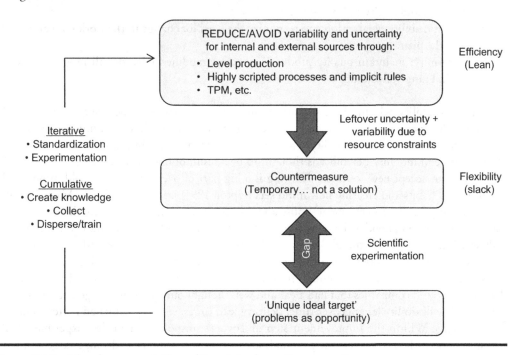

Figure 10.5 Visual representation of Toyota's absorptive capacity process.

The ambidextrous exploitation and exploration mechanisms, along with the absorptive capacity found in the cumulative "feedback loop" of reflection-review and the iterative experimentation/standardization-training steps, may help establish strong organizational processes for dealing with uncertainties and volatilities in a Lean environment. The success of these organizational competencies lies in the specialization of those who actually performs the work. Ohno (1988) describes a business organization as a human body where major body functions, such as heart rate, are automatic, without input from the brain (autonomic nerve). He states that in a production system, this "autonomic nerve means making judgements autonomously at the lowest possible level" providing "reflexes that can respond instantly and smoothly to small changes in the plan without going to the brain." By enabling the lowest possible level to create flexibility capabilities through these strong organizational processes automatically, "without direct management intervention," response time in addressing uncertainties and volatilities is reduced, leading to an increase in customer satisfaction. Over time, a Lean organization will "shift to adapt to the nature and frequency of the problems they encounter" (Spear and Bowen 1999) in the pursuit of the "ideal production system" that is specific and unique to each company.

10.2.2 Human Resources/Labor Competency

Despite labor's importance as a flexibility competency, "conceptual and empirical literature tends to emphasize equipment flexibility and to neglect the potential impact of labor" (Zhang et al. 2003).

Based on Upton's flexibility classifications, labor flexibility is defined as (Zhang et al. 2003):

■ Range variety: number of tasks an associate can carry out with consideration for speed of execution and ability to learn quickly
■ Mobility: ability of labor force to recognize the need for change in the work plan and implement the plan
■ Uniformity: maintain quality/productivity across modified jobs for full range of products and full range of volumes

Labor flexibility within these classifications vary with worker experience (Upton 1995b). Workers with longer service have an increase in range/variety flexibility (number of products), but a decrease in mobility flexibility (ease of product changeover) in a non-Lean environment. This decrease in mobility flexibility is thought to be a result of older workers who are too "set-in-their-ways" to accept new routines. Training is a big part of overcoming those old mind sets by breaking old habits and creating new mind sets (Upton 1995b). In Toyota (NUMMI case study), the iterative process of experimentation/standardization-training discussed in the organization competency section provides that new mind-set (Adler et al. 1999) and is contained in an implicit ruleset within Toyota (Spear and Bowen 1999). These tacit rules help create and standardize how processes are designed, operated, and improved. Within the design step, work-specific processes are standardized for easy and thorough training at the operational level (Spear and Bowen 1999). Upton also found companies that had clear and well thought out operations targets for both range and mobility flexibility (changeover time, delivery lead times, etc.) typically had better labor flexibility results. Within the improvement step of Toyota's unspoken four rules, experiments take place, with well-defined targets for gap analysis, such as the mobility and range targets of labor flexibility (Adler et al. 2009).

Some of the literature has focused on the positive effects of longer employment service on flexibility. As stated earlier, longer service also correlates to greater range flexibility (Upton 1995b) due to a worker's deeper knowledge or experience of a plant's processes at outlying ranges. This experience is the accumulation of an individual's absorptive capacity over time. Again, this is in line with observations of past literature findings that absorptive capacity was found to be important at the individual level (Patel et al. 2012). To ensure longer term employment within Toyota, job security and trust between senior management and process operators are part of Toyota's core cultural assumptions. Greater worker experience at Toyota is also achieved through a policy of promoting from within its own ranks, appointing floor associates into line-management roles. These core cultures, in turn, strengthen training and "organizational memory" that accumulates within these long-term Toyota employees (Adler et al. 1999). Narasimhan et al. (2004) wrote how deep experiences that provide workers with the skills to work at the far range of a process can be thought of as tacit skills, similar to the "organizational memory" of implicit process knowledge that motivates Toyota (Spear and Bowen 1999).

Labor skill in a flexibility competence context also has been discussed in literature. Labor skill sets are typically categorized under broad-based and specialist for a given manufacturing process. Process specialization development is achieved through training, as discussed earlier. In-depth knowledge found in process or product specialization skills allows for the creative thinking necessary for changes that bring about flexibility capabilities (Narasimhan et al. 2004). Broad-based skills are "complex and difficult to replicate" without the proper environments found in job rotations, special projects, and cross-functional teams (multi-level and multi-discipline) (Bhattacharya et al. 2005). A proper mix between these broad-based skills and specialized skills contributes to a company's flexibility. Rather than trying to predict what future skill sets will be needed, a true variety of labor skills is the best solution for increasing a company's chances at reducing the effects of future environmental uncertainty (Bhattacharya et al. 2005). Efforts in developing those necessary skills, that result in higher flexibility, is best concentrated on process-training rather than equipment-training and includes higher levels of job-rotation training (Sawhney 2013). Toyota develops both specialized and broad-based skills through the four organization mechanisms discussed in the organizational section: meta-routines, job enrichment, switching and partitioning (ambidexterity). Where meta-routines and job routines strengthen process specialization, switching and partitioning helps round out broad-based skills. An example of partitioning within Toyota occurs during new model development where cross-functional pilot teams are created to develop processes for new products. The pilot teams are multi-discipline and include key team leaders from the floor. Skill development here is an iterative and cumulative process (Adler et al. 1999), similar to the absorptive capacity process discussed earlier:

1. Floor leaders bring specialization knowledge of individual processes to cross-functional teams. Team members have typically contributed to past pilot teams (staffing continuity and depth of expertise = organizational memory).
2. Team provides opportunity for broader based skill development from interaction with multi-disciplined team. The setting and collection of knowledge here is suitable for innovation/exploration types of improvement over previous (flexible) processes.
3. New set of specialized skills developed for new process. Pilot team members return to the floor to train new team members who will be performing work.

In addition to labor skill, two additional dimensions to labor flexibility have positive effects on profitability and productivity—labor behavioral flexibility and human resource (HR) flexibility

(Bhattacharya et al. 2005). Behavioral flexibility is different from skill flexibility in that an employee may possess the skill, but lack the motivation for change. HR flexibility includes flexibility of labor policies. While Bhattacharya et al. (2005) do not specifically classify behavioral plus HR flexibility, they may be considered the implementation portion of labor flexibility. Sawhney's (2013) study has shown that plant performance is positively associated with acquired labor flexibility (range + mobility) if it is properly implemented.

10.2.3 Slack Competency

Slack as a flexibility competency includes the use of open capacity or inventory to overcome internal (e.g., machine downtime) and external uncertainties (e.g., volume) (Jack and Raturi 2002). However, slack in larger amounts in a Lean manufacturing environment is considered waste. In a Lean context, a less wasteful manufacturing flexibility solution is required to negate uncertainty (Anand and Ward 2004). Upton (1995b) also noted in a study of the US paper industry (and industry in general) that the customers' demands of product proliferation has made inventory slack uneconomical. Hasik (2006) notes the same trend for OEM automakers, as customer market demands drive an "increased product proliferation and decreased average volumes."

For Toyota, slack is typically seen as a temporary countermeasure to unique and individual problems. In this sense, they do not "pool" all in-house work-in-process (WIP) into one location, but rather separately match each countermeasure stock to each unique problem. This separation provides clear instruction that workers "own" this problem and the temporary countermeasure (stock). Ultimately, they are responsible for removing this slack through their targeted improvement efforts. (Spear and Bowen 1999). Countermeasures may be necessary for internal (e.g., cycle time variability, machine downtime) and external reasons. For the latter, Spear and Bowen (1999) noted special circumstances within Toyota where: "in some cases, variations in customers' needs are so large and unpredictable that it is impossible for a plant to adjust its production to them quickly enough."

Capacity as a slack flexibility includes open available production time and can be considered a "soft scaling" flexibility due to the minimal delay time to implement (Deif 2012). Toyota uses capacity slack as a quick solution for volume uncertainty. Manufacturing is typically constrained to two shifts so that overtime production (early start on days, late ending on afternoon shift) can fulfill unexpected volume demand. This third shift is also reserved for preventative maintenance time to reduce internal uncertainties (Autoweek 2014).

10.2.4 Supply Base Competency

In the literature, there is a difference in opinion on the role of the supply base in a firm's flexibility competency. One strategy involves reserving high complexity parts for in-house manufacturing, where in-sourcing allows workers to develop the specialized skills of processes and products necessary for a high level of flexibility competency (Narasimhan et al. 2004). The opposing strategy supports outsourcing as a means of increasing a company's flexibility. Here, a supplier's resources and deep product knowledge is leveraged to support mass customization, with respect to part cost, design and manufacturing complexity, and shrinking product development timelines (Alford et al. 2000). In NUMMI's case, Toyota sees a benefit in outsourcing complexity where supplier process and product innovation is deemed an asset to address cost, complexity, and timing. The success of Toyota/Supplier codependence is built on trust and coordination, using the same four organization mechanisms to promote ambidexterity. In fact, suppliers of highly complex and integral components are considered an extension of the Toyota team, sometimes participating in pilot team exercises with Toyota team members (Adler et al. 1999). Adler balances his statement by acknowledging that offloading complexity can also result in a loss of core competencies (that build human resource skills) and loss of bargaining power with suppliers.

Ultimately, there exists an optimal balance between manufacturing cost, maintaining control of a supply chain, and balancing the risks of outsourcing (Alford et al. 2000). While Adler et al. (1999) presents a case study of supply base outsourcing for a Lean OEM manufacturer, this literature review does not go any deeper. Further investigation may provide insight into different strategies within the context of supply chain position/depth (OEM, Tier 1, and Tier 2), product type, level of Lean implementation, logistics complexity, and manufacturer/supplier relationships.

10.3 The Beginnings of a Flexibility Strategy Framework for a Lean Operation

Based on Zhang's "Flexibility Manufacturing Competence on Capability and Customer Satisfaction" framework presented earlier, next a company must fully understand its flexibility requirements:

1. What flexibility capabilities are necessary to satisfy the customer (product range/mix and/or volume)?
2. What balance/mix of flexibility competencies are necessary to achieve those capabilities?

Additionally, over the course of achieving customer satisfaction, a firm also must consider and justify the effects of flexibility based on costs, resources, production performance, and timing (e.g., delivery) (Upton 1994). Currently, there is no framework to assist in choosing the right flexibility capabilities and competencies to address environmental uncertainties/volatilities in a Lean manufacturing context. As with the flexibility competency section, we will attempt to find flexibility in the literature, with strong empirical studies in non-Lean contexts, and logically link those results with the literature on Lean manufacturing practices and case studies as confirmation. Both Zhang and Upton's considerations and the previously discussed competencies together form the beginnings of this framework.

Literature has two general approaches to answering the two questions for establish a company's flexibility requirements (He et al. 2011):

1. Linking flexibility requirements to uncertainty in environment—adaptive in nature, follow market trends, capability of speed.
2. Linking to corporate strategy—proactive, setting trends, capability of surprise.

In terms of a planning timeframe, the adaptive approach seems more immediate. Adaptive and reactive are used interchangeably within the literature and both speak to the need for speedy capabilities, found in the earlier definition of flexibility. Proactive hints at a longer planning timeframe. Proactive and strategic are often used interchangeably within literature. However, proactive flexibility has taken on different definitions within literature. These multiple definitions seem to indicate a lack of consensus within research. In one case, proactive flexibility is used for uncertainty avoidance where tools such as total productive maintenance (TPM), statistical process control (SPC), design for manufacturing (DFM) are administered (Hallgren and Olhager 2009). Uncertainty avoidance is similar to Toyota's use of the Heijunka tool for proactively controlling volume variability day-to-day (Spear and Bowen 1999). The other take is in line with He's (2011) corporate strategy definition where proactive flexibility considers a long-term timeline, involving "significant change and commitment" (resources, capital) and occurring infrequently (Upton 1995a). Yet another definition of proactive flexibility contains both a strategic element (redefinition) and an uncertainty avoidance element (reduction) (Gerwin 1993).

While the strategic approach does lend itself to a longer time frame in Upton's (1995a) and He's (2011) definitions, the uncertainty avoidance or reduction portion of proactive flexibility can be timeless. Another approach is needed to establish a "flexibility timeline." To help further define timing within a flexibility framework Upton (1995a) has considered the following: operational, tactical, and strategic timelines. The auto industry, for example, has three distinct time periods: short (weeks), medium (months), and long (between generation of vehicles) (Hasik 2006). For a Lean production system, we will consider short as Heijunka period to 20 week forecast, medium as 5 months to 2 year forecast, and long-time periods as values between generations of vehicles.

To understand which approach (proactive vs. adaptive) is appropriate for which environmental circumstance, Ketokivi (2006) proposes a contingency theory approach, stating that a "better fit between the type of environmental dynamism and type of flexibility pursued is associated with better business performance." Ketokivi uses Gerwin's (1993) flexibility categories of banking (slack), adaptation (reactive/adaptive), redefinition (setting trends) and reduction (uncertainty avoidance). The data suggests that companies with a relatively more predictable (low uncertainty) environment seem to take a more proactive approach (redefinition and reduction), while companies in a low-predictability (high uncertainty) environment seem to take a more reactive approach (banking and adaptation). Here proactive speaks to both a longer planning timeframe with redefinition (strategic) and planning that is either short or long term with reduction (uncertainty avoidance).

Hallgren and Olhager (2009) study operational performance with respect to flexibility levels and flexibility output for various flexibility sources. The results provide two insights. First, volume flexibility and mix flexibility are two different and separate types of flexibility capabilities. Second, mix/variety flexible plants that use a higher level of proactive strategies perform better, whereas volume flexible plants that use a combination of both proactive and adaptive strategies perform better.

Anand and Ward (2004) approach the fit between environment (uncertainty, volatility) and flexibility differently than Ketokivi (2006). From empirical studies, Anand and Ward's results show that companies that have strong range-flexibility capabilities (manage product or process mix/variety) in volatile (fast changing but relatively predictable) environments will have higher performance. Companies that have strong mobility-flexibility capabilities (ability to quickly change product and/or volume) in unpredictable (uncertain) environments will have higher performance.

When considering Lean applications/practices that support these studies of flexibility/environment fit, one must first consider how TPS was created and evolved with flexibility capabilities of both range and volume in mind. On range/mix flexibility, Ohno (1988) discusses the need for diversification to satisfy the consumer, but also a need for level production to minimize downstream variability. However, "leveling becomes more difficult as diversification develops." To overcome this difficulty to "keep diversification and production leveling in harmony and still respond to customer orders in a timely manner" Ohno emphasizes the need to improve mobility by reducing lot sizes and reducing set-up time as well as improving process range with "specialized, yet versatile production processes through the use of machines and jigs that can handle minimal quantities of material." He uses an example of multiple vehicle platforms on the same line using leveling and small lot: "one sedan, one hardtop, then a sedan, then a wagon, and so on." This sort of planning hints at a strategic timeline at a model/process development stage.

A MacDuffie et al. (1996) study of OEM automakers in North America noted that Japanese plants had the highest level of option variability, due to their high level of model mix complexity, with no negative effect on productivity or quality as compared to their US counterparts. Anand and Ward (2004) refer to a 1990 Womack study that suggests Lean manufacturing provides a good environment for achieving range flexibility. As a large portion of a plant investment is required to accommodate complexity resulting from greater product mix, automakers must consider a manufacturing strategy across and within all plants "balancing the number of vehicle entries (number of unique body styles) with the capabilities of its assembly plants, both in terms of volume and product mix capacities." Mobility flexibility, during this process, has two meanings (Hasik 2006):

1. Ability of manufacturing systems to quickly change mix or volume within a certain expected customer timeframe
2. Ease and speed of model development and changeover between generations of vehicles

In the NUMMI study by Adler et al. (1999), Toyota promotes "front loading mutual adjustment" organizational coordination to help find the best solution between design considerations and reality. This is true for both product and production processes. This strategic, proactive, and concurrent approach in product and process development leads to a reduction in the time needed to changeover between models, and a reduction in the number of engineering changes after launch. This is the mobility that Hasik (2006) spoke of and Gerwin (1993) referred to as having strategic competitive importance. The organizational structure is a separately managed "pilot team"—a multi-disciplinary and ambidextrous group that includes key floor leaders with specialized skills from their respective departments. The pilot team cross-functional environment promotes sharing of knowledge that creates more broad-based skills for all team members. After the pilot team exercise is complete, floor leaders would then return to the floor and train their team members on the new processes/standardized methods as part of the iterative processes of absorptive capacity as they move to production. To ensure the lessons learnt from each model changeover is cumulative, team members often are carried over to subsequent model changeovers (Adler et al. 1999).

On volume flexibility, Ohno (1988) points out that any process that requires a fixed number of workers is a "major handicap in any factory that has to respond to a change in production." To remove this constraint for changes in volume, equipment/processes must be able to accept various number of workers with no loss in productivity and "multi-skilled training for workers must be instituted." Ohno remarks that these labor and equipment improvements for volume flexibility must occur "while times are still normal," a steady state of sorts to make the scientific experimentation of gap analysis easier to conduct.

This steady state in an uncertain environment can be attained through Toyota's temporary slack countermeasure of inventory (Spear and Bowen 1999) or open shift capacity for overtime (Autoweek 2014). Slack is temporary in the sense that once the gap between current and target condition is met, the slack is removed. The target condition in this case would require a flexibility competency solution to meet a new long-term customer demand. Whether the "gap is large and strategic or small and operational," experimentation (PDCA: plan do check act) requires a balance of exploitation and exploration (Patel et al. 2012) that is unique to the problem/gap (Adler et al. 2009). The larger and more challenging the gap (e.g., ideal target), the greater the need for innovative solutions brought on by exploration. However, Toyota avoids the idea that one must choose between exploration and exploitation to avoid trade-offs. Instead, Toyota instills an overriding culture of "continuous learning" (Adler et al. 2009). In terms of absorptive capacity opportunities for volume flexibility capability, Ohno (1988) considers the challenge and learning experience of raising productivity for negative growth. He states that anyone can improve productivity and efficiency by increasing production quantities "but few people in the world can raise productivity when production quantities decrease." Ohno's commonly spoken "unreachable goal" to spur on innovative thinking in this context: "I always say production can be done with half as many workers."

A visual representation for the beginnings of a "flexibility strategy framework in a Lean manufacturing environment" is depicted in Figure 10.6. The inspiration for this framework comes from a remark made by Hajime Ohba (a General Manager at Toyota supplier support center): How to plan for change is as important as the change itself (Spear and Bowen 1999). This framework for flexibility selection and balance I am proposing is built on Lean's strength of formalization and "routinization," using Toyota's absorptive capacity process as the starting point or seed. Unique flexibility capability solutions within this framework are created through a company's strategy, organization, Lean practices, labor, slack, and manufacturing processes/equipment by customizing Lean's strengths in iterative operational routines and cumulative learning processes/worker knowledge for a given timeframe and customer need.

10.4 Case Study: Targeted Use of Flexibility to Manage Pull Uncertainty in a Lean Internal Supply Chain

10.4.1 Introduction

A high-ranking member from the parent company of TRQSS had just visited their plant. On a tour of TRQSS' injection molding (IM) department, he discovered a problem: the production system lacked process standardization, a well understood source of poor quality and non-value-added work. A team was quickly assembled and tasked with standardizing all IM manufacturing processes. At the same time, another issue was raised by management: excessive IM production weekend overtime. The large amount of direct labor* overtime on the IM production floor led senior management to suspect something was wrong with the "pull" between IM (the supplier) and assembly (the internal customer) (Figure 10.7). TRQSS, as a keiretsu partner of Toyota, had employed TPS from its original formation nearly 20 years ago. Within TPS, demand pull signals form downstream "internal customers" in the form of "kanban" cards form the critical information signals that coordinate production across the facility as well as the broader supply chain.

This case study follows how an investigation of a seemingly small overtime issue uncovered much deeper problems, leading to a complete overhaul of a 12-year-old, broken Heijunka system.

10.4.2 Background

Quality Safety Systems (QSS), a manufacturer of automotive seat belts, was established in 1987 as a joint venture with US auto supplier TRW and Japanese auto supplier Tokai Rika Japan (TRJ), which is 35% owned by Toyota Motor Company (TMC) as part of their "keiretsu." The original

---

* Direct Labor here refers to labor that is used in actual parts production.

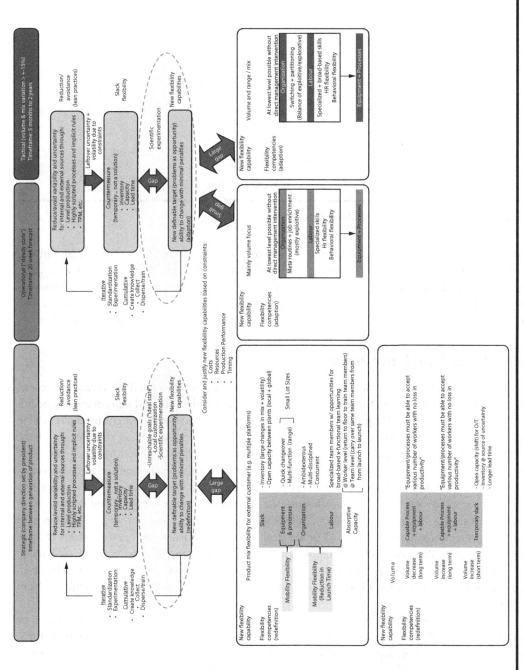

Figure 10.6   Flexibility strategy framework in a Lean manufacturing environment.

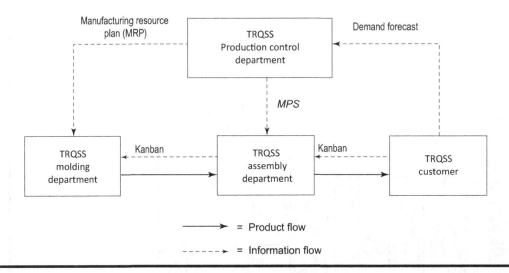

Figure 10.7 TRQSS internal "pull system" overview.

joint venture agreement restricted QSS to supply only Japanese auto "transplants" that had just begun sprouting up in North America in the mid-1980s. Although TRW and TRJ were competitors in automotive safety restraints, both had little experience in operating a North American plant for Japanese customers. The joint venture sought to strengthen those weak points. In 2005, TRW sold their stake in QSS to TRJ, which also led to renaming the company as TRQSS.

10.4.3 *The Initial Investigation*

Fourteen years' prior, the IE Manager Gillian Anderson, led a newly created TPS team in successfully launching a brand-new from scratch TPS pull system with a Heijunka production scheduling on the assembly side. Heijunka, or "level production," provides a consistent production plan that is necessary for standard work. The Heijunka volume is calculated as the average of the customer forecast over a given period. In TRQSS' case, the Heijunka period for assembly was 1 week's worth of customer forecast data. Every day, the production line is required to build to this Heijunka volume. When the actual customer order (or pull) is above Heijunka, fluctuation safety stock is used to cover the difference. When the actual customer order is below Heijunka, fluctuation safety stock is rebuilt (Figure 10.8). When it came time to rolling out TPS to the molding area, the parent company and the IM group decided to create a new pull system themselves in 2005. As a result, Anderson was not too familiar with the system, nor the issues they were having.

The weekday "no kanban" audit for the 55 molding machines also revealed that the "pull system" problem was not confined to just a few machines. This seemed to be a systemic problem (Figure 10.9).

In particular, one machine stood out from the rest in the audit. Machine 165–4 was supposed to be loaded with enough customer demand volume to produce parts on only two shifts, but in reality, it was running three shifts on most weekdays. This machine also was one of several machines that was running overtime occasionally on weekends (Figure 10.10). The maintenance logs showed no machine issues that could have explained the weekday downtime.

The next step was to check if kanbans were returned from assembly back to IM immediately after parts were consumed by assembly. To understand where the kanbans travel in the plant, the

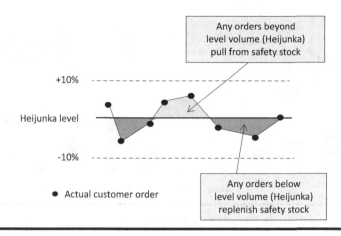

Figure 10.8   Heijunka production scheduling.

	No. of machines	% of total	
No kanbans on weekday + weekend O/T			
Machine loading < 100%	16	29.1%	40% of all machines ran unplanned O/T
Machine loading > 100%	3	5.5%	
Weekend O/T			
Machine loading < 85%	3	5.5%	
Legimately running weekend O/T			
Machine loading >100%	19	34.5%	34.5% of all machines ran planned O/T
No concerns	14	25.5%	25.5% of all machines ran no O/T

Figure 10.9   "Saturday overtime" audit results.

"kanban loop" between IM and assembly was mapped (Figure 10.11). At TRQSS, two types of kanbans existed. Production instruction kanbans (PIK) are used to provide instructions to a production line on what to produce (which machine and quantity). Once production is complete, the PIK is placed on the full box (Figure 10.12).

A second type, part withdrawal kanbans (PWK), are used to instruct material handlers which parts to retrieve for the next downstream production area (e.g., the immediate downstream customer). As the next full box is pulled off the warehouse shelf by the material handler, as instructed by the PWK, the PWK is placed onto the tote with the PIK and is mailed back to the IM production area. The full box with PWK then travels to the internal customer for use. When a full box of parts is consumed by the internal customer, the PWK once again instructs the material handler to pick another full box from the warehouse. This "kanban loop" logic used at TRQSS ensured that IM parts are only produced to replenish what is used by assembly, what TPS refers to as a "pull system."

So why were machines that were fully capable of running production during the week becoming idle? The root-cause seemed to be more complicated than a simple kanban return issue that some had initially thought. How complicated? Figure 10.13 conveys the complexity of TRQSS' internal production flow.

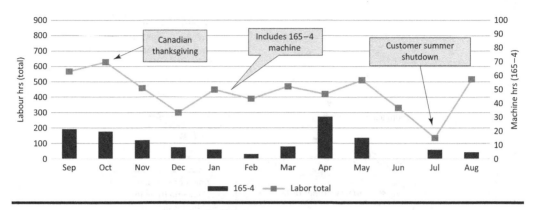

Figure 10.10 Injection molding machine overtime.

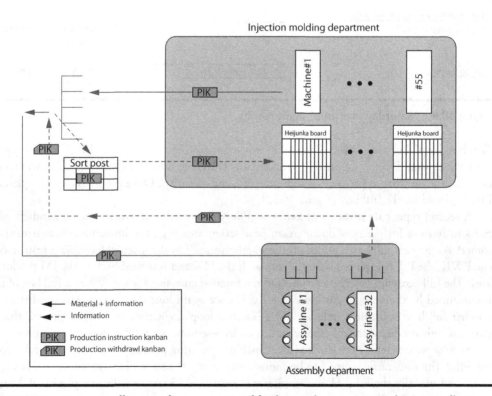

Figure 10.11 Current pull system between assembly (internal customer) and IM (supplier).

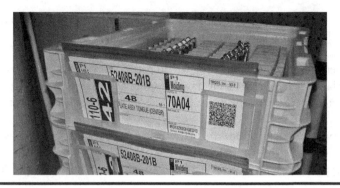

Figure 10.12 Example of a re-usable PIK attached to full boxes of injection molded parts (48 pcs.).

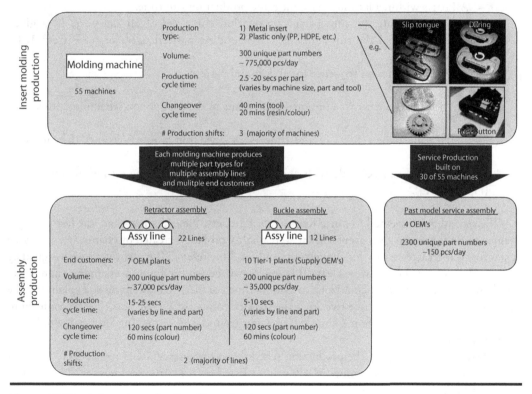

Figure 10.13 Internal production flow chart.

10.4.4 *The Deep Dive*

Anderson turned to the person who was most familiar with IM production scheduling. Davis Reiss had worked in IM for nearly 20 years, the last 15 as the injection molding scheduler. He was there, 12 years prior, when TPS Heijunka was rolled out to IM, with the help of the Japanese parent company. A form of Heijunka was developed by the parent company called "pattern and lot." However, in those 12 years there was no improvement to the system.

Reiss explained how pattern and lot is used to separate higher volume parts ("pattern" parts) from lower volume parts ("lot" parts). While pattern part PIKs were produced every day, lot parts only ran when accumulating PIKs hit a predetermined reorder point. When asked how he applied "pattern and lot" in his IM scheduling job, Reiss revealed there was no process documentation on IM Heijunka. "It is just me. I am the only one that does this. Besides, there's so much to the job that it is not something that is easy to put down on paper." However, despite the lack of documentation, Reiss declared "I have never shut down assembly for lack of parts." To understand Reiss' process, a list of steps needed to schedule each of the 55 machines was compiled:

1. Determine which parts fall into the "pattern" category—high usage parts produced daily at the same scheduled time every day.
2. Remaining parts are "lot"—lower usage parts whose build frequency is less than one time per day.
   - A "lot" is a group of lower usage parts, designated by a letter (lot A, lot B, …).
   - Each part is assigned to one lot only.
   - All parts within a lot must have the same production run time.
   - Lot assignment: the sum of the production run time of all the parts in a given lot should equal the run time for corresponding pattern part. lot A = Pattern 1, lot B = Pattern 2.
3. Determine a production sequence for all lots and patterns.

Reiss also had to consider two additional constraints in the production scheduling process:

■ 90%/10% rule (where 90% of the time is assigned for production and 10% for part changeovers).
■ No changeover can coincide with another changeover (at the same time) within a zone (Figure 10.14).

The second point seemed to cause Reiss a lot of anxiety. He explained that "the last manager wanted to fix the changeover events. There were quality problems created by changeover errors, so a new role was created strictly for changeovers and machine resets." The new roles were assigned by zone so that responsibilities were clear. This zone coverage required non-overlapping changeover for those machines in a particular zone to avoid a time conflict. Reiss went on to explain that he spent a large amount of his time tweaking the reorder points (ROPs) of "lots" just to conform to this constraint. As Reiss called it, "I just keep playing around with it, making lots smaller or larger, until it works."

Asked when a change to the production schedule was necessary, Reiss responded, "I look at the material requirements planning (MRP) volume based on the customer forecast 20 weeks out" (Figure 10.15).

If there is a large volume change, I might have to change the lot or pattern size. If the volume change is significant enough and long term, a part tool may have to move to another machine due to a machine capacity concern." Once completed, the production schedule boards consisted of two different boards for each machine—a "PIK return board" (Figure 10.16) and a "Heijunka scheduling board" (Figure 10.17).

As each molding machine is loaded with different part numbers, the board design is different for each machine. Considering that a schedule contained over 300-part numbers, across 55 machines, and 6 different machine groups, the entire manual process seemed extremely complex and time consuming. Wanting to know how this "pattern and lot" Heijunka system actually performed, a study began with the 165-4 machine. It provided a good starting point given that there

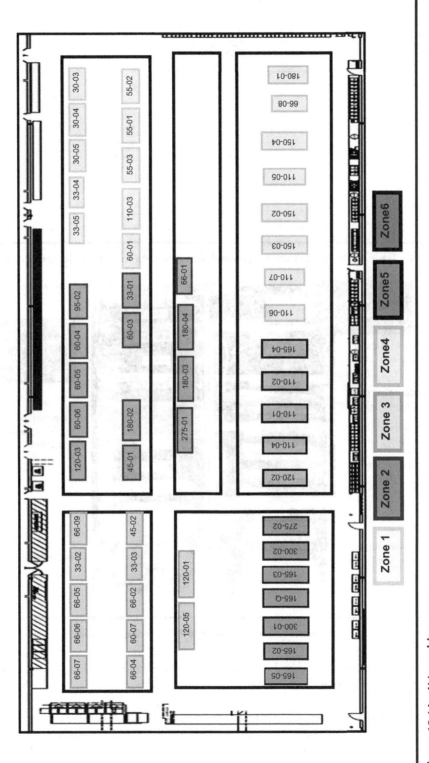

Figure 10.14   IM machine zones.

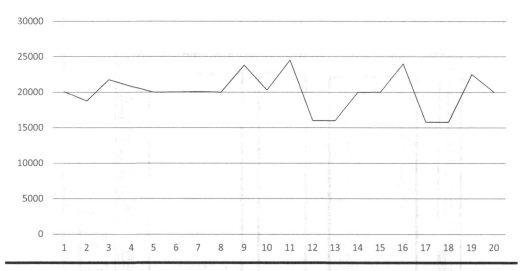

Figure 10.15 Typical TRQSS customer's 20 week forecast data for a high demand part.

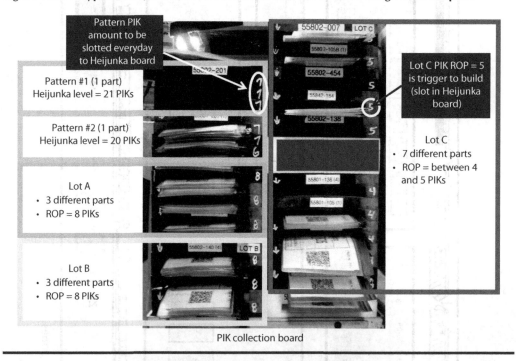

Figure 10.16 Current "PIK return board" example (60-4 molding machine).

was little reason for running weekend overtime. The pull from this machine also was one of the simpler ones, producing parts for a small number of assembly lines (four in total) with only two end customers.

Since a pull system originates from the end customer, this is where the investigation began. The Toyota pull from assembly was first studied (Figure 10.18). The data showed no surprises. The customer pull variation for volume and product mix from their 4-week forecast (Heijunka) was within expected limits for Toyota (±10%) in a given week. Because assembly carried fluctuation

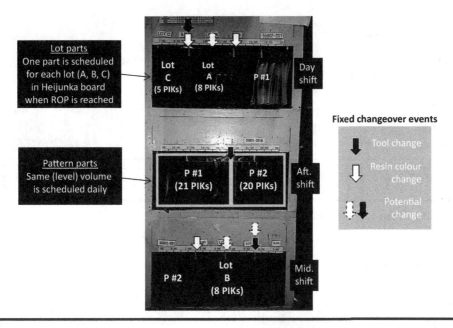

Figure 10.17 Current "daily Heijunka scheduling board" example (60-4 molding machine).

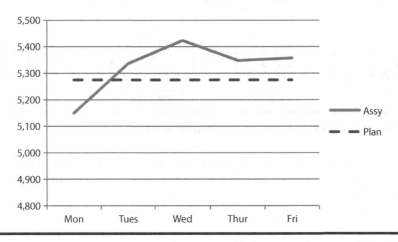

Figure 10.18 Typical customer daily pull from assembly compared to assembly Heijunka plan.

safety stock to cover this ±10% in the form of finished goods, the downstream supply chain (e.g., IM) should not see this pull variation.

Next, the assembly pull from IM was investigated over the same 1-month (Figure 10.19). Even with consistent customer pull from assembly, assembly production has some volume variation in volume greater than the customers' ±10% in a few instances. This variation was attributed to internal machine downtime and labor shortages.

The plan and actual IM production in response to that assembly pull also was charted (Figure 10.20). Again, there was some machine and tool downtime, but that could not totally explain the large day-to-day variation. After breaking down the same IM production into pattern and lot types, a surprising detail emerged. The one pattern part that should have had consistent weekday production was instead showing massive volume variation.

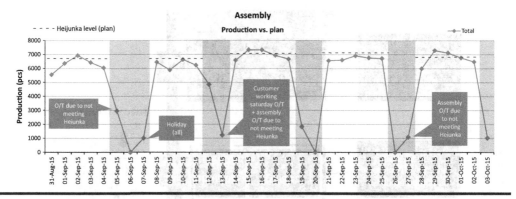

Figure 10.19   Plan versus actual assembly build.

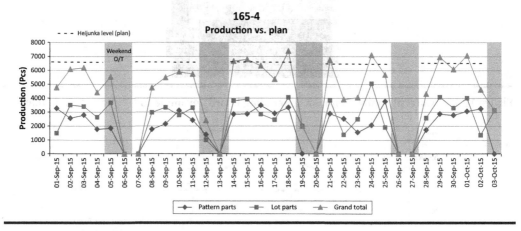

Figure 10.20   Plan versus actual IM production volumes.

Smaller volume IM lot parts composed of a lot A (2 parts), a lot B (2 parts), and a lot C (7 parts), were also displaying the same behavior. A quick check verified that the assembly pull of pattern and lot parts did not exhibit this same variation (Figure 10.21) for the 15 finished goods that consumed the one pattern part and the 31 finished goods that consumed the 11 lot parts. While the total lot consumption by assembly was consistent, further breakdown uncovered some variation for each lot that exceed 10% (Figure 10.22).

The numbers confirmed that IM was not building to replenish what assembly pulled. Anderson asked Reiss why he thought IM production varied so much. Reiss said that it probably stemmed from the fact that, "Production associates move kanbans around in the scheduling board to keep the machine running or if they think that inventory is getting low. They sometimes even print extra kanbans. They are scared that they are going to shut down assembly."

After some digging it was discovered that PIKs were being pulled ahead in the schedule. For instance, even after building Monday's PIKs, a portion of Tuesday's kanbans were pulled ahead and built on Monday. Why would the IM production group not follow the Heijunka plan? Was IM holding too little inventory to support the assembly pull, or was it something else? And why was there a significant difference in Heijunka planning volumes between assembly and IM? Whatever was causing these issues and the excessive unplanned overtime, it would take more than just two people looking at it to solve.

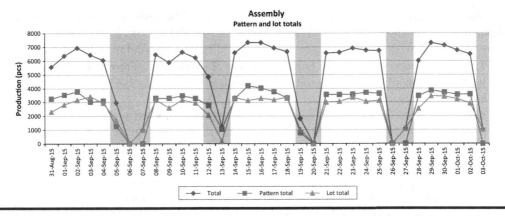

Figure 10.21   Assembly pull from IM broken out into pattern and lot parts.

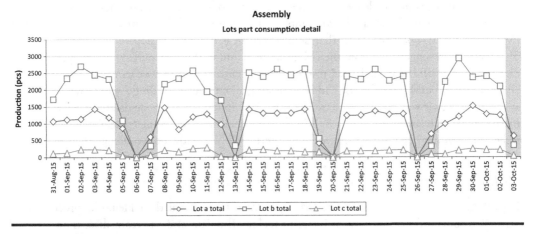

Figure 10.22   Breakdown of assembly pull of lots.

10.4.5 The Kaizen Team

Anderson had been having on-going conversations with Danielle Lewis about the IM situation. A decade earlier Lewis reported to Anderson and together they had launched TPS in assembly. That experience gave them some insight into the IM data and what it meant—the IM group needed help. Forming a team would be the next step.

10.4.5.1 First Impressions

Reiss started off the first meeting by presenting the findings. The data was an eye opener for the new team and kicked off a long and varied discussion on what was wrong with the current system. One point in particular seemed to be echoed by many in the IM group: "If we are already running some machines on a weekend, the floor supervisor will say, 'Why not run this other machine too with no extra labor?' Yet, come Monday, the machine that would normally run is shut down because there are no kanbans." This lack of discipline was troubling. It also seemed to indicate a trend since Reiss had made a similar comment earlier. However, those actions were somehow explained again by the fact that "IM has never shut down assembly." They did what they needed to do to keep parts on the shelf so that assembly kept running.

The discussion continued and the list of issues grew. Danielle Lewis was quick to point out the differences between assembly's and IM level plans. "Assembly's Heijunka level is based on the next 4 weeks' worth of customer demand forecast while IM's planning window is 20 weeks. IM looks too far out." An investigation into TRQSS customer's 20-week forecast revealed that only the data for weeks 1–8 were of any use for production planning, while weeks 1–4 were actually 10–15% within actual orders. (Figure 10.15).

Lewis also was very concerned with IM's lack of rationality when planning inventory for both production and fluctuation safety levels. Assembly's inventory levels are based on historical data from customers' order fluctuation and internal downtime. IM just uses a 'one size fits all approach'." Reiss acknowledged that IM's inventory was just a blanket number of 1.5 days for the majority of their part numbers—more than enough to cover assembly's production pull. "I have to do that," Reiss stated. If a machine gets behind, I have no way of knowing because the supervisors will just move the PIKs in the Heijunka board to compensate instead of leaving them at the original time. Production is constantly changing my production plan around."

The picture became a little clearer to the team: many of the standard and logical Heijunka processes that existed on the assembly side simply did not exist for IM's Heijunka. However, many in IM were skeptical—perhaps, other than some overtime issues, the IM department system worked? There were even suggestions from the IM group to abandon the TPS pull system altogether. "Just give me a list of all the parts I need to build for the entire week and we can figure out the most efficient way to build them." Reiss had been talking about batch building a week's worth of parts at one time. Lewis was quick to squash the idea. "We follow TPS—replenish only what is pulled in as small a batch size as possible." Walking back to her desk after the meeting, Anderson thought to herself, "IM has been isolated for so long in terms of TPS. How do we change their minds?"

10.4.5.2 Finding the Need

Even if Anderson could convince the IM department to overhaul their Heijunka process, there was still a long and complex list of issues to tackle. The data and the team discussion revealed several sources of variation and pull imbalances between assembly and IM. A trend toward greater customer customization was one source of variation uncertainty. The past few years saw a large increase in technologies and total technology variations, with little change in volume demand (Figure 10.23).

If the team was going to make sense of it all, they would need tools that would simplify all that complexity. Anderson remembered reading about Toyota's iterative problem-solving process and how they used flexibility, in the form of slack, to control leftover variation (Figure 10.5).

For the experiment portion, the company's president had recently been indoctrinating the need for bottom-up problem solving through the scientific and logical approach of "The Improvement Kata" process:

1. What is the target condition?
2. What is the current condition?
3. What obstacles are preventing from reaching the target?
4. What is your next step? (use controlled experiments to overcome obstacles)

Using the two problem-solving processes in tandem would form the basis for the team's roadmap. So how to convince the IM team that change is necessary? Anderson kept thinking about how several IM managers over a 16-year period had failed to yield any significant improvements.

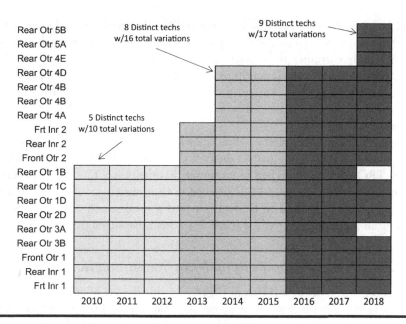

Figure 10.23 Technology history and forecast.

Why? What was missing? Every Kaizen must have a need or a reason to improve, an underlying problem to solve. The IM teams had failed to see those problems. To them, a "no part shortage" situation was a sign that their Heijunka system was working. They had missed the true reason for a level production plan.

"The IM department has been lacking a well-defined need for improvement," Anderson thought. And for the need to have any urgency in the eyes of the team it needed to be driven by the president and VP's direction. "Well, the president and VP both want standard work in IM, so …that's the need!" (Figure 10.24).

10.4.5.3 A Tale of Two TPSs

Anderson was not sure what kind of reaction she would receive from senior management. The idea of overhauling the IM Heijunka system was way beyond the scope of the initial IM overtime problem. Those worries were put to rest once the president and VP quickly gave their full support with little concern. The only question: "Why were we using this pattern/lot system in the first place?" No one could really offer a good explanation. Perhaps TRQSS' parent company believed that their pattern/lot system, which functioned properly in Japan, would have an identical outcome in North America. Both TRQSS' and their parent's production systems

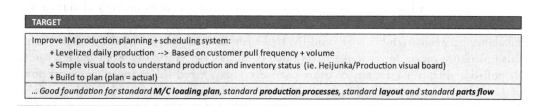

Figure 10.24 Heijunka kaizen target.

were established on TPS. However, the Japanese and North American production environments were quite different in some ways. For example, customer pull rates were much more frequent in Japan. More frequent customer pulls corresponded to much more frequent pulls inside the plant. The parent's production areas were set-up to respond to those pull rates. These differences were attributed to geography—North American customers were much further away from their supply base than Japan. Further logistics distances in North America translated to fewer customer pickups over the course of a day.

These sorts of distinctions, among others, may have explained differences in internal supply chain pull variances and pull rates within the two TPS systems. While the difference may not be fully known, TRQSS' TPS group had to recognize that their own TPS system, firmly rooted in Toyota Lean principals, still needed to be tailored to their customers' behaviors and production environments. The data collected so far had provided a good record of the unique production behavior. Now all the team need to do was create a system that managed that behavior.

10.4.5.4 Something Old, Something New, Something Borrowed

Over the next series of meetings, the team began to tackle the list of current issues and identify any obstacles that stood in the way. The team decided that several of the issues had solutions easily borrowed from the Heijunka on the assembly side. "Commonization" of processes between the two areas made sense. The pull system between assembly and IM departments should be thought of as one system, not two separate entities. The standardization through common processes would help seamlessly join the two production areas.

One of the bigger impacts of standardization included a formal calculation for the number of PIKs in the system, including inventory levels. Where IM used a "one number fits all" approach to inventory, the assembly side was thoughtfully and logically broken out by specific needs:

1. Production kanbans—scheduled production for the day
2. Safety stock kanbans
   - Customer fluctuation—inventory to overcome customer order variations
   - IM production downtime—inventory to overcome unplanned IM downtime
3. Lead time kanbans—kanbans waiting to be scheduled

IM was lacking an analytical approach in all three categories. Even with an acceptable 10–15% pull variation from assembly, there was no way of establishing level production in IM without proper safety stock levels. However, the team was getting ahead of itself. According to the problem-solving roadmap, the first step in creating a Lean, level pull system was to manage uncertainties without mobility slack. Inventory was the temporary countermeasure for absorbing uncertainties that could not otherwise be managed or eliminated in that pull production system.

What would an improved IM Heijunka look like? Borrowing assembly's Heijunka processes was deemed a poor fit. There were large differences in pull attributes, such as the imbalance between assembly usage and IM replenishment rates driven by the 90%/10% rule. This imbalance meant lower usage parts (lots) could not be built daily, even though assembly pulled and consumed many of those parts every day. Fixed IM changeover events posed an even bigger challenge. Finding a method for a level production schedule while satisfying those constraints proved to be a daunting task for the team. A lack of understanding of the current system did not help matters. Much of the meetings were spent trying to grasp how

Reiss' made it all work. He tried explaining to the group, but the explanation usually came down to "trial and error." A new, innovative approach was needed if a workable solution was going to be found.

Anderson knew that Reiss, who had been doing the same job for so long, was having a very difficult time contributing. New ideas and concepts were met with replies of frustration from Reiss. "I'm so used to doing it this way that I can't picture it being done any other way." But as the IM Heijunka process "owner," Reiss had considerable knowledge of the production floor. This was the sort of knowledge needed to find a solution that worked both on paper and on the floor. To help Reiss overcome this "rut," the two of them began meeting informally between meetings to bounce ideas off one another.

They began to look deeper into the problems of the current pattern/lot system. There was one issue that kept coming up in conversation—IM productions' consistent need to alter the daily schedule plan. Sometimes PIKs that were meant for the next day were pulled ahead to fill idle time (open slots in the Heijunka board). Other times there were too many PIKs (well over 15% fluctuation plan) that had to be delayed. Why did the production crew feel the need to do that? Assembly's pull from IM for high-volume pattern parts was consistent. Lot volumes did have some variation, but that variation was not consistent.

Given the pull variation within the lot parts, they began a closer look there. What made the current IM Heijunka system so difficult to understand was the randomness of lot parts hitting their ROPs. Because ROPs were decided by a common run time to meet a fixed changeover schedule (Figure 10.25), lot parts production schedules became erratic (Figure 10.26). Was the root of the problem with lot scheduling?

They went back to the original definition of pattern and lot:

- Patterns were parts with high volume and consistent pulls (built daily).
- Lots consisted of parts with low volume and inconsistent pulls (built on ROP).

After examining the assembly pull data once again, Anderson and Reiss believed that the majority of the parts seemed to fit a pattern based on their pull consistency alone. However, all but one of the parts for 165-4 were currently designated into lots. "If we assigned more parts to patterns then most of the production time would be spent doing changeover," said Reiss. This was in keeping with the 90%/10% rule. So, if parts did not fit either of the categories perhaps a new category was needed. Or perhaps the existing categories needed to be redefined.

Pat/Lot	M/C No	Part-colour #	No. cavities	Cycle time	Box qty	Daily usage	Time/day (min)	Kanban/day	Lot time	Pcs/lot	Kanbans/Lot	Kanbans in ass'y	Safety rate	DOH	Released kanbans
p	165-4	100-1B	4	34.7	49	2660.00	384.59	54.29	420.00	2905	60	6	1.5	1.60	87
a	165-4	101-1B	4	39.5	80	487.00	80.15	6.09	257.84	1567	20	2	1.5	5.26	32
a	165-4	101-2B	4	39.5	80	433.00	71.26	5.41	257.84	1567	20	4	1.5	6.28	34
b	165-4	100-0B	4	34.7	49	524.00	75.76	10.69	122.31	846	18	5	1.5	2.99	32
b	165-4	102-5B	4	39.1	48	347.00	56.53	7.23	122.31	751	16	2	1.5	3.60	26
b	165-4	103-5B	4	38.3	48	347.00	55.38	7.23	123.14	772	17	2	1.5	3.87	28
b	165-4	101-4B	4	39.5	80	300.00	49.38	3.75	123.14	748	10	2	1.5	4.53	17
c	165-4	102-2B	4	39.1	48	92.00	14.99	1.92	123.14	756	11	1	1.5	9.39	18
c	165-4	103-2B	4	38.3	48	92.00	14.68	1.92	123.14	772	11	1	1.5	9.39	18
c	165-4	102-4B	4	39.1	48	15.00	2.44	0.31	123.14	756	11	1	1.3	51.20	16
c	165-4	103-4B	4	38.3	48	15.00	2.39	0.31	123.14	772	11	1	1.3	51.20	16
c	165-4	101-4B	4	39.5	80	4.00	0.66	0.05	123.14	748	5	1	1.3	140.00	7

Figure 10.25   Current pattern/lot schedule construction for Machine 165-4.

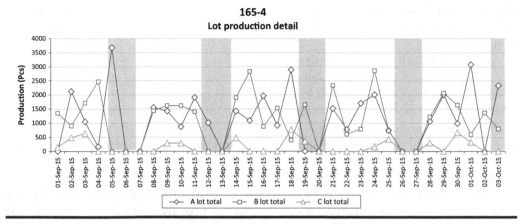

Figure 10.26   Actual IM lot production detail for Machine 165-4.

To resolve the issues with the current "lot" parts, they concluded that two improvements were needed:

1. If some of the current "lot" parts weren't behaving as "lots," then they must be "pattern" parts. To avoid violating the 90%/10% rule, pattern frequencies would have to be altered to conform to that constraint.
2. For the remaining "lot" parts that fit a "lot" definition, the current fixed ROP resulted in a non-level production schedule. A new production trigger would be needed to help achieve the "level production" requirement of Heijunka.

These "lot" improvements, when paired with the targeted improvements (visual production status, build to plan and appropriate inventory/PIK levels), formed the complete solution. A new pattern/lot schedule (e.g., Heijunka plan) (Figure 10.27) and new Heijunka board design (Figure 10.28) were then proposed to address all of these necessary improvements.

In the case of 165-4, the newly redesigned Heijunka plan and board consisted of (Kaizen items in italics):

▪ Pattern A: high-volume part built daily, leveled with fluctuation PIKs and *"lot" PIK's*
▪ Patterns B and C: medium volume parts built on 2 or 3-day frequency, leveled with *"lot" PIKs*
▪ Lots: low volume parts built on a variable ROP *(green = inventory ok, yellow = caution/ should run, red = critical/must run)*

Reiss spent the next few weeks creating a similar plan for additional molding machines, each with different customers that ordered different part technologies and displayed different levels of pull variation. He remarked that, while he still had some difficulty "forgetting the old system," he began to gain confidence. As the new system experiment was brought on-line for more machines, overtime began to trend downward by nearly 35% while overall IM parts inventory was lower. The experiment seemed to be a success.

			Assy Heijunka				IM Production Heijunka Kanbans			A	Safety Stock Kanbans				B	Lead Time Kanbans	C	Total Kanbans =A+B+C
Pat/lot	Part-colour #	No. cavs	Cycle time (s)	Box qty (pcs)	Daily usage (pcs)	Prod'n time (min/day)	Freq (# per day)	Kanbans/pattern	Kanbans/lot	Production run (# Kanbans)	Fluctuation (%)	Fluctuation stock (# Kanbans) x	Downtime stock (# days)	Downtime stock (# Kanbans) y	Total safety stock (# Kanbans) x+y	Slotting lead time (Hrs)	Total slot lead time (# Kanbans)	Total released (# Kanbans)
p (a)	100-1B	4	34.7	49	2717.80	392.95	1.00	55.47		55.5	15%	9	1	55.5	64.5	12.0	27.73	148
p (b)	101-1B	4	36	80	1013.95	152.09	0.50	26		26.0			0.5	6.3	6.3	24.0	12.67	46
p (b)	101-2B	4	36	80	572.40	86.86	0.50	15		15.0			0.5	3.6	3.6	24.0	7.16	26
p (b)	101-0B	4	36	80	301.70	45.26	0.50	8		8.0			0.5	1.9	1.9	24.0	3.77	14
p (c)	100-5B	4	34.7	49	528.50	76.41	0.50	22		22.0			0.5	5.4	5.4	24.0	10.79	39
p (c)	102-5B	4	39.1	48	331.30	53.97	0.50	14		14.0			0.5	3.5	3.5	24.0	6.90	25
p (c)	103-5B	4	38.3	48	330.80	52.79	0.50	14		14.0			0.5	3.4	3.4	24.0	6.89	25
L (a)	102-2B	4	39.1	48	93.60	15.25	Variable		12	12.0			0.5	1.0	1.0	24.0	1.95	15
L (a)	103-2B	4	38.3	48	93.65	14.94	Variable		12	12.0			0.5	1.0	1.0	24.0	1.95	15
L (a)	102-4B	4	39.1	48	10.95	1.78	Variable		12	12.0			0.5	0.1	0.1	24.0	0.23	13
L (a)	103-4B	4	38.3	48	10.95	1.75	Variable		12	12.0			0.5	0.1	0.1	24.0	0.23	13
L (a)	101-4B	4	36	80	2.20	0.33	Variable		7	7.0			0.5	0.0	0.0	24.0	0.03	8

Figure 10.27 New Heijunka plan (pattern/lot) for Machine 165-4.

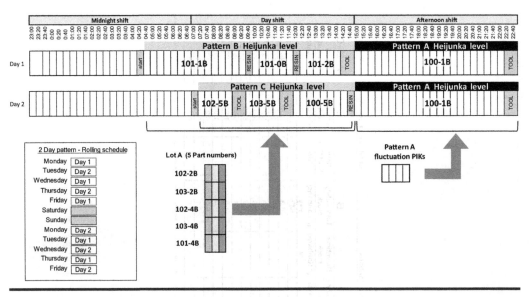

Figure 10.28   New Heijunka board for Machine 165-4.

10.5 Final Thoughts

The case study discussed in this chapter touched mostly on a strategic timeframe. As there was no continuous improvement tied to long-term company strategy, the Kaizen team had to start by completely redefining the entire Heijunka process. New scheduling process flexibility helped manage volume and product mix variability to maintain a level production volume within the allowable ±10%-15% range needed for Heijunka. The Kaizen team displayed organizational and labor flexibility through a mix of multi-disciplined and specialized team members, while also providing opportunities for broad-based cross-functional team learning. Since there is a large difference between production rates and changeover times between assembly and IM departments, slack provided a temporary buffer. Strategically, management must close this gap over the long term with the ideal target of a one-for-one pull/replenishment. While this target may seem unreachable due to many difficult constraints, it provides a hard to reach goals that may spur on innovation in both efficiency and flexibility at all levels of an organization.

10.6 Conclusions

By creating the beginnings of a flexibility framework that is based on Toyota's iterative and cumulative problem-solving process, Lean manufacturers have a systematic and proven set of tools to help select and balance flexibility competencies:

- Reduction/avoidance: Eliminate and reduce variation and uncertainty through foundational Lean practices.
- Mobility flexibility: Temporarily suspend leftover variation and uncertainty due to resource constraints using slack.

■ New flexibility competencies: Set new goals to move toward a more predictable target environment. For Operational and Tactical timeframes, scientific experimentation helps bridge the gap between current and the target made possible through the steady state of mobility flexibility. New flexibility competencies developed to reach the new target in this timeline are typically Adaptation types. For strategic timeframes, ideal targets, local customization and scientific experimentation are necessary to bridge the gap. New flexibility competencies developed to reach new targets in this timeline are redefinition types.

■ Standardize new flexible processes, document and train: Standardize the new processes, document them, train personnel and then repeat from the top.

Going forward, large gaps in Lean/flexibility research exist that need to be addressed. To date, the majority of existing flexibility the literature is concentrated on the adaptive approach with only a small minority focused on the strategic side (Cannon and St John 2007). In the case of flexibility within a Lean environment, the literature gaps are even greater for both adaptive and redefinition categories. The included case study presented an opportunity to address those shortfalls. Further empirical research and case studies are needed to further strengthen the proposed flexibility framework to help Lean companies select and balance flexibility competencies to ultimately satisfy their customers.

References

Adler, P. S., Benner, M., Brunner, D. J., MacDuffie, J. P., Osono, E., Staats, B. R., Takeuchi, H., Tushman, M., and Winter, S. G. (2009). Perspectives on the productivity dilemma. *Journal of Operations Management*, 27(2), 99–113.

Adler, P. S., Goldoftas, B., and Levine, D. I. (1999). Flexibility versus efficiency? A case study of model changeovers in the Toyota production system. *Organization Science*, 10(1), 43–68.

Alford, D., Sackett, P., and Nelder, G. (2000). Mass customisation—An automotive perspective. *International Journal of Production Economics*, 65(1), 99–110.

Anand, G., and Ward, P. T. (2004). Fit, flexibility and performance in manufacturing: Coping with dynamic environments. *Production and Operations Management*, 13(4), 369–385.

Autoweek. Greimel, H. (2014). Toyota drops resistance to 3-shift plants. http://www.autonews.com/article/20141027/OEM01/310279965/toyota-drops-resistance-to-3-shift-plants

Beach, R., Muhlemann, A. P., Price, D. H. R., Paterson, A., and Sharp, J. A. (2000). A review of manufacturing flexibility. *European Journal of Operational Research*, 122(1), 41–57.

Bhattacharya, M., Gibson, D. E., and Doty, D. H. (2005). The effects of flexibility in employee skills, employee behaviors, and human resource practices on firm performance. *Journal of Management*, 31(4), 622–640.

Cannon, A. R., and St John, C. H. (2004). Competitive strategy and plant-level flexibility. *International Journal of Production Research*, 42(10), 1987–2007.

Chang, A.-Y. (2011). Prioritising the types of manufacturing flexibility in an uncertain environment. *International Journal of Production Research*, 50(8), 2133–2149.

Deif, A. M. (2012). Dynamic analysis of a Lean cell under uncertainty. *International Journal of Production Research*, 50(4), 1127–1139.

Gerwin, D. (1993). Manufacturing flexibility: A strategic perspective. *Management Science*, 39(4), 395–410.

Hallgren, M., and Olhager, J. (2009). Flexibility configurations: Empirical analysis of volume and product mix flexibility. *Omega*, 37(4), 746–756.

Hasik, M. J. (2006). An analysis of motor vehicle assembly plant complexity: Developing a framework to evaluate the existence of a complexity threshold. Massachusetts Institute of Technology.

He, P., Xu, X., and Hua, Z. (2011). A new method for guiding process flexibility investment: Flexibility fit index. *International Journal of Production Research*, 50(14), 3718–3737.

Jack, E. P., and Raturi, A. (2002). Sources of volume flexibility and their impact on performance. *Journal of Operations Management*, 20(5), 519–548.

Ketokivi, M. (2006). Elaborating the contingency theory of organizations: The case of manufacturing flexibility strategies. *Production and Operations Management*, 15(2), 215–228.

MacDuffie, J. P., Sethuraman, K., and Fisher, M. L. (1996). Product variety and manufacturing performance: Evidence from the international automotive assembly plant study. *Management Science*, 42(3), 350–369.

Narasimhan, R., Talluri, S., and Das, A. (2004). Exploring flexibility and execution competencies of manufacturing firms. *Journal of Operations Management*, 22(1), 91–106.

Ohno, T. (1988). *Toyota Production System Beyond Large-Scale Production*. Productivity Press, 1–130 Portland, OR.

Patel, P. C., Terjesen, S., and Li, D. (2012). Enhancing effects of manufacturing flexibility through operational absorptive capacity and operational ambidexterity. *Journal of Operations Management*, 30(3), 201–220.

Sawhney, R. (2013). Implementing labor flexibility: A missing link between acquired labor flexibility and plant performance. *Journal of Operations Management*, 31(1–2), 98–108.

Spear, S., and Bowen, H. K. (1999). Decoding the DNA of the Toyota production system. *Harvard Business Review*, 77, 96–108.

Upton, D. M. (1994). The management of manufacturing flexibility. *California Management Review*, 36(2), 72–89.

Upton, D. M. (1995a). Flexibility as process mobility: The management of plant capabilities for quick response manufacturing. *Journal of Operations Management*, 12(3–4), 205–224.

Upton, D. M. (1995b). What really makes factories flexible? *Harvard Business Review*, 73(4), 74–84.

Zhang, Q., Vonderembse, M. A., and Lim, J. S. (2003). Manufacturing flexibility: Defining and analyzing relationships among competence, capability, and customer satisfaction. *Journal of Operations Management*, 21(2), 173–191.

Index

9781138032217